W9-BZO-582

A GLOBAL AFFAIR

Copyright © 1995 Jones & Janello

Published in 1995 by Jones & Janello
267 Fifth Avenue New York, NY 10016

This book would not have been possible
without the support of the Ford Foundation
and Rockefeller Family and Associates.

Printed in Hong Kong by Toppan Printing Co.
Bound in China

ISBN 0-9646322-0-9

In northern Afghanistan, 1990.

PROCESSED

A GLOBAL AFFAIR

An Inside Look at the United Nations

Edited by Amy Janello and Brennon Jones
Introduction by Brian Urquhart

Jones & Janello

UN headquarters under construction. September 1949.

Contents

OUR OBJECTIVE IN CREATING A GLOBAL AFFAIR IS TO GIVE readers, particularly those unfamiliar with the United Nations, a sense of the people behind the organization and its worldwide activities. The UN's popular depiction—like that of many large institutions today—is defined largely by immediate events and by what is deemed newsworthy. This often obscures invaluable history and leaves unsung the contributions of some exceptional people.

A Global Affair is not a comprehensive history—some of the UN's myriad agencies and activities are mentioned only in passing—instead, it attempts to capture, in an impressionistic manner, the spirit and personality of the United Nations as it has evolved since 1945.

UN checkpoint on the Cairo–Suez Road, 1973.

In 1970 the journalist Richard Hudson wrote in The New York Times, *"Every time I walk into the United Nations, I am struck by the fact I am leaving the United States....the swirl of international politics here would always give me this strange, exhilarating feeling of being in a uniquely cosmopolitan atmosphere."*

We hope A Global Affair *conveys that sense of energy, a hallmark of the United Nations for most of its history, and brings to life those UN involvements that are far from head-quarters but from which the world organization's ultimate successes and failures can be most clearly gauged.*

The Editors

Introduction

Brian Urquhart

I WAS 14 YEARS OLD WHEN ADOLF HITLER CAME TO POWER IN 1933. The Japanese were already in Manchuria. The free nations of the world failed to use the League of Nations to stop this international banditry. Two years later Mussolini invaded Abyssinia, and the humiliating descent to World War II began. As a teenager I, along with many others, felt that something should be done to stop the slide to disaster. Our governments, however, sat on their hands.

It was this bitter early experience that gave me a passionate desire to work for a world organization dedicated not only to peace, but to resisting evil. Six years' service in the British Army during the war, and especially the spectacle of the rape, ruin and disgrace of Europe under the Nazis, only strengthened this ambition. To this day, working for the United Nations seems to me the most interesting job—and the highest privilege—that a reasonable person could ask for. It is, of course, a frustrating and often disappointing vocation, but who ever expected working for a better world to be easy?

The United Nations and its galaxy of specialized organizations were created in a fervent reaction to the human race's greatest collective disaster, the Second World War. The system was set up by national leaders who had experienced that disaster firsthand and were determined that nothing like it should ever happen again. The UN Charter was their blueprint for a more just and peaceful world and, at the beginning at any rate, they all seemed determined to make it work.

It was not long, however, before nations began to re-arm and to threaten one another all over again. Even worse, the growing enmity of the UN's two most powerful members, the United States and the Soviet Union, caused the world to be divided into two hostile, nuclear-armed

9

camps for more than 40 years. Despite the chilling international climate, the organization forged ahead. Having presided over a surprisingly peaceful process of worldwide decolonization, the UN developed the technique of peacekeeping—using soldiers as intermediaries between hostile forces—to fill dangerous power vacuums and contain regional conflicts. The organization provided a sort of safety net to prevent a sudden lurch to nuclear war. Although there were many small wars in the first 50 years of the UN, there was no third *world war.*

In other fields as well the UN did pioneering work, again despite the Cold War. It put human rights on the international map as a criterion for national and international behavior, and turned its attention to a new generation of global problems—development, the environment, women's rights, population, poverty, to name a few—that will help determine the future of the human race. It moved into virtually all major fields of human activity and made substantial progress in many of them.

"L'ONU, c'est quelle tribu?"—(The UN, what tribe is that?)—a provincial Congolese administrator inquired when we arrived in the chaos of the Congo in 1960, shortly after the nation had won its independence. His question is not as odd as it might seem. The United Nations—the largest collection of foreigners in the world (currently comprising 185 member states), yet with no sovereign power of its own—is often viewed with suspicion and a good deal of skepticism. Its true value is best seen in great international crises, when it can provide an acceptable escape from a major calamity. History, however, may well judge as more significant its less spectacular, longer-term work in international law, in economic development and on social issues.

Only a few of the men and women who do the real work of the UN and its agencies are well known, or known at all. The young people saving lives and caring for children in a refugee camp in Rwanda, the soldiers sheltering civilians under fire in Sarajevo, may be glimpsed on the television screen, but none will be known by name. Their colleagues who devote their lives to developing international law, devising development programs or engaging in the endless exchanges of preventive diplomacy will remain invisible and anonymous. And yet, without them, the best-laid plans of governments and international organizations would remain nothing but brave phrases in diplomatic documents.

Few people now remember the veteran foot soldiers of the international world, the people who represented the true spirit of the United Nations as it was conceived 50 years ago. Even Ralph Bunche, the world's champion mediator and the father of peacekeeping, is almost forgotten. Who remembers Maurice Pate, the American investment banker who founded UNICEF; or General E.L.M. Burns of Canada, the first commander of a peacekeeping force; or René Cassin of France, Eleanor Roosevelt's partner in establishing the Universal Declaration of Human Rights; or Robert Jackson of Australia, the greatest of humanitarian relief operators; or Colonel S. S. Maitra of India, who, 35 years ago in the Congo, provided a perfect example of the peacekeeper as humanitarian and military man combined; or David Owen of Britain, who masterminded and built the UN Development Programme; or Raúl Prebisch of Argentina, the great economist of Latin America? Even less remembered are the countless faithful workers who served them.

I remember a difficult evening in Africa in November 1961. I was then the head of the UN operation in Katanga, the Congo, and I had been rather forcefully kidnapped from a dinner party in Elizabethville, the capital of Katanga, by the thugs of the secessionist regime. As I sat, in considerable anxiety and discomfort, in some godforsaken camp in the bush, I asked myself what on earth I thought I was doing. The answer, curiously enough, was comforting and invigorating. I was trying, as an objective and disinterested civil servant, to sort out a particularly messy and violent episode in the short history of a newly independent nation. That is what I had been sent to do, and maybe the idea would eventually get through to my captors. Fortunately, it did. I am sure that this experience has been shared many times in different ways by those who have chosen to serve the United Nations.

This book commemorates some of the dedicated civil servants and national representatives who have striven to make the United Nations work in its tumultuous first 50 years. It gives vivid glimpses of them at various stages of what Dag Hammarskjöld once described as "a venture in progress towards an international community living in peace under the laws of justice."

The Early Years

The Early Years

Kathleen Teltsch

T HE MOOD IN SAN FRANCISCO'S WAR MEMORIAL OPERA HOUSE was one of high hopes and exhilaration. President Harry S. Truman, preparing to address the delegates who had gathered for the signing of the United Nations Charter on June 26, 1945, summed up the mood when he raised his hands and spontaneously exclaimed, "Oh, what a great day this can be in history!"

The delegates had spent more than two months drafting the charter. On the day of the signing, newspapers carried reports of ground battles and air strikes against enemy targets in the Pacific; the war in Europe had been over for less than two months. The world was weary of war. Many of the delegates had lived for years with blackouts, rationing and other privations; some bore the scars of war. For them, the birth of the United Nations seemed to mark the beginning of a shining new era, a time in which wartime allies would work together to preserve the peace.

There was reason to be optimistic. Whereas a quarter of a century before, the United States had held itself aloof from the League of Nations, thus spelling the organization's doom, now it was committed to making sure that the United Nations—a name proposed by President Franklin D. Roosevelt—worked and endured. The Allies, who had fought so hard together, would surely now work equally hard to preserve the peace.

The first threat to the new charter came not from a recalcitrant government but from the hordes of eager photographers who rushed toward the document. A UN official, moving quickly, wrapped his arms protectively around the charter while yelling for guards to keep back the press.

The actual signing of the charter took many hours. It was delayed a bit, among other reasons, because the members of the Chinese delegation needed time to grind a stick of dry ink in a mortar backstage before Foreign Minister Wellington Koo, using a calligrapher's brush, affixed the first signature. Fifty governments were signatories; Poland had to be

PREVIOUS SPREAD *Escorted by New York's finest, outgoing UN Secretary-General Trygve Lie (center left) welcomes Dag Hammarskjöld, the newly appointed UN secretary-general, at Idlewild Airport in April 1953. Hammarskjöld, a Swede, had flown in from Stockholm.*

ABOVE *Elated Russian delegates at the San Francisco conference savor war's end in May 1945.*

RIGHT *Arriving at the San Francisco conference, US President Harry S. Truman greets spectators and the press. In a radio address to the nation, Truman said of conference delegates, "[You] are to be the architects of the better world. In your hands rests our future."*

TOP *Delegates from the League of Nations listen to Hitler's envoy defend Germany's militarization of the Rhineland in 1936. The promises and failures of the League, the first international organization—formed in the aftermath of World War I and dissolved in 1946—were a constant reminder to the architects of the United Nations.*

ABOVE LEFT *Roosevelt and Churchill sign the Atlantic Charter aboard the USS Augusta in 1941.*

ABOVE *Churchill, Roosevelt and Stalin agreed on the voting formula for the UN Security Council at Yalta in 1945.*

LEFT *US, Chinese and British delegates at the Dumbarton Oaks conference, where the outline of the UN Charter was agreed upon, have an informal lunch in September 1944.*

It seems to us that the President's death, instead of weakening the structure at San Francisco, will strengthen it. Death almost always reactivates the household in some curious manner, and the death of Franklin Roosevelt recalls and refurnishes the terrible emotions and the bright meaning of the times he brought us through. By the simple fact of dying, he has again attacked in strength. He now personifies, as no one else could, all the American dead—those whose absence we shall soon attempt to justify. The President was always a lover of strategy: he even died strategically, as though he had chosen the right moment to inherit the great legacy of light that Death leaves to the great. He will arrive in San Francisco quite on schedule, and in hundredfold capacity, to inspire the nations that he named United.

The delegates to San Francisco have the most astonishing job that has ever been dumped into the laps of a few individuals. On what sort of rabbit they pull from the hat hang the lives of most of us, and of our sons and daughters. If they put on their spectacles and look down their noses and come up with the same old bunny, we shall very likely all hang separately—nation against nation, power against power, defense against defense, people (reluctantly) against people (reluctantly). If they manage to bring the United Nations out of the bag, full blown, with constitutional authority and a federal structure having popular meaning, popular backing, and an over-all authority greater than the authority of any one member or any combination of members, we might well be started up a new road.

The pattern of life is plain enough. The world shrinks. It will eventually be unified. What remains to be seen (through eyes that now bug out with mortal terror) is whether the last chapter will be written in blood or in Quink.

—E. B. White, excerpts from *The New Yorker*, 1945

added later, after it was decided which political faction was the real Poland.

Then the charter—encased in a container, secured with four straps and provided with its own parachute—was flown to Washington in the custody of Alger Hiss, the conference's secretary-general.

The conference produced an enduring symbol: the United Nations emblem, a graphic rendering of a map of the world clasped by two laurel branches, signifying peace. The design, intended only as an identifying badge to be worn by authorized participants, was subsequently adopted as the official insignia. The first model used San Francisco as its focal point; this was changed later to the Greenwich meridian, supposedly at the suggestion of a British representative.

"…and in conclusion, Mr. President, I say that if after this great war we are to have a federation of all nations of the earth, where would it be more fitting to have the seat of government of this great brotherhood of free and friendly peoples than right here in God's country?"

From a cartoon US Senate, one representative gives President Roosevelt his views on the future United Nations in June 1944.

The charter-drafting sessions had not been free of bickering: The Soviets and the West accused each other of reneging on an agreement between President Roosevelt and Soviet Premier Stalin about limiting the veto's use. Even small issues proved thorny. The French, who were told that there were not enough French interpreters, surprised the American hosts by ingeniously placing their own people around a conference room. As a result, US Secretary of State Edward R. Stettinius, Jr., had to speak against an annoying murmur of whispered translations.

Although Trygve Lie was a participant at the San Francisco conference as foreign minister of Norway's government-in-exile, he was not one of its stars, either as a speaker or as a particularly skilled negotiator. He left early, rushing home after news came of Germany's surrender, on May 7, and thus missed the signing ceremony. Then, in London—where the General Assembly held its first session in January 1946—the Big Powers picked Lie as their compromise choice for UN secretary-general.

Lie's immediate preoccupation was getting "this machine," as he sometimes called the organization, into working order. The hastily

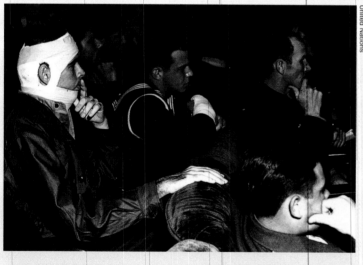

TOP *South African delegate H. T. Andrews (left), and Viscount Cranborne of the United Kingdom (right) wrestle with wording on a draft of the UN Charter.*

ABOVE *Bearing the wounds of the Second World War, uniformed veterans were among the most intent spectators at the UN founding conference.*

RIGHT *Leaving the rostrum at the UN founding conference, President Truman, accompanied by US Secretary of State Edward R. Stettinius, Jr., acknowledges the conference secretary-general, Alger Hiss.*

BELOW *While taking in the San Francisco sights, Prince Faisal ibn Abdul Aziz, head of the Saudi Arabian delegation to the UN conference, attracts the attention of a four-year-old aspiring sailor.*

BOTTOM LEFT *Dr. Mary McCleod Bethune of the National Association for the Advancement of Colored People represented just one of the 42 nongovernmental organizations from the United States invited to San Francisco as consultants.*

BOTTOM RIGHT *In the plush seats of the San Francisco Opera House, delegates debated the precise language of the UN Charter for hours at a time.*

BELOW *Lester Pearson of Canada, who went on to win the Nobel Peace Prize in 1957 for his peacekeeping efforts during the Suez Canal crisis, addresses a meeting during the conference. Seated at his left is Bertha Lutz of Brazil, one of just four women delegates at the conference.*

AP/Wide World Photos

United Nations

United Nations

UPI/Bettmann

Hulton Deutsch Collection

ABOVE *It's a long queue for spectators anxious to enter Central Hall for the UN's first session.*

BELOW *The ornate Central Hall at Westminster in London was chosen as the meeting place for the first session of the General Assembly, held in January 1946.*

TOP RIGHT *A final touch-up in preparation for the tide of international delegates attending the third UN General Assembly at the Palais de Chaillot in Paris in 1948. A devaluation of the franc made France the economical choice to host the Assembly that year.*

BOTTOM RIGHT *Norwegian statesman Trygve Lie was secretary-general for the UN's first eight years.*

United Nations

In 1946 the British Government was looking for a building situated close to the Houses of Parliament for the inaugural meeting of the United Nations. Few areas of London had been left unscathed by the bombing of the Second World War, but Westminster Central Hall had sustained only minor damage, and so was chosen to be the venue for this historic event.

Built at the turn of the century, Central Hall is UK headquarters for the Methodist Church and stands opposite Westminster Abbey. In addition to the Great Hall, which seats more than 2,300 people, the building houses extensive exhibition space and smaller conference rooms.

Westminster Central Hall underwent a transformation for the Assembly. Approximately half of the seating was removed, glass-fronted cabinets for the translation services were installed, and wall-to-wall carpeting laid down. The church sanctuary was boarded up and boxed in to create a modern square appearance and, outside, a great striped awning was erected bearing the flags of the participating nations.

And the church? The church moved out for the only time in its history, first to the Victoria Palace Theatre and then, when that proved too small, to the 2,500-seat London Coliseum, now the home of the English National Opera.

The leaders of the Methodist Church were honored to allow the Hall to be used to launch the UN organization. As Reverend W. E. Sangster, the superintendent minister of Central Hall, commented at the time: divine providence had preserved the building for the establishment of world peace, for in 1946 it was rare to find a hall still intact in the center of London.

—Peter Tudor, general manager, Westminster Central Hall

Bill Bruce and I met in November 1945 at Church House in London where we worked on the conference staff preparing for the first session of the UN General Assembly in London in February 1946. Bill was on loan from the US State Department. I was hired from the staff of the Royal Institute of International Affairs (Chatham House) which for the duration of the Second World War was absorbed into the Foreign Office as the Foreign Office Research Department. We both began our UN careers in November 1945...

In 1942, Bill had been hired by the War Relocation Authority to assist in the administration of a relocation camp at Manzanar, California, where Japanese were interned after the attack on Pearl Harbor. Disturbed by the internment of the American-born Japanese, Bill went to Washington attempting to secure their release and reinstatement in American society. He was hired by the US State Department where he served two years, before attending the founding conference of the UN in 1945...

I came to the UN in part because of my experience living in London during the war, but primarily because of what I had seen and heard during brief visits to Nazi Germany as a teenager. These visits, which included staying with a family where the mother was Jewish, and another in which the son was a member of the SS, and the Munich crisis period of 1938, convinced me that war was inevitable to deter Hitler, and that the atrocities of the Nazi regime, some of which I had witnessed firsthand, should not be permitted to recur.

Bill and I believe that our shared sense about injustices committed, albeit to a very different degree and in very different circumstances, brought us together in London in 1945, and ultimately led to our marriage which continues into the fiftieth anniversary year of the United Nations and hopefully many years beyond.

—Margaret Bruce

recruited staff was an odd mix: Some were veterans of the League of Nations; many more came out of governments or the armed services. Several interpreters had served in underground resistance movements. One declared that he would fight again just for the privilege of being present.

UNTIL 1952, WHEN IT settled in its permanent headquarters on the East River, the United Nations was a transient in search of a home. In its first few years, it moved from temporary quarters in a midtown Manhattan hotel to quarters at Hunter College in the Bronx, then settled for four years in the former Sperry Gyroscope plant on Long Island. Those who put stock in omens should have been pleased with the symbolism: the peace organization occupying a site that had housed a supplier of war material and whose postal address was Lake Success. Assembly sessions were held in a converted indoor skating rink at Flushing Meadow, with diplomats and staff members shuttling between the two sites.

Big Power relations were deteriorating ominously. Still, there was a heady excitement about the United Nations. At least in the early years, New York was pleased to be looked on as the world's capital, especially during the fall 1946 Assembly session, which brought thousands of foreign dignitaries to the city. Crowds would gather outside the Waldorf-Astoria for a glimpse of the Saudi princes in their robes and the motorcades whipping through midtown.

The converted plant was an ugly, sprawling collection of jerry-built offices and miles of corridors. There was a cafeteria, which everybody used at times, and a diplomats' lounge, which was more than a mere watering hole. Here diplomacy was conducted in quiet corners. Meeting rooms and offices were all on one floor, creating a certain intimacy—and a chance for a close-up look at men and women engaged in a historic adventure.

Where the United Nations would make its permanent home was a major preoccupation for the delegates and for Lie and his staff. A search committee toured Westchester towns and found that some were downright hostile to the notion of playing host to the organization. The members considered San Francisco fondly. Too far for the Soviets. Philadelphia? "How can you put the capital of the world in a town that has both baseball clubs in last place?" quipped Herbert Evatt, the Australian foreign minister. A proffered gift from John D. Rockefeller, Jr., of

Objects to Selection: Prescott Bush acted as moderator of a stormy two-hour meeting in Greenwich [Connecticut], as a wave of protests arose today from the area tentatively picked as headquarters of the United Nations Organization. Bush said his neighbors "feel the site might be better in an area where it is wanted."

—*New York Journal-American,* **1946**

The Secretariat is a masterly example of the power of architecture to express monumentality by the use of the rectangle alone. It is a triumph of unadorned proportion.

—**George Howe,** *Architectural Forum,* **1950**

I will say that the Secretariat building seems to me a superficial aesthetic triumph and an architectural failure....Whereas modern architecture began with the true precept that form follows function, and that an organic form must respect every human function, this new office building is based on the theory that even if no symbolic purpose is served, function should be sacrificed to form.

—**Lewis Mumford,** *The New Yorker,* **1951**

TOP LEFT *A 1946 drawing by Hugh Ferriss of Walter K. Harrison's concept for X-City, a development William Zeckendorf of Webb and Knapp was planning for the East River site prior to the UN purchase. Elements of the self-contained city—though not the futuristic airstrip and dock—were incorporated into the UN headquarter's final design.*

BOTTOM LEFT *Members of the UN site selection committee for the permanent headquarters survey the Blue Hills reservation near Boston, one of 16 US sites considered before New York City was chosen in December 1946.*

ABOVE *An international team of renowned architects, who considered more than 50 designs, shows its final model for the new UN headquarters. From left to right: G. A. Soilleux, Australia; Howard Robertson, United Kingdom; Gaston Brunfaut, Belgium; Jean Antoniades, Greece; Wallace K. Harrison, director of planning, United States; Ernest Cormier, Canada; Julio Vilamajo, Uruguay; Oscar Niemeyer, Brazil; and Josef Havlicek, Czechoslovakia. Charles Le Corbusier of France is not pictured.*

RIGHT *A 1946 sketch by Charles Le Corbusier for New York headquarters hints at the final design.*

This memorandum sets forth the terms and conditions of the offer made by me in my letter to you dated December 10, 1946. I have acquired a firm offer from Webb and Knapp, Inc. to sell to the United Nations within thirty days from December 10, 1946 at $8,500,000, the following property between First Avenue and Franklin D. Roosevelt Drive: 1) The western portion of the block between 42nd and 43rd Streets. 2) All of the four blocks between 43rd and 47th Streets. 3) Two small parcels in the block between 47th and 48th Streets.

In addition representatives of the City of New York have assured me of the desire and willingness of the City to acquire and give to the United Nations the balance of the block between 47th and 48th Streets.

To make possible the acquisition of this property by the United Nations, should they decide to accept said offer and to make it the site of their permanent headquarters, I hereby offer to give to the UN the sum of $8,500,000 on the following terms and conditions: a) That the gift shall be made at the time of the closing of the purchase of said property. b) That the City of New York shall agree to give to the UN 43rd, 44th, 45th, 46th and 47th

Streets between First Ave and Franklin D. Roosevelt Drive upon terms which shall permit the UN to close any or all thereof to passage and otherwise to use them for its own purposes without restriction or limitation. c) That the City of New York shall agree to acquire to give absolutely to the UN all the balance of that city block bounded by First Ave, 47th, 48th Streets and Franklin D. Roosevelt Drive not covered by the firm offer of Webb and Knapp, Inc. d) That the City of New York shall agree to give to the UN all rights to bulkheads and piers along the river frontage of the East River between 42nd and 48th Streets. e) That each of the said agreements of the City of New York shall have been concluded in form satisfactory to the parties in interest at or prior to the time of the making of my said gift. f) That prior to the making of my said gift, assurances satisfactory to my attorneys shall have been given to me that the said gift from me will be free and clear of all taxes of the United States, the State of New York, or any other taxing authority having jurisdiction with respect thereto.

—John D. Rockefeller, Jr.

$8.5 million to purchase an 18-acre site on Manhattan's East side resolved the issue.

Designing the structures was another matter. For months speculation ran riot. There were reports that the theme would be Mayan. An Egyptian artist offered a design for a capitol with its own riverside dock, and sketched in a few feluccas. Wallace K. Harrison, the architect in charge of planning, drew a rough pen sketch on a tablecloth. A newsman whipped the cloth off and photographed the drawing, and the picture ran in *The New York Times*. The soaring Secretariat building, flanked by a low-lying domed Assembly, was recognizable in the crude sketch.

LEFT *Clearing the way for construction of the 39-story headquarters meant tearing down old slaughterhouses on the Turtle Bay site. To close the purchase deal, UN officials had to sign a clause promising not to kill cattle at their new location.*

BOTTOM LEFT *A simple, typewritten letter from John D. Rockefeller, Jr., completed an $8.5-million deal for title to the UN headquarters site in New York.*

ABOVE *New York City Mayor William O'Dwyer (right) presents UN Secretary-General Trygve Lie with the deed for seven acres of land that completed the future site of UN headquarters. New York power-brokers Robert Moses (second from left) and Francis Cardinal Spellman (fourth from left) are among those looking on.*

RIGHT *After depositing copies of the UN Charter and the Universal Declaration of Human Rights inside, Secretary-General Trygve Lie (left) and chief architect Wallace K. Harrison seal the cornerstone at the new UN headquarters during a ceremony marking the fourth anniversary of the United Nations in October 1949.*

SOMETIMES THE UNITED NATIONS SEEMED LESS ABOUT GOVERNMENTS and issues than about people. And what personalities they were! What a thrill to watch Eleanor Roosevelt hurrying along, usually trailed by two young State Department advisers.

When foreign diplomats addressed her in formal sessions, they frequently spoke of the United Nations as her late husband's legacy to the world, and she would acknowledge the tribute with a nod. But she was very much her own person—sometimes too much so for the American delegation of which she was a member.

There was the day she made the impromptu observation, in a small committee discussion, that aid to Chiang Kai-shek was "water down the

drain." The press, which had been covering more important sessions or just dozing, caught up with her in a corridor. While American advisers tried to explain away this seeming break with Washington policy, she stood listening and then said quietly, "If I said it, I guess I said it."

She also took on a Soviet spokesman who, during a debate on freedom of information, attacked the "war-mongering American press" and demanded a treaty to curb their evil ways. When he had finished talking, she leaned across the conference table to explain to her "young Soviet friend" that, while the free press might have its failings, "the controlled press is like an egg—part bad, all bad."

On another occasion, she was compelled to explain Washington's view that the United Nations International Children's Emergency Fund, which had done admirable work in relieving suffering, was no longer in an "emergency" situation and should begin winding up its work. The position infuriated Pakistani diplomat Ahmed Bokhari, who retorted angrily that, with the European war over, the United States was willing to see Asian children die of malnutrition.

Mrs. Roosevelt looked shaken and conveyed her dismay to Washington; reports had it that she threatened to resign. In any event, the United States backed away from its demands, and the organization known as UNICEF remains one of the gems in the international aid system. Mrs. Roosevelt's personal contribution was the unanimous approval of the Universal Declaration of Human Rights, which she had seen through committee, at an Assembly session in Paris in 1948.

There were many others who made their impact in those early years. Pakistan's Bokhari, a professional dancer in his youth, went on to become an under secretary-general, a rather unconventional one, who could make brilliant conversation but also enjoyed shocking his listeners. Often, after a long meeting, he would turn up at a dinner party wearing a rough peasant's cloak pulled over his head and spend an hour sitting on the floor, reciting verse or playing tunes on a shepherd's pipe.

The Philippines for years was represented at Assembly openings by its ebullient foreign minister, Carlos P. Romulo, who had more friends in the press than any other diplomat. (One American newsman named his son in Romulo's honor.) Informal and gregarious, General Romulo on occasion didn't mince words. Once, after a meeting with Latino delegates whose conduct he thought had been less than statesmanlike, he wagged his finger at them and admonished them to shape up. "Other-

"You know why they built it that way, like a match box on end"? said a taxi driver approaching the UN building in New York, "They did it so that, when they want to, they can strike a match down its side and the whole thing will go up in smoke."

The UN building does resemble a match box. And, unfortunately, many Americans *would* like to see the whole organization go up in smoke. But if they knew it as I do, if they could see its accomplishments with their own eyes, I think they would feel differently....

[T]he UN *is* a sounding board for communist propaganda, and for anticommunist propaganda, too. That is what it was designed to be: a place where political opinions of all kinds could be expressed in words, rather than bullets. The hope was that differences among nations could be resolved by words, rather than bullets.

Possibly there are "spies and foreign agents" in the Secretariat and the delegations, although an astute intelligence office could surely think of more useful tasks for its operatives....

Each member nation is allowed a certain number of permanent employees on the UN staff. The number assigned to Russia is between 120 and 130. But the actual number of Russian representatives employed in the UN secretariat is *twenty!*

Despite repeated requests, the UN has been unable to inveigle more "spies and foreign agents" out of Moscow. During World War II, the USSR lost so many experts of various sorts that it cannot spare any more for the UN.

—Eleanor Roosevelt, *See,* **1952**

TOP LEFT *Soviet Premier Nikita S. Khrushchev's appearance at the 15th UN General Assembly in 1960—with his fist-pounding, shoe-banging antics—is one of the best-remembered moments in UN history.*

ABOVE *Eleanor Roosevelt and Nikita Khrushchev at
UN headquarters in 1959.*

AP/Wide World Photos

wise," he said, "you'll be just banana republics." On another occasion, when he was serving as president of the Assembly, he told Soviet Foreign Minister Andrei Vyshinsky that his drawn-out speeches were losing the audience: "Anything important should go into the first 10 minutes, because no one really listens after that."

The India–Pakistan conflict over Kashmir went down in United Nations annals not only as a successful exercise in tamping down war, but also as one of the longest debates by two equally matched disputants—Krishna Menon of India and Sir Mohammed Zafrulla Khan of Pakistan.

It was during this debate that Menon noticed the British delegate, Sir Pierson Dixon, scribbling, and snapped, "You could at least listen to my words. I've listened to your boring speeches."

A few hours later, a somewhat chastened Menon took the floor and, in a quivering voice calculated to express humility, extolled

ABOVE In search of a permanent home: Movers shuttle office furniture from the UN's temporary headquarters at Hunter College in New York City to a new facility in Lake Success on Long Island in 1946. The UN remained there until 1950.

TOP RIGHT Jan Smuts, South African prime minister (center), arrives at Flushing Meadow, NY, in 1946 for a session of the first UN General Assembly. An unidentified military attaché is at left.

RIGHT The UN staff at Lake Success gives Secretary-General Trygve Lie a warm homecoming after his five-week trip to meet with European leaders in 1950.

28

rior to the first vote ever cast by the United Nations, in the gymnasium of New York City's Hunter College in the spring of 1946, an inspection of the simple wooden ballot box revealed a handwritten note:

"May I, who have had the privilege of fabricating this ballot box, cast the first vote? May God be with every member of the United Nations Organization, and through your noble efforts bring lasting peace to us all—all over the world."

—Paul Antonio, Mechanic, March 22, 1946

the British delegate. The effect was lost when the microphone picked up a brisk aside to his aide: "What else do I have to take back?"

The same debate also produced an oft-told blooper: Pakistan's chief delegate, ticking off the alleged misdeeds of Indian troops, charged that sikhs had come down from the hills, plundering and killing, and had raped 3,000 women.

A stenotypist, recording the charge, turned "sikhs" into "six," which an editor then "corrected" to read "600 men."

It didn't take the public long to discover that there was a show going on that could be interesting watching. Early on, in 1946, Soviet delegate Andrei Gromyko became a drawing card with visitors by marching out of a Security Council session that was considering Iran's charges of Soviet interference. This was the first outright show of Soviet intransigence and seemed to both shock and intrigue the public. Gromyko—typically described by the press as dour, scowling, veto-wielding and stubborn—remained a leading attraction, and "*Nyet*" became a favorite tabloid headline.

The public came to watch Gromyko, but it came to listen to the American delegate, Adlai E. Stevenson, widely regarded as one of the body's most eloquent orators. Few of his admirers were aware that Stevenson often suffered bouts of anxiety before making a major speech and would claim to be losing his voice. A UN aide discovered it was

wise to keep throat spray around, just in case. Stevenson liked to recall that he was one of the UN's "jubilant midwives" at the San Francisco conference and that he had watched the organization through its toddler days in London and New York. Years later, returning to the United Nations as American ambassador, he was a party to one of its most memorable events—the 1962 Council session called after the United States charged that the Soviets were secretly installing missiles in Cuba that could deliver nuclear warheads. Stevenson, equipped with aerial photographs, made a blistering reply to the Soviet denial by Valerian Zorin. "Do you, Ambassador Zorin, deny that the USSR has placed and is placing medium- and intermediate-range missiles and sites in Cuba? Yes or no? Don't wait for the translation. Yes or no?"

The Soviet delegate, who had been listening to the Russian translation of Stevenson's words, retorted that he was not in an American courtroom. "You are in the courtroom of world opinion," said Stevenson. "I am prepared to wait for my answer until hell freezes over."

The crisis was eventually resolved by a direct exchange between President John F. Kennedy and Premier Nikita S. Khrushchev, with the United Nations helping both sides to back away more or less gracefully.

Leo Rosenthal Collection/UN Archives

As the Cold War grew icier, it became all too clear that the United Nations would not be able to function as its planners intended. But this was not readily apparent in the early days, when world leaders came to the Assembly each fall and assigned some of their top diplomats as ambassadors.

THE FIRST WAR TO PREOCCUPY THE UNITED NATIONS BROKE OUT TWO years after the organization's founding. In 1947 Britain decided it could no longer cope with rising violence in its Palestine mandate and dropped the crisis on the General Assembly, which approved a partition plan calling for separate Arab and Jewish states with an internationalized Jerusalem. In a dramatic meeting, Arab members walked out of the Assembly hall. A few months later, the new Jewish state of Israel was proclaimed. Egypt invaded, and the war was on.

AP/Wide World Photos

Over the years (and four Arab-Israeli wars), the Palestine issue was a major preoccupation. "The Palestine problem has twisted the organization's image and fragmented its reputation and prestige as no other issue has," wrote UN Under

The United Nations does sometimes behave like a four-year-old. More than one Honorable Delegate, oblivious of the fact that he has all the world for a stage, has walked out of meetings in a huff. Some have used the rostrum of the Assembly itself as a vantage point from which to hurl verbal abuse at nations, ideologies and sometimes even at mere mortal men, mostly fellow-delegates who have aroused their ire or called them names other than their own. Not so long ago, we were treated to an unedifying spectacle when some delegates, who shall here be nameless, refused to take part in the discussion of an issue on which they were called upon to state their side. They ignored the whole proceeding, sulking in their seats like children who, finding that they can't have things their own way, refuse to abide by the rules of the game.

—Carlos P. Romulo, *United Nations World,* **1950**

A pro at reducing international tension: A quip from General Carlos Romulo, Philippine ambassador to the UN (center), triggers smiles from Soviet Foreign Minister Andrei Vyshinsky (left) and Secretary-General Trygve Lie after a stormy meeting of the General Assembly in 1949.

BOTTOM LEFT *Sir Zafrulla Khan of Pakistan (second from left) and Prince Abdallah of Yemen (right) sign the papers admitting their countries into the United Nations in 1947, with Secretary-General Lie (left) and UN Legal Counsel Hanna Saba (second from right) on hand for the ceremony.*

TOP RIGHT *Just before making an impassioned 1956 address to the General Assembly calling for the withdrawal of foreign troops from his country, Egyptian delegate Omar Loufti debates a point with India's ambassador to the UN, Krishna Menon.*

BOTTOM RIGHT *Sir Selwyn Lloyd, British delegate to the United Nations (left), shortly before a heated debate with Soviet Foreign Minister Andrei Vyshinsky (right) for trying to dictate policy in Korea in 1953.*

Secretary-General Brian Urquhart in 1987 in *A Life in Peace and War*.

But it also led to the organization of the UN observers to supervise truces, which became a key mechanism of the later armistice arrangements and the basis for UN peacekeeping operations. Ralph Bunche, an American who came to the United Nations via the State Department, was the main architect of the Middle East peacekeeping operation and in 1950 won a Nobel Peace Prize for the achievement.

Although remembered chiefly for these accomplishments, Bunche was influential years earlier in the behind-the-scenes negotiations that led to the creation of the Trusteeship Council, whose mission was to oversee 11 colonial territories and guide them toward independence. What emerged was the UN's first real involvement in encouraging decolonization, a process that would spur nationalism in Africa, changing forever the balance of power in the United Nations.

Creating the council involved laborious negotiations over paragraphs, sometimes over a few words, which dragged on late into the night. Occasionally, Bunche would slip over to the nearly deserted press area for a furtive cigarette until the weary diplomats, in rare unanimity,

voted solemnly to drop the smoking ban.

The same year Bunche won his Nobel Peace Prize, the UN found itself caught up in war—one that damaged its standing in non-Western eyes and impaired the credibility of its secretary-general. Like many delegates, Trygve Lie regarded it as an anomaly that China's seat was occupied by the nationalists, who controlled only Taiwan, rather than by the mainland Chinese, and he tried futilely to get Western ministers to discuss the issue. The Soviets had demonstrated their objection to the nationalists by walking out of the Security Council and other bodies.

Their absence proved to be a gross miscalculation. When the North Koreans invaded the South, Lie called on the Council members to act against the aggressor. President Truman had already ordered American forces to come to the South's aid when the Council met, and

without a Soviet veto to block it, the Council voted for military action against the Northern aggressors. The Soviets never forgave Lie for his role and blocked his re-election, although he managed to stay on for a three-year "extension" of his term. Lie later said that he had "often wondered whether there might have been any Korean War at all if the Peking government had been permitted to represent China in the spring of 1950."

His last years in office were

ISRAEL

TOP LEFT *Ralph Bunche, acting UN mediator in Palestine (center), confers with General A. Lundström, the UN's chief military observer in Haifa, in 1948.*

LEFT *Delegates from the Arab countries huddle in 1947 to discuss a compromise plan on Palestine. Left to right: Victor Khoury of Lebanon, Faris El-Khouri of Syria, Royal Prince Faisal ibn Abdul Aziz of Saudi*

Arabia, Charles Malik of Lebanon, Mahmoud Hassan Pasha of Egypt and Ali Jawdat of Iraq. Fadhil Jamali of Iraq is hidden behind Jawdat.

ABOVE *Elated Israelis, including Abba Eban, seated center, beam as their country becomes the 59th UN member by a vote of 37 to 12, with nine abstentions, in May 1949.*

ABOVE *Nasrollah Entezam of Iran (left), Sir Benegal Rau of India (center) and Mohamed Fawzi Bey of Egypt huddle just prior to the General Assembly's overwhelming vote in February 1951 to label the People's Republic of China an aggressor in Korea.*

LEFT *In October 1950 the UN sponsored a blood drive at the UN's Lake Success headquarters for international forces in Korea. Andrew Cordier, executive assistant to the secretary-general, was among the first to give. Nurse Margaret Callaghan checks his blood pressure before taking a pint.*

made difficult by charges leveled by Senator Joseph McCarthy that spies were operating in the United Nations. Lie hoped to defuse the crisis by allowing McCarthy's people to interrogate the American staff and to enter into the building and fingerprint them. Abe Feller, one of Lie's trusted legal advisers, broke under the strain and committed suicide—a victim, said the secretary-general, of the McCarthy witch-hunt. Lie resigned in 1953, saying "it was time for a change."

Lie was a man of volatile temperament whose emotions were readily visible. His successor, Dag Hammarskjöld, was the opposite. Even to staff members who worked with him for years, the impassive Swedish diplomat remained an enigma. But everyone seemed to agree that he was brilliant, with talents that might help restore the crumbling image of the United Nations.

The staff Hammarskjöld inherited had been badly demoralized by McCarthy's tactics. He set about trying to rebuild confidence. Although visibly embarrassed by the effort, he visited staff members in their offices and arranged for a Staff Day celebration before the busy Assembly, using the occasion for a serious talk,

ABOVE *In April 1953, at Stockholm's Brumma Airport, Dag Hammarskjöld boards a flight bound for New York, where he will be sworn in as the UN's second secretary-general.*

RIGHT *The first UN Secretariat Staff Day was celebrated in 1953 with an evening of music and entertainment that included performances by (center), Danny Kaye, and singers Marion Anderson and Enzio Pinza. UN Secretary-General Dag Hammarskjöld is at left.*

which staff members welcomed. They said it made them feel they were truly sharing in the United Nations' operations.

To the surprise of many, he cast himself as master of ceremonies at the 1953 annual staff party, introduced Danny Kaye and almost managed to look as if he enjoyed it all. On another occasion, a staff member with the manner of a British nanny approached and insisted he take a turn on the dance floor. As they waltzed stiffly by, she could be heard whispering, "One-two, one-two. Pick up your feet."

About all that was known about the new secretary-general was that he came from a family of diplomats, had a reputation as a financial wizard and negotiator and had cultivated tastes in music and art. He was unmarried, had few close associates and preferred privacy. "The private man should disappear...the international civil servant should take his place," he said. Private diplomacy was his forte.

His reports and his responses at news conferences were often a puzzlement and sometimes a disaster to those searching for news. He preferred it that way. Trygve Lie was pleased when some of the clumsy remarks he made in speeches were polished before appearing in print. Not so Dag Hammarskjöld, who at times indulged in deliberate obfuscation. "I know you're good," he once told staff writers, "but don't change a word."

Because President Eisenhower found it expedient to use Hammarskjöld's talents, he was able to expand the authority given to the secretary-general far beyond that of his predecessor. At Washington's request, Hammarskjöld went to Peking in 1954 to try to free American pilots shot down in the Korean War and sentenced as spies. The airmen were eventually released, and he received worldwide acclaim. Then the United States asked his help in shoring up the Middle East armistice agreements, which led him to undertake "shuttle" diplomacy, traveling back and forth between meetings with President Gamal Abdel Nasser in Egypt and Prime Minister David Ben-Gurion in Israel.

But a new Middle East crisis loomed after the United States ceased helping Egypt to build the Aswan High Dam. President Nasser, national pride at stake, retaliated by seizing the Suez Canal Company from its British and

United Nations

French owners in the summer of 1956. An Israeli reprisal raid on Egypt gave Britain and France the orchestrated opportunity to move in with air forces. The General Assembly ordered a cease-fire and supervisory measures and gave Hammarskjöld 48 hours to put together an international contingency to do the supervising. Hammarskjöld turned to Bunche, saying, "Now go get a force together."

No sooner had the United Nations succeeded in preventing an escalation of the conflict over the canal than it was confronted with reports of an uprising in Hungary against the Soviet Union's presence. The Assembly called for the UN to send investigators to Hungary, but within a week the Soviets had crushed the revolt, and the Soviet-controlled regime in Budapest refused them entry.

It was not until 1960 that Hammarskjöld, like Trygve Lie, came into open conflict with Moscow. This time the issue was the newly independent Congo. After a trip to Africa, Hammarskjöld had returned convinced that the United Nations must help the new state survive and sent Bunche to attend the Congo's independence day celebrations and assess the country's needs. Within days, the Congolese troops mutinied and the former Belgian colonial authority used the occasion to send in troops to protect the European population. The Congo's mineral-rich Katanga province seceded, obviously with European support.

Again, the United Nations mustered a force to restore order, but Hammarskjöld refused to allow it to be used to quell the Katanga revolt. The Soviets opened an all-out attack on the secretary-general, demand-

ing his replacement with a three-member directorate. The Africans rallied behind Hammarskjöld, giving him a standing ovation when he boldly refused to quit. But not long after, Hammarskjöld died in an air crash on his way to meet Katangese officials in a renewed effort to resolve the Congo's difficulties.

Years after his death, UN staff members still felt his influence. "You would think he left us a presence," said one official who worked with Hammarskjöld. The word "presence" was a deliberate choice, because it was the term Hammarskjöld used to describe the element he tried to employ to defuse each crisis he tackled.

IN ITS 50 YEARS OF LIFE, THE UNITED NATIONS HAS UNDERGONE PROfound changes. One obvious change is its size. From an organization of 51 members, its ranks have swelled to 185. Foundations have been laid for nine additional flagpoles outside the UN enclave. (Hammarskjöld, who suggested placements for 100 poles when the Assembly Hall was undergoing expansion in 1961 would have been astonished at today's numbers.) Early on, UN diplomats informally agreed that an applicant had to have a population of at least 100,000 to be considered. Today tiny Palau, with about 16,000, is a member.

ABOVE *Secretary-General Dag Hammarskjöld briefs the press in 1955 on his return after an historic trip to China to meet with Premier Chou En-lai about American airmen and other UN soldiers held captive in that country.*

RIGHT *In Uppsala, Sweden, Secretary-General U Thant pays his respects at the grave of predecessor Dag Hammarskjöld, in May 1962.*

When Dag Hammarskjöld and 15 others died, I raced to Salisbury from my post in Geneva to help arrange for the return of all the victims.

Facing tight deadlines arising from scheduled plans for funerals, including a Hammarskjöld service in Sweden to be attended by world leaders, we at last managed to ready a huge chartered aircraft, converted into a flying funeral chapel. Each of the 16 caskets was covered by the appropriate national flag, and the pitifully meager packets of personal effects were clustered nearby.

The pilot and I worked feverishly on flight plans, often with only the sketchiest information. In a bizarre exchange, he acknowledged that he had no information on the length of runways at Malmo Airport, in southern Sweden. When I found a reference in my World Airways Guide, he was pleased: "Good. Sounds as if we can get in okay, and maybe even get out again."

The long and arduous flight across half the world then began. The first stop was Leopoldville, base for the United Nations Operation in the Congo. Hundreds of UN troops and staff, Congolese leaders, and the diplomatic corps had gathered at the airport for a simple and moving ceremony of homage for the secretary-general and his companions who had left from the same spot only a few days before. Only 30 minutes after landing, we headed north in the African night, bound for Geneva where thousands waited at the airport to pay tribute and where the first of the flag-draped caskets would be transferred to the family of the secretary-general's brilliant young legal adviser.

A few hours later, in the small hours of the morning, we were airborne again, headed for Malmo to bring home the crew of the ill-fated aircraft. The stop was very brief, but again marked by a simple ceremony, after which we headed for Stockholm, where the world's attention was now centered.

Soon after taking off, six Swedish fighter planes took up position around our aircraft as an escort of honor. As we descended to the Stockholm airport, we saw that all of Sweden had come to a complete halt, all traffic frozen in place. Touching down precisely at noon, as planned, we found the huge airport completely still, the only sound coming from the muffled drums of the honor guard which quickly surrounded the plane.

—John A. Olver

Financial problems are not new, only more serious than ever before. Members owe $1.9 billion for peacekeeping operations alone. The budget for the Secretariat has grown to $1.3 billion. There just is not enough money for needed repairs, and the United Nations these days looks, frankly, in need of an overhaul. Even the murals by Portinari look faded. New gifts are being discouraged: The UN is running out of wall space.

Meanwhile, security needs have imposed tight restrictions on visits, particularly since the 1993 bombing of the World Trade Center and evidence that the United Nations was on the terrorists' list. For the same reason, the meditation room is locked and access to it restricted. The gardens—once a favorite site for delegates, staff members and visitors—have been closed so that massive repairs, necessitated by leaks and crumbling concrete, can be carried out below ground. Workmen are racing, hoping to finish before the anniversary.

There still are staff members around who remember the early years. The Mohicans, a club of Secretariat members whose service began at Hunter College, has about 100 members. And many have held on to their commitment to the United Nations' vision.

Oliver Lundquist was busy the day the UN Charter was signed. He had come from Washington after preliminary preparation, on loan from the Office of Strategic Services, to help with the preparations for the signing ceremony.

Diplomats had to be rehearsed for their roles. A sheet of parchment was produced on which they practiced their signatures. Lundquist still has it. Collectors have offered impressive sums. Universities would love it. Lundquist has other plans. The paper will go to the Franklin D. Roosevelt Library in Hyde Park, he says, adding, "That's where it belongs."

CHAPTER TWO

Keeping the Peace

Keeping the Peace

Michael J. Berlin

TODAY WHEN PEOPLE AROUND THE WORLD VISUALIZE THE UNITED Nations keeping the peace, they share a common image—the blue helmets worn by soldiers of many nations. But what has become a global symbol was created in a moment of inspired improvisation at the outset of the UN's first large-scale peacekeeping operation, one that prevented a regional conflict from igniting a major war.

The year was 1956. Egypt, stung by the cancellation of Western financing for the Aswan High Dam, nationalized the Suez Canal Company. The British and French, eager to regain control of an economic lifeline they had overseen for decades under an international agreement, forged a secret pact with Israel, which wanted to secure its southern flank against *fedayeen* raids from Egyptian-controlled territory. The Israelis attacked on October 29; two days later the British and French demanded that both sides pull back, then dispatched their own troops and began bombing Egyptian installations near the canal. Moscow hinted at intervention; Washington, taken by surprise, looked for diplomatic ways to defuse the crisis.

When British and French vetoes blocked the UN Security Council, Canada's Lester Pearson proposed on November 4 that the General Assembly authorize a UN Emergency Force that would go beyond previous UN military observation missions by interposing entire military units between combatants. Secretary-General Dag Hammarskjöld negotiated an agreement for the multinational UN troops to replace invading Israeli, British and French soldiers in the Sinai Peninsula and Gaza Strip. This deft piece of diplomacy enabled the invaders to leave Egyptian territory while saving face. It also eased pressure on Moscow and Washington to intervene.

Negotiating the agreement was one thing, making it work on the ground was another. How could the United Nations generate a flow of supplies to 6,000 troops from nine countries? The improvised solution

LEFT *A UN military observer stops to ask for directions to the cease-fire line separating Pakistani and Indian forces during a territorial dispute over Kashmir in 1955.*

ABOVE *US Ambassador Henry Cabot Lodge, Jr. (center), confers with Secretary-General Dag Hammarskjöld during a Security Council meeting on the Middle East crisis in July 1958. Meanwhile, Dr. Tingfu Tsiang, ambassador from the Republic of China to the UN (left), catches up on the news.*

PREVIOUS SPREAD *One of the earliest peacekeeping missions: A 1947 UN Balkan Commission of Inquiry, including members from Norway, the USSR and France, investigates border violations in Greece. The group traveled to the Greek frontier to meet Albanian, Greek, Bulgarian and Yugoslavian parties involved in the dispute.*

TOP *Norwegian UN peacekeepers arriving in Port Said, Egypt, in 1956 are welcomed by departing British soldiers, who were leaving as part of a cease-fire agreement in the Suez.*

was to buy goods from the 17 ships blocked inside the Suez Canal. Meanwhile, to distinguish the neutral Canadians from the invading British (who wore identical uniforms), the United Nations borrowed thousands of American helmet liners and spray-painted them UN blue—and so, 11 years after the founding of the United Nations, its most dashing symbol came into being.

THE PRINCIPLE THAT THE GENERAL ASSEMBLY CAN ACT TO KEEP THE peace—as it did in creating the Emergency Force—had been established in 1950, when North Korea invaded South Korea. At the time, the Soviets were boycotting the Security Council to protest the majority's refusal to give China's seat, held by Chiang Kai-shek's nationalist government in Taiwan, to the newly established People's Republic. When Soviet Ambassador Yakov Malik returned to the Council and vetoed further action on Korea, Washington turned to the General Assembly, which adopted a "Uniting for Peace" resolution. Drawn up by American Secretary of State Dean Acheson, the resolution spelled out the Assembly's authority to take action if the Council cannot deal with a threat to

ABOVE *Making way for the peace-keepers: A troop train arrives in Port Said, Egypt, in 1956.*

RIGHT *With a refinery burning in the distance, UN peacekeepers arrive in Port Said by ship in November 1956, just as the UN-administered cease-fire went into effect.*

On Dag Hammarskjöld's first visit to his UN Emergency Force troops in the Gaza strip during the Christmas holiday of 1957, he was taken directly from the Gaza airstrip, where he landed, to visit the Brazilian company which had the responsibility of oversight of the Gaza/Israel line which actually crossed the airstrip. The Brazilian company commander had an overlay chart and gave a short talk in heavily accented English about the duties of his company. When he was through, he asked the secretary-general if he would like a cup of coffee, adding, with deliberate modesty, "As you know, we're from Brazil and we hope you'll like Brazilian coffee."

The SG's party was surrounded by liaison officers from other national contingents making up UNEF and by representatives of local information media. The SG smiled appreciatively at the Brazilian Captain and indicated his pleasure at the prospect of coffee. A bright young liaison officer from the Colombian battalion spoke up: "Yes sir, Mr. Secretary-General, here you will have the second-best coffee in the world! When you visit the Colombian battalion, you will be able to compare our *arabica* coffee with the Brazilian *robusta*!"

And one of the TV fellows from Egypt pitched in: "And of course you know that you are in the land famous for its so-called Turkish coffee." Hammarskjöld kept nodding and smiling and was silent.

But then another newsman shouted, "By the way, Mr. Secretary-General, which type of coffee do you personally prefer?"

We in the UN Secretariat were fascinated by the question and eager to see how the SG would handle this one. He said simply that in his opinion "good coffees are like fine wines—each appropriate to its own occasion!"

—R. Bruce Stedman

peace because of a veto by one or more of the five permanent members (Britain, China, France, the US and the USSR). The Korean War saw the first use of force by troops under the UN flag, when the Security Council created a "UN Command." The troops were in fact not under UN command at all; the US was in full control.

IN ITS EARLIEST YEARS, THE SECURITY COUNCIL WAS THE FOCAL POINT for efforts to keep the peace by fact-finding and mediation. It sent commissions to Indonesia and Kashmir to investigate complaints brought before it and to negotiate differences. The General Assembly sent similar commissions to the Balkans, Korea and Palestine.

The Assembly partitioned Palestine, a British mandate, into Jewish and Arab sectors in 1947. Fighting erupted when surrounding Arab countries rejected the UN decision and invaded the newly proclaimed state of Israel.

To monitor one truce in the fighting, the Security Council created the United Nations Truce Supervision Organization, the first full-fledged UN peacekeeping operation, with military officers on the UN payroll and under control of the secretary-general. Although that truce did not last long, UNTSO became the longest-lived and most versatile of the 35 peacekeeping ventures established in the United Nations' first half-century.

The initial round of Arab-Israeli fighting was ended by UN mediator Ralph Bunche, an American who was instrumental in drafting the UN Charter provisions for trusteeship and decolonization at San Francisco in 1945. His tactic in dealing with Middle East conflict was to isolate the negotiators in the cold, damp and remote Hôtel des Roses on

the island of Rhodes, with its execrable food and bad communications. There, Arab and Israeli officers ate together and sometimes sat across the table in direct negotiations. But it was Bunche who made the proposals. With a keen sense of what each side needed and could live with, he drafted and redrafted armistice texts that were impeccably balanced. Israeli delegate Walter Eytan wrote that Bunche "was gifted, some thought almost a genius, at drafting; sooner or later he was able to contrive a formula to defeat almost any problem."

At one point Bunche wrote to his wife, Ruth: "I talk, argue, coax and threaten these stubborn people day and night....This is killing work. I haven't been out of the hotel for two weeks now."

The only evening recreation was billiards and Ping-Pong, and Bunche, a master at both since his student days at the University of California at Los Angeles, established psychological domination by beating all comers. He orchestrated pressure by calling in sanction threats from the Security Council or the major powers when he needed them, and by issuing his own threats to quit or go public over unreasonable demands.

Bunche, who came to personify the impartial international civil servant, ran the UN's peacekeeping operations from 1948 until his death in 1971. For the 1949 armistice agreements between Israel and its neighbors, he won a Nobel Peace Prize.

THE MOST POLITICALLY AND LOGISTICALLY COMPLEX OF ALL UN PEACE-keeping operations began in 1960 in the Congo, which slid toward anarchy shortly after Belgium granted it independence. After an army mutiny prompted the return of Belgian troops, Secretary-General Hammarskjöld—with joint Soviet and American backing—won Security Council authorization for a UN force. The UN operation in the Congo, which mustered almost 20,000 troops at its peak in 1961, did much

United Nations

more than keep the peace. Thousands of UN civilian "advisers" actually managed the country. "We ran the ministries, ensured the water supply, brought in Haitian judges, organized a central bank, kept the airport open, provided vaccinations and flew in food supplies," recalls George Sherry, the UN civilian representative in Elizabethville at the time.

ABOVE *Mustang fighter pilots from Australia—one of 16 UN member nations that sent troops to defend South Korea from the North—plot a mission in 1951.*

TOP RIGHT *A Thai soldier bids farewell to his family before boarding a troop ship in Bangkok destined for the Korean conflict. A large part of early peacekeeping units were made up of troops from smaller nations.*

MIDDLE RIGHT *Just freed by the North Koreans, American POWs await processing at Freedom Village in South Korea. They were among the first released in a 1953 prisoner exchange arranged by the United Nations.*

RIGHT *The Korean conflict formally ended with the ceremonial signing of a truce by Lieutenant General William K. Harrison of the United Nations Command and General Nam II of North Korea in an austere structure in Panmunjom. The communists had built it just for the occasion.*

51

LEFT *Sporting new uniforms and high spirits, United Nations guards, part of the UN observer group being established in Palestine, leave New York for their new Middle East assignment in June 1948.*

BELOW *Stunned on hearing the news of Count Folke Bernadotte's assassination in September 1948, members of the Security Council listen to eulogies. From left to right, in front: two unidentified delegates, Yakov Malik of the Soviet Union, Secretary-General Trygve Lie, Sir Alexander Cadogan of Great Britain and Assistant Secretary-General Arkady Sobolev of the Soviet Union.*

UN officials negotiated the withdrawal of foreign forces, pressured rival Congolese politicians to come to terms and ultimately imposed by force an end to the secession of the mineral-rich Katanga province under Moise Tshombe.

It was the UN's first venture into what later came to be called "nation-building," and also the first time that troops under UN command used force. By the time the United Nations left in 1964, 234 of its soldiers had been killed in the line of duty—the largest death toll in the UN's first half-century in an operation fully under its flag and its control.

While the United Nations succeeded in preserving unity in what is

now Zaire, it did so at an immense political cost. First the Soviets (who backed Patrice Lumumba, who had been overthrown as prime minister) and then the Western powers (who backed Katanga) were alienated by Hammarskjöld's insistence on supporting the central government.

ABOVE *UN peacekeepers help restore calm during a demonstration that turned violent outside UNEF headquarters in Port Said, Egypt, in March 1957.*

RIGHT *UN Under Secretary-General Ralph Bunche (center) meets with Major General E.L.M. Burns (left), commander of the first UN Emergency Force, and his staff, over a modest lunch at UNEF headquarters in Gaza in 1957.*

At one time there was trouble in one of the provinces, Kasai, and quite extraordinary measures had to be taken in order to save people from starving to death. At that time the UN was very bad off as far as transportation facilities. We had to have trucks. So, what we did was steal trucks from the Congolese army, who used them for mischief anyway, and painted them with the UN emblem. This, of course, was highly unorthodox, and you can imagine when the UN auditors started getting close to this sort of operation they became, should I say, a bit confused. For years...someone was writing to me about it and asking for receipts and checks and so forth. So, I said to him quite simply, "We stole them. We saved people and that was what the whole thing was about." We had to get the food to the people. If we had gone along with protocol they would have died, quite simply.

—Sture Linner, UN Oral History Collection

Hammarskjöld died in a plane crash in 1961, while on a mission to mediate a dispute, but the conflict lived on to plague his successor, a Burmese diplomat named U Thant. France, the Soviet Union and others refused to pay the costs of the operation (the total came to more than $600 million) and demanded that peacekeepers operate under Security Council command rather than under the secretary-general.

The issue was—and remains—how much sovereignty nation-states, especially those that are major powers, will yield to the United Nations. If, once a UN force is created, a major power cannot use its veto to control day-to-day operations, then the secretary-general or his field commander will have gained a significant degree of freedom and the institution will have become a major player in its own right.

A committee set up to resolve peacekeeping principles produced some common ground but failed to reconcile views on financing and control. The dispute nearly tore the United Nations apart in 1964–65, when the United States first forced—then backed away from—a showdown on whether those withholding their dues should lose their vote in the General Assembly. After 1965 there were no peacekeeping initiatives for eight years.

TOP LEFT *On his arrival in October 1962 at headquarters for UN forces (in background) in Leopold-ville, the Congo, Ralph Bunche is met by Officer-in-Charge Robert K. A. Gardiner (left). Bunche once described the Congo as "the toughest spot I've ever been in."*

LEFT *Reinforcements arrive in Elizabethville, the Congo, to back up UN troops under attack by the Katangese in December 1961. In back of the truck at rear are Katangese who are being detained for questioning.*

ABOVE *With his forces detaining 190 UN peacekeepers at the Hotel Europe (in background) in Jadotville in 1961, Katangan President Moise Tshombe (second from left) confers with UN Commandant Patrick Quinlan of Ireland (right) and another UN officer. Notebooks at the ready, David Halberstam (with dark glasses) of* The New York Times *and Peter Lynch of United Press observe. The UN troops were later released.*

The Congo in July was like the Marie Celeste—a large, fully equipped ship from which the crew had vanished and in which fear and utter disorder had already caused the breakdown of many essential services....In some cases, stenographers and office boys had overnight become chiefs of services without any real training for the job; nursing orderlies had become chief surgeons, and truck drivers had become directors of transportation....

Those of us lucky enough to take part in the first months of ONUC will certainly never forget it. To say that it was, and is, a unique operation is an understatement. For most of us it became an obsession—a constant source of enthusiasm, fascination, amazement, exasperation and sometimes, it must be admitted, of hopeless laughter. There was plenty to do, it was never dull; the words "usual" and "normal" had no meaning or currency whatsoever.

This group worked out of Room 410 in the Stanley Hotel and in spite of the size of the room in relation to the 24-hour-a-day crowd which filled it, a firm grasp had already been established on the tangled and writhing skein of Congo events.

Although a single over-worked telephone, which often disintegrated under the strain and at best led only to a capricious hotel switchboard, and the public telegraph service from an entirely disorganized post office were the group's only link with the outside world, indomitable resource and energy made such disadvantages seem trivial. This small group seemed to be, and perhaps was, the only fixed point in an otherwise totally fluid and changeable scene. Thus, ministers, ambassadors, refugees, journalists, soldiers and everyone else in Leopoldville with something on their mind (and most people had) converged like homing pigeons on Room 410. It was, on one occasion, the scene of an armed incursion by the mutinous army and on others the place where orders were given to the commanders of outgoing UN contingents. It was also Dr. Bunche's bedroom.

—**Brian Urquhart,** *Secretariat News*, **1960**

AP/Wide World Photos

Like all secretaries-general, U Thant took diplomatic initiatives on his own authority. His most successful was his first—during the 1962 Cuban missile crisis. When Washington announced a naval "quarantine" of Soviet ships ferrying missiles to Cuba and demanded that the missiles being installed there be withdrawn, Thant appealed to both superpowers to defuse the potential nuclear confrontation.

Soviet Premier Nikita S. Khrushchev agreed to Thant's appeal to hold back Soviet vessels, rather than to President John F. Kennedy's demand that he do so. Thant had saved Soviet face and created a breathing space. A later offer of UN inspections to verify the withdrawal of missiles was turned down by Cuban President Fidel Castro, and the crisis was ultimately resolved bilaterally by Washington and Moscow.

The most enduring controversy for Thant and the United Nations stemmed from the decision to withdraw the United Nations Emergency Force from the Sinai in 1967, at the demand of Egyptian President Gamal Abdel Nasser. There was no doubt that Egypt had the legal right to demand the withdrawal of UNEF—a withdrawal that led directly to the Six-Day War. Nasser also had the practical ability: Two UNEF contingents—the Indians and the Yugoslavs—had already pulled back from crucial zones without UN orders, and Egyptian units had already bypassed other UNEF troops and moved up to the Israeli border. Since UNEF had been created by the Assembly, Thant didn't take the issue to the Security Council. For that, and for failing to give diplomacy more time to work, he was blamed by Western critics.

TOP LEFT *Preparing for the worst: UN observers ready for a mission at the first training course held for UN peacekeepers in Strängnäs, Sweden, in 1965. Participants include: (from left) Major A. Linde of Denmark, Major Alpo Kantola of Finland, Lieutenant Colonel Leif Aarset of Norway, Major Reino Ritasaari of Finland and Captain John Norrlinder of Sweden.*

ABOVE *On United Nations Day 1964 in Gaza, Colonel Lazar Musicki, acting UN commander-in-chief of emergency forces, takes a salute from UN planes and members of a Canadian squadron.*

ABOVE *A Ghanaian soldier, one of 7,000 UN peacekeepers from 12 countries who set up a buffer zone in the Sinai just days after the violation of a cease-fire by Arab and Israeli troops in 1973.*

RIGHT *At a UN surveillance site—part of an "early warning" system established in the Sinai in 1975—an Indonesian peacekeeper monitors oil tanks near the Gulf of Suez while his Finnish colleagues keep up appearances.*

At the same time, the UN's reputation as a peacekeeper suffered, because a UN force had failed to serve its purpose at a critical moment. The reason for its failure is to be found in the very nature of peacekeeping: UN peace forces are invited guests; they can do their job only if the disputants wish to avoid a fight. If one side wants to do battle, and the big powers fail to twist its arms, peacekeepers are merely in the way.

IN 1973 SUPERPOWER CONFRONTATION LOOMED ONCE AGAIN WHEN A new outbreak of fighting between Israel and Egypt violated the cease-fire imposed by the Americans and Russians to end the Yom Kippur War—the fourth and biggest Arab-Israeli conflict. On October 24 there were reports that Soviet troops might be dropped into the battle zone to save Egypt's Third Army from encirclement. Washington responded that evening by declaring a military alert. Early on the morning of October 25, the eight Security Council members belonging to the non-aligned movement caucused and Yugoslav Ambassador Lazar Mosjov proposed a new UN peace force as an alternative to direct military action by the superpowers. The non-aligned group agreed to the US condition excluding troops of permanent members of the Security Council from being allowed in what became UNEF II—a deliberate attempt to prevent Soviet troops from participating in any military force. In return, US Secretary of State Henry Kissinger agreed to 36 Soviet officers joining the UN Truce Supervision Organization in Egypt and allowed the use of a Polish logistics contingent by UNEF II—the first time a Soviet-bloc nation contributed to peacekeeping. The resolution was adopted the same day.

Because of the continuing superpower dispute over financing and control, the Secretariat could make no contingency plans for peacekeeping operations. "If word got out that we were planning ahead," says Brian Urquhart, who succeeded Bunche as director of peacekeeping operations, "the Russians and French would have marched into the secretary-general's office and raised hell." So once again, as in the Sinai and the Congo, everything was improvised. In drawing up the ground rules for UNEF II, the peacekeeping staff—Urquhart, George Sherry and F. T. Liu—achieved in three hours, on the night of October 25, what Russian and American negotiators had failed to work out over a decade. They put on paper the definitive blueprint for a peacekeeping operation. The first UN units—Austrians, Finns and Swedes

borrowed from the UN force on Cyprus—were in the field in 17 hours.

That UN report essentially resolved the political battle over command and control of peacekeeping. It gave a degree of control to the secretary-general, leaving him in day-to-day command. But it granted the Security Council a short leash, requiring its consent to the appointment of the UNEF II commanding general and a Council vote every six months to renew the force's mandate. The mission of UNEF II was also spelled out in detail, as was its right to use force if necessary to resist "attempts by forceful means to prevent it from discharging" the duties set by the Security Council. The UNEF II blueprint became the model for all future peacekeeping operations.

The UN peacekeeping staff—a handful of impartial civil servants insulated over the years from governmental pressures and from politicized departments elsewhere in the Secretariat—was aided by a logistics genius, George Lansky, the Director of the UN Field Operations Service. Unlike a nation, the United Nations has no resource reservoir of its

ABOVE *On a trip to the Mideast, UN Secretary-General Kurt Waldheim winds up a meeting with, left to right: Roberto Guyer, under secretary-general for special political affairs; James Jonah, principal officer in the office for special political affairs; Brian Urquhart, under secretary-general for special political affairs and Major-General Ensio Siilasvuo, chief coordinator of the UN peacekeeping mission in the Middle East.*

RIGHT *In February 1977 UN Secretary-General Kurt Waldheim gets a tour of a heavily damaged section of Beirut from Abbas Hameih, chief of protocol for Lebanon's foreign ministry.*

In the early years, UN peacekeeping operated on a shoe-string budget. The Field Operations office, with a small staff of mostly former military personnel, coordinated the action. We knew what had to be accomplished, but had no directives, rules or regulations. Nor were there any warehouses, equipment or supplies. We had absolutely no experience to guide us in the logistics of supplying multination peacekeeping operations.

Our first requirement was to establish a reliable, independent communications network. The UN recruited radio operators and technicians from throughout the world. Two of these chaps were sent to the used radio equipment market in lower Manhattan with the limited funds at our disposal to purchase the most essential second-hand equipment they could get.

Problems arose at every turn. The chief ones were the lack of funds, and the difficulty, at times impossibility, of acquiring from commercial companies the supplies and components we so desperately needed.

We finally began demanding, urging, begging countries contributing peacekeeping forces to supply everything they would need on mission including vehicles, weapons, internal radio equipment and rations for an extensive period.

With each country bringing its own equipment and supplies, other problems arose, including incompatibility of spare parts for all the different makes of jeeps, trucks and weapons.

We had to supply a multitude of items for the UN troops, all in UN blue. There was the headgear—helmets and liners, berets and caps, shoulder patches and scarfs, decals, for all types of vehicles and buildings, and UN flags, of different sizes.

We received the most extraordinary requests: snow chains for vehicles in the Sinai deserts that would get bogged down in sand; shields for our troops in the Congo who were being pelted with stones by women protesters.

—George Lansky

own, so success lies in knowing where to get things fast. Lansky operated like a supercomputer. At the critical organizing meeting for UNEF II, Urquhart was told in a call from the field that the last item on the equipment list before the force could be deployed was trained dogs to track down the bodies of Egyptian dead, which the United Nations had agreed to recover. Urquhart recalls: "I said, 'George, 20 teams of tracking dogs.' He always carried this bulging folder, and he flipped through it, pulled out a paper and said, 'Could I use your phone?' In five minutes the dogs were on the way to Sinai."

Negotiations then began where the Egyptian and Israeli lines met, in tents on the Cairo-Suez Road. They took place under the guidance of the UNEF commander, Major-General Ensio Siilasvuo of Finland, and Urquhart's aide, James Jonah of Sierra Leone. Quite soon negotiations went far beyond the initial objectives of prisoner exchange and supplies for the encircled Egyptian Third Army. By November 26 Israeli Major-General Aharon Yaariv and his Egyptian counterpart, General Mohamed El-Gamasy, were close to a disengagement agreement. Under it, Israel would pull back from the canal in return for Egyptian troop reductions in the area. The Israelis broke off the dialogue, however, under pressure from Kissinger. He wanted to achieve a disengagement agreement himself as the first fruit of the peace talks scheduled to open in Geneva one month later. The first disengagement pact was eventually completed by Kissinger in January 1974.

FROM 1974 UNTIL THE THAWING OF THE COLD WAR IN 1987, THE ROLE of the United Nations in keeping the peace was limited. Those years marked the high point of developing nation dominance within the institution, a time when the major powers (and smaller ones such as Israel and Egypt) did most of their problem-solving outside the Security Council or General Assembly.

Since its first years, the United Nations headquarters had been used as a neutral meeting ground where private diplomacy by the superpowers and others helped to keep the peace. The most vivid example occurred in February 1949, when the American and Soviet delegates to the Security Council, Philip Jessup and Yakov Malik, had a not-so-chance encounter (some accounts say in the delegates' lounge; others, at adjoining men's room urinals) that led to the ending of the Soviet blockade of West Berlin.

Israel's Abba Eban used to tell reporters that when he was foreign minister he achieved more in two weeks at the United Nations than his entire foreign service did the rest of the year. He could meet in secret with people who had the power to make decisions, including those who had no formal relations with Israel. It was at UN headquarters that Israeli leaders negotiated with Soviet officials and eventually diplomatic relations, which had been broken off in 1967, were re-established.

Many other nations used the United Nations even more secretly as a venue for dealing with governments (or liberation movements) they did not officially recognize.

In June 1984, with civil war raging in Lebanon, Mr. Pérez de Cuéllar undertook a risky mission to the Middle East. Prospects for peace were slight, but an attempt at tackling this most explosive of issues was obligatory for the UN's chief. Accompanied by a small group, including Under Secretary-General Brian Urquhart, his special assistant Gianni Picco, and myself, as press spokesman, he met with President Gemayel in a bunker-like hotel at Yarzeh on 10 June.

The same day, his flight from Yarzeh to Jordan had to be cancelled in the face of heavy shelling of the foreign military heliport. He was driven to the port of Jounieh where Lebanese army helicopters awaited to ferry him to Damascus and thence to Amman via UN aircraft. The Lebanese pilots, dashing and confident in their best uniforms, lulled our group into a mood of trust and security. Meanwhile, they had forgotten to notify the Syrian Army Command of their flight plan. When our unidentified aircraft was spotted by Syrian radar over the Bekaa Valley, missile launchers were ordered into action.

We landed in blissful ignorance, to be greeted by a panic-stricken array of Syrian and UN officials. The order to fire had been cancelled at the last second by Damascus. Mr. Pérez de Cuéllar dismissed our experience with his customary shrug of the shoulders. Deeply fatalistic, he always stubbornly refused to play the hero. Not so the rest of us. From then on, we took it upon ourselves to remind flight crews of our healthy lust for life and, to their intense annoyance, never stopped regaling them with tales of their fellows' failures.

—François Giuliani, director of media division, UN Department of Public Information

LEFT *US Ambassador to the UN Daniel Patrick Moynihan emphasizes a point to US Secretary of State Henry Kissinger during a session of the UN General Assembly in 1975.*

RIGHT *UN Secretary General Pérez de Cuéllar confers with Giandomenico Picco, UN assistant secretary-general for political affairs in 1982.*

BELOW *UN Secretary-General Javier Pérez de Cuéllar (standing with glasses) meets with Austrian peacekeepers at their headquarters in Camp Faouar, Syria. He was accompanied by Under Secretary-General Brian Urquhart, signing the visitor's log, and Chef de Cabinet Virendra Dayal (third from left).*

THE TURNING POINT FOR THE UNITED NATIONS, AS FOR THE WORLD, was the advent of Soviet President Mikhail S. Gorbachev. It became clear—first to the European leaders and UN officials; eventually to Washington—that Gorbachev not only wanted to disengage from Cold War contests (and costs), but also wanted an activist United Nations to pick up the slack and neutralize regional disputes and tensions. He put his money where his mouth was by paying $200 million in past peacekeeping debts. (At about the same time, under the Reagan administration, Washington began withholding peacekeeping dues and other UN obligations, fueling a new UN financial crisis that persisted through the organization's 50th anniversary.)

Although the Reagan administration remained cautious, Secretary-General Javier Pérez de Cuéllar seized the moment, pressing United Nations mediation in Central America, Cambodia, the Iran-Iraq war and Afghanistan. At a press conference in January 1987, he went a step farther, pushing the ambassadors of the Council's five permanent members to meet privately and map out their common ground on those issues.

In so doing, he restored the system intended by the founders of the United Nations, who foresaw a global hegemony of the major powers, exercised through the UN Security Council, to impose

solutions on disputants and thus maintain or restore international peace.

Those who were involved look back on the years 1988 through 1991 as the golden age of UN problem-solving and peacekeeping. Whereas only three peacekeeping operations (in the Sinai, Golan Heights and Lebanon) were initiated between 1966 and 1988, 17 were launched between 1988 and 1995.

The first mediation to bear fruit was the complex package of agreements that extricated the Soviet army from Afghanistan. It was patiently negotiated by the flamboyant, Havana-smoking Ecuadoran Under Secretary-General Diego Cordovez and was signed in April 1988.

Pérez de Cuéllar took the lead in ending the long war between Iran and Iraq. When the fighting began, in 1980, the Security Council adopted a series of pro-Iraq resolutions, impairing the UN's ability to mediate. To compensate for the Council's tilt toward Iraq, the secretary-general listened to both sides; he then issued a report substantiating Iran's claims that its soldiers were victims of poison gas and negotiated a halt in the use of ballistic missiles against civilian populations. He lined up the Big Five to support his own balanced peace terms. Finally, in July 1988, when Washington and Moscow tacitly signaled Iraq that it could postpone a truce for several months to press on and seize Iranian territory, Pérez de Cuéllar got Saudi Arabia (the main banker of Iraqi President Saddam Hussein) to warn Iraq to end the fighting.

During Pérez de Cuéllar's tenure, too, Namibia, which South Africa had governed for decades in violation of UN resolutions, won its independence through negotiations conducted outside the United Nations. When factional fighting broke out and the election process was in danger of collapse, the UN Transition Assistance Group (UNTAG)

As the helicopter lifted off from Metubane village on the island of Quilua, Mozambique, a large crowd closed around the bemused figures of two United Nations election observers—me, an English journalist, and my colleague, a Bangladeshi army major—and our embarrassingly large pile of provisions.

Cases of bottled water, two weeks supply of army rations, a tent, a shovel, a machete, a plastic bucket, sleeping bags, camp beds, a non-stick frying pan with two spatulas (but no cooker), two torches (with broken bulbs) and a gas lamp (with no filament). Mosquito nets fluttered from a nearby flagpole and coconut tree, carried there by the helicopter's vortex.

An impromptu speech about how we had come to see the 1,282 registered voters of Metubane make their mark freely and fairly in Mozambique's first ever-popular elections was greeted with a flattering amount of clapping and smiles, quite probably of incomprehension, as only a small number of villagers speak Portuguese.

Our arrival had clearly come as a big surprise. Apart from the recent registration of voters, Metubane had been effectively cut off from the outside world for the duration of Mozambique's long civil war. The last they saw of a white man was the back of a Portuguese colonial administrator as he sailed away 20 years ago.

Three days later, with the votes counted and results posted on the great mango tree (ten out of ten for procedure on the UN checklist!), the people of Metubane professed themselves well-pleased with the democratic process. "We like the idea of democracy here," the eldest son of the village chief said, "and we hope it will bring us the things we need. And, by the way," he added, "if you get the chance, you couldn't send us a couple of footballs, could you?"

—Adrian Penninck

played a crucial role in assuring a fair and safe election in 1989.

The UN role in Namibia, as earlier in the Congo, went beyond peacekeeping. The Transition Assistance Group, in which the UN deployed about 4,500 troops, 1,500 civilian police and 2,000 civilian administrators and monitors, set the pattern for future UN operations of similar complexity in Cambodia, El Salvador and Mozambique, where mediation led to nation-building.

The Reagan administration actively opposed a UN role in Central America, but Pérez de Cuéllar and his deputy, Alvaro de Soto, persevered. They played a peripheral part in Nicaragua but were crucial in negotiating the agreement between the Salvadoran government and the Farabundo Martí National Liberation Front on December 31, 1991, at the very moment Pérez de Cuéllar left office. It was de Soto who drafted the text of the final agreements and overcame deadlocks, using innovations such as the creation of a civilian police force and the establishment of a UN team to monitor human rights.

Cooperation among the Big Five, plus other "players" such as Japan, Australia, Vietnam and six members of the Association of Southeast Asian Nations, was responsible for the agreement on Cambodia, signed in October 1991. Once again, the United Nations was

Paul John Miller/Black Star

LEFT *Yasushi Akashi, the UN secretary-general's special representative in Cambodia (center left) greets voters during assembly elections the UN conducted in 1993. UNTAC also supervised the cease-fire ending the country's civil war and launched reconstruction efforts.*

BELOW *A Russian helicopter delivering troops and supplies in Cambodia during UN Transitional Authority in Cambodia (UNTAC) operations in 1992.*

responsible for running the country during a transitional period. Between March 1992 and the end of 1993, the UN Transitional Authority in Cambodia deployed 22,000 soldiers and civilian workers to supervise elections and provide training and humanitarian assistance. One armed faction, the Khmer Rouge, opted out of the coalition, but most of the country was stabilized by the time the United Nations left.

THE FINAL ACHIEVEMENT OF THE NEGOTIATIONS LAUNCHED BY PÉREZ de Cuéllar—this one with no authorization from any UN body—was the freeing of 12 Westerners and 91 Lebanese held hostage by extremist groups in Lebanon. It was achieved in secrecy by Giandomenico Picco, a member of the secretary-general's staff who had established contacts in Iran during talks on Afghanistan and the Iran–Iraq war.

Most of the effort, which began in 1989, involved meetings in Iran to pave the way for contacts with the pro-Iran hostage-takers in Beirut. Like the Iranians, they distrusted the Security Council because of its domination by the major powers. Picco went to Beirut nine times, journeying, as he calls it, "from the world of the living to the world of the Islamic jihad."

He was handled like any hostage—eyes covered, locked into a car, changing cars three times. After being walked out of a car, through tunnels and up stairs, always blindfolded, he was stripped for a search and seated in a chair. When the blindfold was removed, he saw three masked people. The walls of the room were covered with sheets so it could not be described. Picco began to negotiate.

The very first time, he was asked, "Are you here for the Security

Council or the secretary-general?" When he said he represented only the secretary-general, his chief interlocutor (believed by Israeli intelligence to have been Imad Mugnieh, the supposed head of Islamic jihad) told him: "Good answer. If you'd given us the other one, we would have killed you now."

That first time, in August 1991, was the most frightening for Picco. The last time, in June 1992, when he brought the last two Western hostages out of Beirut, was the most dangerous, because the people holding them had threatened to kill Picco. During previous visits, he had been sure there were unseen protectors near him. Not so that last time, Picco said: "I was flying solo in every respect. What really happened [to convince the kidnappers not to kill him] I will never know."

In the Persian Gulf War of 1991, mediation by Pérez de Cuéllar failed to avert confrontation. The Iraqi occupation and annexation of Kuwait in August 1990 was almost universally perceived as a blatant violation of the norms of international behavior. The Security Council became involved immediately and soon imposed harsh economic sanctions. The Bush administration decided to use force and won Council approval to do so. As was the case in Korea in 1950, the Council signed a blank check made out to Washington, which directed the military operation under the UN flag but outside UN control.

Chris Steele-Perkins/Magnum Photos

After the war the Council provided an observer mission to patrol the border, experts to delineate it and a commission to monitor Iraq's compliance with the UN-mandated dismantling of its nuclear, biochemical and missile capabilities. The Council also set up a UN mechanism to market Iraqi oil and dole out reparations. It has yet to be activated, although some funds from release of frozen Iraqi assets have been disbursed.

DURING THE LAST THREE YEARS OF ITS FIRST HALF-CENTURY, THE United Nations—designed to deal only with differences between nations—was repeatedly called upon to keep the peace, or restore it, in disintegrating nations. Since March 1992 it has launched peacekeeping operations in the former Yugoslavia, Somalia, Angola, Mozambique, Georgia, Liberia, Haiti and Rwanda. But in all those situations, when mediation failed, traditional peacekeeping—which depends on the consent of the feuding factions—was inadequate.

The United Nations tried to use peace enforcement under Chapter Seven of the UN Charter, which deals with the collective use of force by the international community to preserve or restore world peace. The object was to separate combatants who were unwilling to stop fighting

ABOVE *UN peacekeepers from Pakistan guard a supply truck delivering food to a distribution center in Mogadishu, Somalia, in 1993.*

RIGHT *One of the luckier ones: A young Rwandan gets help from a UN medic from Australia outside the Central Hospital in Kigali in 1994. As many as 300,000 children were killed during the Rwandan turmoil that year.*

ABOVE *UN Commander General Philippe Morillon of France (center) with Serb General Ratko Mladic (left) and Bosnian Serb President Radovan Karadzic (right) following peace negotiations in May 1993.*

TOP RIGHT *UN Secretary-General Boutros Boutros-Ghali and special envoy Cyrus Vance paying a visit in 1992 to a wounded Bosnian in Sarajevo.*

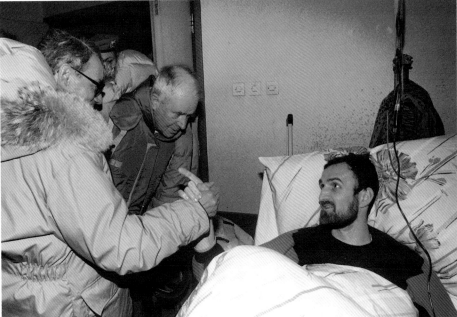

or to live up to agreements they themselves had reached. The problem was that enforcement depended on the willingness of the United Nations and the troop-contributing governments to take casualties. And most governments lacked that will.

Brian Urquhart, the former head of UN peacekeeping operations, and others proposed a standing UN military force, which would allow the international community to take immediate action until other troops could be recruited, equipped and moved. But governments were reluctant to accept an idea which would give greater power to the United Nations and might also be expensive, even though it would be under the control of the Security Council.

Meanwhile, a major problem facing the international community in the 1990s has been the sheer volume of peacekeeping. At the end of 1994, the United Nations was directing 17 operations simultaneously, and its headquarters staff was swamped. The nearly 70,000 troops in the field exhausted the reservoir of contingents from contributing governments, which numbered 77. The costs skyrocketed to $3.5 billion per year. Governments were in arrears by $1.2 billion; about half that tab was owed by the United States.

As the 50th anniversary approached, the Secretariat was trying to grapple with these problems. It increased the staff of the peacekeeping division. It set up a "situation center" in the Secretariat building, filled with maps and communications gear, staffed by 26 officers and operating around the clock. It intensified efforts at "preventive diplomacy," to identify and mediate international or internal disputes before they reached a crisis. In the first attempt at "preventive peacekeeping," a

force of more than 700 troops was stationed in Macedonia as a deterrent and a tripwire. Governments were asked to commit, in principle, military resources to UN operations, and the United Nations began training some of those troops.

Kofi Annan of Ghana, who, like Urquhart, rose through the UN staff ranks to become head of the peacekeeping department, recognizes that in peace operations the ideal is that "outsiders should come in perceived as neutral" and should maintain that neutrality whenever possible. But, he says, there must be better "threat and risk assessments, and if force is foreseen, you don't put peacekeepers on the ground." If force is needed, he adds, "it is up to governments to warn the public that UN operations are not risk-free."

Storm clouds loomed over the future of peacekeeping as the 50th anniversary approached. Pressures grew in nations serving as the principal contributors to peace operations—the United States in particular—to limit participation in multilateral military activities. The inherent strength of the institution lay in the fact that, as never before, the UN was the forum in which political discourse could be generated for collective action to keep the peace. Failures in the former Yugoslavia, Somalia and Rwanda stood as vivid lessons that the price of inaction was far higher—in terms of political reality as well as money and lives—than the price of collective involvement at an early stage.

LEFT *UN peacekeepers dodge sniper bullets on a Sarajevo street. More than 400 UN soldiers have been abducted in former Yugoslavia since 1992, and some 159 have been killed.*

BELOW *Former Yugoslavia, 1993: UN peacekeepers mind the rules of the road, giving livestock safe passage near Vitez.*

ABOVE *One of the wounded residents of Gorazde who was evacuated by UN helicopters after Serbian troops ignored UN ultimatums and pounded the Muslim city for three weeks in 1994.*

RIGHT *The carcass of a Sarajevo bus gets a lift. After three years of siege, much of the city's transport has been brought to a standstill by a shattered economy and shrapnel.*

The taboo against UN actions that interfered in the internal affairs of nation-states was already broken. The problem of peace enforcement remained, but the models for solving it were available. The major powers could yield a modicum of sovereignty to the United Nations, as in the Congo, or enforcement could be contracted out, as in the Persian Gulf.

For half a century, the people who have worked for the United Nations and those who have used it to help keep the peace invariably have found innovative ways to achieve their ends. Improvisation has become a UN trademark, and it is still in demand.

A Look at Some Peacekeepers

Karl Maier

KUITO WAS THE MOST DANGEROUS CITY IN THE MIDDLE OF THE WORST war in Africa, and Hans Peter Vikoler was the only UN worker in town. He had been coming to Kuito since late 1993, when the UN helped to negotiate a cease-fire in Kuito between rebels of the National Union for the Total Independence of Angola (UNITA) and troops loyal to the government controlled by the Popular Movement for the Liberation of Angola (MPLA). At the time, thousands of corpses lined the city's streets, victims of the fighting or of simple starvation.

At first, Hans could not spend nights in the city, which was literally divided into two by the warring armies. The fear was that if the truce was broken, as it routinely was, mortar shells would rain indiscriminately. For expatriate workers, as for the Angolans they were there to serve, there would be no way out. So each day Hans would fly in with the first transport plane and out with the last.

After 10 days of fierce shelling in February 1994, the cease-fire held, and Hans, who worked for the World Food Programme (WFP), became the first UN aid worker to live in Kuito. He was joined by 10 international relief workers from Médecins sans Frontières-Belgium, the International Committee of the Red Cross and OXFAM. But unlike them, he had no bunker at the back of his house.

He went to the airport several times a day, depending on how many UN cargo planes were allowed to land. There he monitored the unloading of relief goods, mainly food, blankets, medicines and soap, before making his way back to a UNITA checkpoint manned by young soldiers armed with AK-47s and rocket-propelled grenades. At the checkpoint, the local commander, Captain Pepe de Castro, made sure that half the goods went to his side and the other half to the government-controlled part of town. That done, Hans drove his battered Toyota Landcruiser across a one-mile no-man's-land into the government-held area—right into another checkpoint. Here, too, he encountered well-armed young soldiers. Their loyalty, however, was to the MPLA government of President José Eduardo dos Santos. After a soldier questioned him again pointlessly—Hans came through this checkpoint five, sometimes ten times a day—a piece of string that constituted the checkpoint was lifted, and Hans was allowed to proceed.

Before him spread the center of Kuito, once a picturesque colonial town, now reduced to big piles of rubble by thousands of bullets and hundreds of mortar shells. Hungry women and children filled the streets and waved as Hans passed in his Landcruiser, one of a handful of vehicles still in working order. As the provider of WFP aid, the principle source of food for the 25,000 people in Kuito, Hans was a celebrity. Everyone had trouble pronouncing his name, so they just called him "Anstee," after the former UN Special Representative to Angola, Margaret Anstee.

As he visited dozens of refugee camps and feeding centers for malnourished children, the same numbing questions were fired at him. "Anstee, when will more food come?" "Can you help us build a new feeding center?" "We have no soap, we have no oil, and the salt is running out. What can you do?"

Hans took it all in stride, patiently answering the pleas with promises to do what he could.

Kuito might have been one of Africa's most destroyed cities—it was where UNITA and the MPLA had engaged in 18 months of mortar duels and street fighting that had killed up to 25,000 people. For Hans, though, it was home. He flew the 500 miles to the capital, Luanda, only on weekends. Invariably he could be found on the Atlantic Ocean beaches of the nearby peninsula of Ilha. Hans loved to swim for hours at a time—to escape, for a while, the tragedy of Kuito.

Cynicism became second nature to most aid workers in Angola, where civil war, land mines and famine had claimed the lives of hundreds of thousands of people. Hans knew that food aid was no solution, but the alternatives were even bleaker. "No one cares a damn about these people, but if we stop feeding them, they will die for sure," he said.

That knowledge drove him to surrounding villages and towns like Cunje, where a government garrison and 10,000 civilians were completely surrounded by UNITA, and farther out into rebel-controlled rural areas, through countless checkpoints and across roads that in the past had been mined. He could never be sure if all the mines had been cleared.

The peril was greatest inside the city, however. In May the mortars started firing one evening at 8:00 as Médecins sans Frontières was preparing to throw a party. For the first night, Hans stayed in his house, the shells landing so fast that it was impossible to count them. The next day he made it to the Red Cross's underground bunker, where he stayed in cramped conditions with four other people for eight nights. At that point a cease-fire held long enough for a UN plane to arrive and evacuate the foreign aid workers. When Hans returned to Luanda, he caught up on some badly needed sleep and then headed out to Ilha. "So many times while I was in that bunker," he said, "I just thought about when I could swim again."

THE PROBLEM WITH INTERNATIONAL PEACEKEEPING IN THE 1990s WAS THAT the United Nations blue helmets on the ground had a tough time finding any peace to keep. It was seldom scarcer than in Somalia, an East African country ripped apart by civil war and starvation. In December 1992 the United States spearheaded a UN effort to protect food convoys destined for hundreds of thousands of Somalis on the brink of famine. In Somalia the line between keeping the peace and starting a war was razor thin.

Originally greeted by most Somalis as saviors, the UN soldiers quickly felt the warm welcome fade. Just two weeks after the American soldiers stormed ashore as part of Operation Restore Hope, troopers on patrol in the center of Mogadishu came under fire from Somali militiamen. Confrontation was looming.

One of the early hotspots in central Mogadishu was along the so-called Green Line, a tense frontier of bombed-out buildings and rubble-strewn streets that separated the militias loyal to the two most powerful faction leaders in Mogadishu—Ali Mahdi Mohamed and General Mohamed Farah Aidid. Perched on a hill overlooking the Green Line were the ruins of what had been Somalia's national parliament. Each day a platoon of young soldiers tramped over piles of shredded papers and patches of broken glass to take up a position behind its bullet-riddled walls and windows.

A decision on how to react to a challenge from one of the warring factions often had to be made in a split second by an officer in his mid-20s who was never sure if his superiors would support the action. The dilemma was spelled out by Lieutenant Andrew Milburn, the platoon commander at the parliament, just days after a heavily armed truck had roared up to challenge the marines. One Somali fired his AK-47 assault rifle into the building, while another, on the back of the vehicle, aimed a 50-caliber machine gun at the soldiers. Milburn gave the order to fire back. One Somali was wounded. "The locals say they know we cannot shoot," Milburn said. "I just got tired of people running with their weapons every time we said, 'Put them down.' "

As a faint red glow over central Mogadishu heralded the coming night, two American corporals, Mark Burnett and Troy Sievers, rode from the ruins of the parliament back to their makeshift base at the city's port. Coming down the hill along Fiat Avenue on the Green Line, they spotted a group of Somali gunmen lurking in the shadows and immediately began shouting, "*Dhig Bundo, Dhig Bundo*," Somali for "put down the gun." While Burnett sat at the steering wheel, Sievers had the unenviable task of jumping out of the American military Humvee vehicle to chase the fleeing militiamen. Theirs was a risky action because they were under orders not to try to disarm militiamen when they were outnumbered. Burnett and Sievers went ahead anyway, and took two rifles before beating a fast retreat.

The shooting at the parliament and the confiscation of the weapons were small incidents by the standards of violence that would later come to characterize the UN operation in Somalia. Such incidents were routine for soldiers from Italy, Pakistan, the United Arab Emirates and a host of other nations participating in the UN peacekeeping force. But they also were symptomatic of the pressures facing the blue helmets as they sought to keep peace where there was none.

By the time Lieutenant Milburn and his troops were packing their bags two weeks later for a return trip to San Diego, frustration was high and nerves were frayed. Milburn disagreed with his superiors' order to pursue a quiet campaign of disarming the gunmen. "The only way to make progress here is to go door to door and get the weapons," he said. "Just picking them up when you see them on the street is not good enough."

IF KEEPING THE PEACE AS A UN BLUE HELMET IN MOZAMBIQUE TAUGHT anything to Botswanan Corporal Tosten Basutlhi, 32, it was the folly of civil war. "It is really dangerous for a country to go into war, that is the main thing I will tell people back home," said Corporal Basutlhi. "We should always be aware that problems leading to war can start anywhere, even in Botswana."

Evidence of what civil war could do to a country was all around. During his eight months in Mozambique, the corporal had seen entire villages that were burned-out ruins, with their residents now living in camps for thousands of Mozambicans displaced by the fighting. They survived on food provided by the UN and international relief agencies. Mozambique, one of the world's poorest countries, was only a few hundred miles from Botswana, one of Africa's richest nations, but it seemed like another world.

The corporal's unit, nicknamed *Mafetsakgang*—"ultimate conflict busters," in the Tswana language—was part of the United Nations' 6,000-strong peacekeeping force. It was sent to Mozambique to maintain peace until the country's first-ever elections, in October 1994. The *Mafetsakgang* unit, stationed at a barracks outside the central Mozambican town of Chimoio, was part of a Botswana Defense Force contingent of 350 soldiers protecting the Beira Corridor, a road, railway and oil pipeline transport artery linking the hinterland of southern Africa to the Indian Ocean port of Beira. The unit's duties included working with the local police to set up armed patrols on the road during the day and occasionally at night. By the time the conflict busters left, they had become the most popular foreign troops among Mozambican civilians.

The 16-year civil war in Mozambique had come to an end two years before, when the government of President Joaquim Chissano and the Mozambique Liberation Front (Renamo) rebel movement signed a peace agreement in Rome. The UN operation in Mozambique began in December 1992 and became one of the world body's most successful international missions. The government and rebel armies were demobilized, the general elections went off almost without incident and Renamo accepted its defeat at the polls.

Prior experience—Botswanan troops had participated in the Somalia mission, Operation Restore Hope—had taught the *Mafetsakgang* unit that international peacekeeping operations can be anything but peaceful. Yet that did not dissuade the troopers from volunteering for a tour of duty in Mozambique. "Most of the guys want to participate in these UN peacekeeping operations," said Lieutenant Colonel Duke Masilo, the contingent's 34-year-old commander. "It is exciting to be stationed abroad, and prestige comes by working with the armies of the world."

The peacekeeping operation in Mozambique, unlike the one in Somalia, was a quiet affair. Relations between civilians and the UN peacekeepers in Chimoio (the capital of Manica province) soured, however, in the wake of allegations that Italian soldiers were involved with child prostitutes. The mood changed when the Botswanan forces moved to Chimoio from Zambezia province.

Tight discipline among the troops and a policy of getting involved with local sports and charity groups earned popular admiration for the *Mafetsakgang* unit. "We are very friendly with the Mozambicans. We are Africans, like them. We are always playing sports, and we have been helping the disabled," said Private Donald Phale. "It is very good for the peacekeeping troops to work on the social side so they can be hand in hand with the civilians," added Corporal Twodays Motingwa. "That way civilians can get used to soldiers."

In July 1994 Lieutenant Colonel Masilo and his men organized a soccer tournament for four Mozambican teams. "We really scored points with the tournament because we provided every player with uniforms, which they were able to keep," he said. "Each team won a trophy no matter how they played, because we did not want anyone to feel like a loser."

It was the self-discipline shown by the *Mafetsakgang* troops, however, that won the highest praise from the Mozambicans. The Botswanan soldiers were not allowed to drink in public or visit local discotheques. "Things like bars and going to discos, it is a very bad habit for a soldier," noted Corporal Motingwa, a 13-year veteran of the Botswana Defense Force. "These are things that will affect you and lead to bad behavior."

The Botswanan conflict busters, for their part, left expressing admiration for the Mozambicans they had come to help. "What impressed me the most was the way the people plow with their hands. They have no tractors or anything like in Botswana," said Sergeant Oitshupile Pule, who also served in Somalia. "The Mozambican people are very tough."

CHAPTER THREE

Nurturing the Children

Nurturing the Children

Francis Wilkinson

THE KING OF MOROCCO WAS LECTURING HIS VISITOR, UNICEF Executive Director James Grant, about the beauty and sophistication of his country, describing it as "the France of the southern Mediterranean." When the King broke off his monologue to sip a drink, Grant characteristically seized the opportunity.

"What you're saying about Morocco is true," Grant agreed, "except for one thing."

"And what is that?" asked the King.

"Moroccan children," Grant said, "die at 10 times the rate of children in France."

Grant, who led UNICEF for 15 years until a week before his death in January 1995, fortunately possessed the kind of subtle political instincts and ready charm that enabled him to deliver such vexing news without giving offense.

If offense was seldom taken as a result of Grant's visits with heads of states, action often was. At the King's subsequent direction, for instance, Morocco made rapid strides in protecting children's health. Between 1985 and 1992, the number of Moroccan children immunized against measles jumped from 42 percent to 81 percent, and the nation's children progressed on other fronts as well. Morocco became a success story in UNICEF's worldwide campaign to eliminate preventable childhood diseases.

For five decades, UNICEF has been encouraging, often prodding, governments to address the causes of children's suffering. Though the organization has striven to achieve its own obsolescence, war, famine and, above all, poverty and disease have conspired to assure UNICEF an ample portfolio well into the next century.

UNICEF was founded as a temporary response to a specific emergency. The idea of a children's relief agency was born from the chaos of World War II, which turned millions of children around the globe into

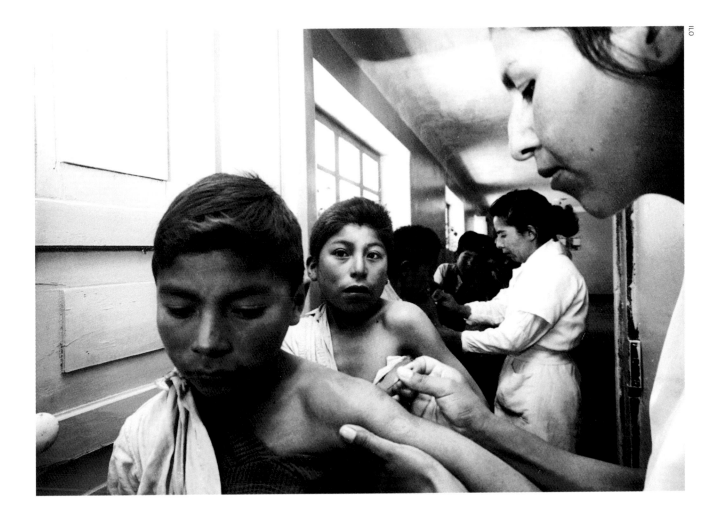

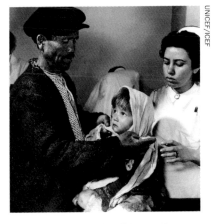

LEFT *UNICEF Executive Director James Grant greets children in Abidjan, Côte d'Ivoire, in June 1994.*

ABOVE *Under his father's watchful eye, a young Turk with a head injury awaits assistance at a UNICEF-supplied medical center in Kizilcahamam. The facility was established to improve health services for mothers and children in the area.*

PREVIOUS SPREAD *A mother and child cross a maize field in northern Malawi in 1993.*

TOP *Bolivian schoolchildren line up for vaccinations as part of a program to aid the Indians of the Altiplano in seven Andean countries. The program received assistance from a variety of UN agencies, including UNICEF.*

ABOVE *Nepalese children in the early 1960s grasp for food at a UNICEF-supported distribution point.*

TOP RIGHT *Despite their disabilities and the ongoing civil war, Greek children play a rousing game of soccer outside a bombed-out school in 1948.*

RIGHT *Offering aid and comfort: A worker for UNRRA helps a Greek woman and her family in 1948. Civil war in Greece had broken up families and forced many to flee their homes.*

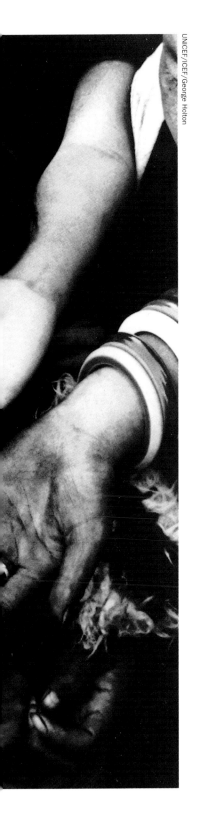

refugees and scavengers. Orphans roamed the burned-out cities of Europe, searching for food amid garbage, and for shelter amid rubble. Even children living with one or both parents often faced an arduous daily hunt for food and clean water. With diets severely constricted and medicine unavailable, tuberculosis, rickets and other diseases struck whole towns full of undernourished, weakened and ill-clothed children.

At the behest of US President Harry Truman, former President Herbert Hoover toured Europe in the spring of 1946, visiting 38 countries in 82 days to assess the need for relief. Hoover's successful organization of European relief during and after World War I had been one of the greatest achievements of his life. Now, accompanied by a small group of loyal aides, he was again charged with saving people who had

just survived the most destructive war in history and were struggling to survive its aftermath. Since 1943, the Allies had been shipping food and medicine to Europe under the auspices of the United Nations Relief and Rehabilitation Administration (UNRRA). But much more was needed. In June, after he returned from his tour, Hoover delivered a radio

address in which he sketched the contours of an international organization devoted to the salvation of children.

"There are somewhere between 20 to 30 million physically subnormal children on the continent of Europe," he informed his radio audience. "There are millions of others in Asia....The redemption of these children should be organized at once."

Hoover envisioned an international body dedicated to children and supported by all nations. The following December, the UN General Assembly created UNICEF—the United Nations International Children's Emergency Fund. In 1947 UN Secretary-General Trygve Lie named a Hoover protégé, American investment banker Maurice Pate, to be the emergency fund's first executive director.

UNICEF's work began immediately out of Pate's Washington office. The quiet but determined son of a Nebraska banker, Pate had no children of his own. But inspired as a young man working for Hoover's Commission for Relief in Belgium during World War I, he possessed a bold sense of mission. The day after his appointment, Pate appealed to the US government for a whopping $100 million contribution to his fledgling organization. (He received $15 million.)

Soon thereafter relief supplies, coordinated by UNICEF, began to flow into Europe. Several thousand tons of cotton cloth were shipped to countries that turned the fabric into diapers, blankets and infant clothing. Enough leather for more than 2 million pairs of shoes was distributed across Europe, allowing impoverished children to trade in the broken shoes and in some cases newspapers and rags that barely covered their feet. Supplies of cod liver oil arrived from Canada, Norway and New Zealand to halt the effects of rickets, caused by Vitamin D deficiency, which had warped the legs and stunted the growth of millions of malnourished children. (Many of the children were so small that relief officials often mistook five- or six-year-olds for toddlers.)

Vast quantities of

ABOVE *Doing their bit for a worthy cause: Yugoslavs retrieve containers after donating milk for a UNICEF-funded program to provide fresh and dry milk to undernourished children.*

BELOW *Former US President Herbert Hoover became a hero to many World War II refugees, like these Warsaw children in 1946, when he spearheaded the drive to feed Europe's children.*

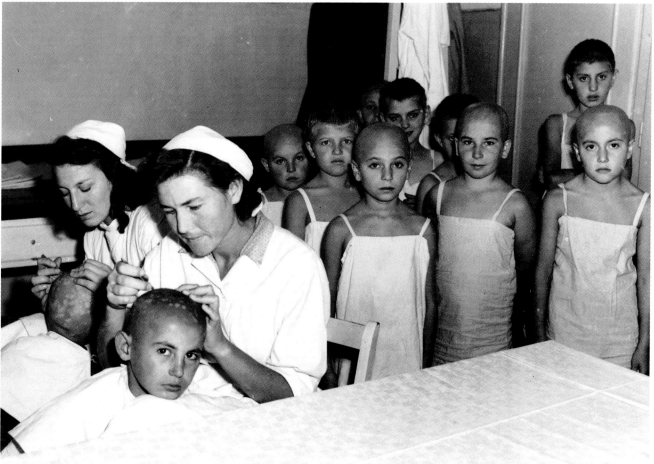

ABOVE *First a shave and then treatment: Yugoslavian youngsters wait to have their scalps treated for sycosis, a skin disease, at a UN-supported hospital in Belgrade.*

milk powder were shipped from Australia, Canada and the US to children's institutions throughout Europe and China. As Judith Speigelman relates in *We Are the Children*, published in celebration of UNICEF's 40th anniversary, "The milk tasted much better hot than cold. Using big vats, volunteers experimented with recipes from UNICEF, adding noodles or macaroni to perk up the liquid. Hungry children were no different from other children; they drank only what tasted good to them."

UNICEF became closely identified with the milk it delivered in such prodigious quantities, gaining fame as the world's "milkman" and even employing the image of a child drinking milk as its international symbol. But the agency did more than just send milk powder to the hungry. It also aided the rebuilding of a shattered European dairy industry so that nations could once again provide for themselves. In doing so, it established a precedent it would follow for the next five decades.

BY 1953 EUROPE'S RECONSTRUCTION WAS WELL UNDER WAY, AND MANY of the UN's industrialized member nations thought the need for an emergency children's fund had passed. As the world settled into the Cold War, funding for UNICEF dropped. Even UNICEF's most avowedly apolitical intentions appeared suspect when viewed through the distorting lens of East–West competition.

In October 1953, the agency received permanent status from the UN General Assembly, at which time it changed its name to the United Nations Children's Fund, but the original acronym was retained. Its role was broadened after it made a hard-fought case for engagement in developing nations, where millions of children died from hunger and disease each year and many millions more were crippled or stunted. This marked the start of a new phase for UNICEF, which set forth on a crusade with the World Health Organization to wipe out preventable childhood diseases throughout the world.

It proved daunting, however, to combat disease in developing countries, where education was limited and the infrastructure for communications and transportation was rudimentary. Although UNICEF often managed to obtain medical supplies at a discount, bringing them to people in need required both ingenuity and energetic commitment from governments, voluntary groups and local communities.

In Thailand, elephants brought healthcare providers carrying penicillin, syringes and equipment to remote villages. Itinerant workers conducted public-information campaigns to assure villagers that bending over to receive a piercing shot in the rear wasn't as crazy as it seemed. Indeed, it wasn't. A single shot of penicillin was sufficient to cure yaws, a painful, contagious and crippling disease that affected tens of millions worldwide.

At one makeshift outdoor clinic in eastern Nigeria, a team of more than two dozen health workers formed an assembly line to examine and treat Ibo villagers. Each villager was inspected carefully for signs of yaws, which often began with blisters on the soles and palms. Using chalk to write on the patient's back, a senior nurse inscribed the dosage of medicine the patient required. Health workers then soaped, disinfected and injected the right buttocks of each patient.

Within two decades, 160 million people in Africa were examined, 60 million were treated for yaws and the disease was eradicated.

Through most of its history, UNICEF has collaborated with other agencies on major health and development undertakings. A case in

ABOVE *Maurice Pate, the first UNICEF executive director, with Swedish children in Stockholm in the early 1960s. Head of the agency for 18 years, Pate traveled to 93 countries spreading the word that the needs of children should outweigh political considerations.*

RIGHT *UNICEF used camel-power to deliver insecticide needed to combat malaria in areas where hundreds of thousands of Palestine refugees were encamped in the early 1950s. The anti-malaria campaign was part of a multiyear assistance effort that involved sending food, blankets and clothing as well.*

BELOW *On a mission to treat yaws in Thailand, a UNICEF medical team found the going a bit rough. With half of the country's people in areas heavily affected by yaws, such mobile clinics were constantly on the move.*

point is the successful battle to wipe out trachoma, an eye disease that blinded millions of children. UNICEF and the World Health Organization worked together in eliminating it by supplying and distributing penicillin and other antibiotics, and educating and raising public awareness about the crippling affliction.

UNICEF's campaign against malaria, which involved the spraying of DDT, was the largest single item in the agency's budget in the mid-1950s. The campaign had mixed results, helping to eradicate the disease in several countries in Europe and the Caribbean but meeting resistance in other parts of the world.

UNICEF also helped build penicillin plants in Chile, India, Pakistan and Yugoslavia, so that those nations could begin producing their own medicine. "It was a typical UNICEF operation," Maurice Pate later said of Bombay's penicillin plant, constructed in the 1950s. "Instead of giving them penicillin, we gave them the tools to make their own."

PAYING FOR SUCH WIDE-spread activities was—and remains—a perennial struggle. Voluntary funding from governments has always been the major source of UNICEF revenues, with the United States supplying the largest dollar amount and, for many years now, Scandinavian countries supplying by far the largest contributions relative to population. Although Sweden's population is only

3.4 percent that of the United States, Sweden contributes nearly as much. In addition, countries receiving UNICEF's assistance contribute to the organization's budget.

UNICEF, however, has long benefited from less conventional sources of revenue. Due to the appeal of UNICEF's unique mandate, the organization receives one-third of its budget from contributions raised by 38 UNICEF National Committees. Then there are UNICEF greeting cards. In 1947 a Czech girl's painting of five girls dancing joyously around a maypole was reproduced as a UNICEF poster. Two years later it was turned into a greeting card, which was sold to employees of UNICEF and the UN. By the early 1950s, UNICEF greeting cards were being reproduced from works donated by some of the world's greatest artists, starting with Raoul Dufy in 1952. Matisse, Chagall, Picasso, Kandinsky, O'Keeffe, Dali and others contributed. Sales in the US soared when trend-setting first lady Jacqueline Kennedy made it known she favored the cards. Initially reproduced for their public-relations value, greeting cards and other products now generate $130 million in revenue, about 13 percent of UNICEF's $1-billion budget.

Aside from cranky Cold War-era critics in the US who considered the United Nations and its agencies a breeding ground for godlessness and espionage, UNICEF has generally had a relatively easy time attracting—and maintaining—public support. That task has been further eased by the deployment of celebrities as UNICEF's Goodwill Ambassadors.

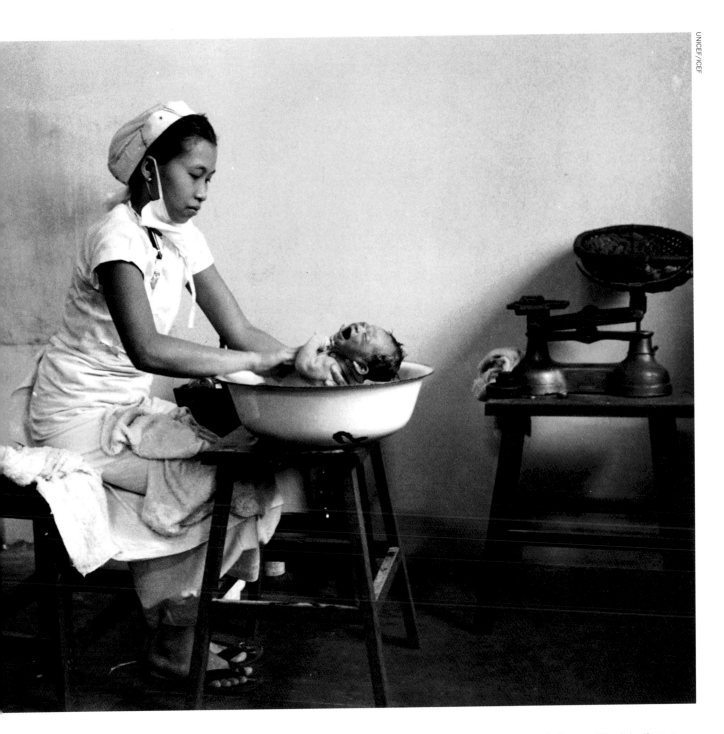

TOP LEFT *In 1955 a man gets an injection against yaws at a Nigerian field clinic—one of many set up in assembly-line fashion to treat whole villages at a time.*

LEFT *Getting the cure: A young Indonesian girl gets a shot of penicillin to fight yaws, the disease that caused the painful blistering of her face. With*

UNICEF's help, the goal of one million injections a year was reached in a three-year period in the early 1950s, eliminating the disease in Indonesia.

ABOVE *A newborn is bathed by a midwife-in-training at a maternity hospital in Rangoon, Burma, in 1955. UNICEF helped rural and urban health centers in Burma rebuild services after World War II.*

Comedian Danny Kaye created the mold, traveling all over the world on UNICEF's behalf and making a 1955 film, *Assignment: Children*, that was translated into 9 languages and seen by tens of millions. The film featured a seven-year-old Thai boy named Boonting, who had yaws and was covered with scabs. Two weeks after receiving a shot of penicillin, courtesy of UNICEF, Boonting was cured, as were six of his brothers and sisters.

Over the years, some of the world's great stars have donated their time and energy to UNICEF. Actors Peter Ustinov and Liv Ullman have traveled through mountains and jungles as UNICEF Goodwill Ambassadors. Others who have generated publicity about UNICEF's work, a prerequisite of successful fundraising, include singer Harry Belafonte.

Japanese television star Tetsuko Kuroyanagi and Greek singer Nana Mouskori.

Audrey Hepburn was a much-admired ambassador for UNICEF at the time of her death in 1994. Hepburn, who had been malnourished as a child in Nazi-occupied Holland, never forgot the benefits provided to

Imo State, Eastern Nigeria: "Ohazoara? You can't want to film in Ohazoara!" The official in his neatly pressed safari suit and his air-conditioned office looked at us in amazement. "Ohazoara is a very backward place, the people are very poor and underdeveloped."

We knew this. That was exactly why the water and sanitation program was in Ohazoara. "We're from UNICEF." On that he signed our permit.

The water and sanitation team and the people of Ohazoara were waiting for us. We had already chosen our sites and "cast" our film. Tomorrow Ngozi Oko, the health educator, would be teaching village women how to treat childhood diarrhea. Grace Ogbonna, the sanitarian, would be out supervising the digging of pit latrines. Felicia Onu, the community health volunteer, would be visiting neighboring compounds. Billy Obasi, the driller, would be maneuvering his great yellow rig onto a rocky outcrop of sandstone. All these activities, and more, awaited our eager film crew.

Before the UNICEF program arrived in Ohazoara, no good water had been found for 30 years. People were forced to rely on dirty infected ponds and every year came cholera and guinea worm. Then came the drilling rig and the miracle of "water struck from the rock." Boreholes and handpumps began to transform people's lives.

On our last evening in Ohazoara we called on *Eze* (King) Solomon Nkwo, who broke the kolanut and called for champagne to honor "his sons and daughters from the UNICEF." Another new handpump had been commissioned that day. To the modern-minded official such an event might seem insignificant. But the *Eze* saw things differently. "The good news is water," he said. "Here in Ohazoara, UNICEF's name is now indelible."

—Maggie Black

TOP LEFT *An Indian street gets a thorough cleaning as part of a community development program assisted by UNICEF and the World Health Organization.*

LEFT *Ecuadoran government workers spray insecticide to eradicate malaria-bearing mosquitos in the Guayaquil region of the country. UNICEF supported the campaign from 1956 to 1958.*

ABOVE *In Uganda's Lake Salisbury, children who were exposed to leprosy in 1961 enjoy a good scrub with medicinal soap supplied by UNICEF.*

European children immediately after the war by UNICEF's forerunner, the United Nations Relief and Rehabilitation Administration. "I auditioned for this job for 45 years," she told UNICEF colleagues, "and I finally got it."

UNICEF's campaign to eliminate the most easily preventable childhood diseases met with early success. Haiti, where roughly half the population had suffered from yaws prior to UNICEF's creation, was essentially rid of the disease by the time UNICEF won the Nobel Peace Prize in 1965. Still, Haitian children were as susceptible as ever to persistent illness—including lethal diarrhea—that was related to poor water quality and sanitation and, ultimately, to poverty. A shot of penicillin could do only so much.

IN THE 1960S, UNDER THE LEADERSHIP OF UNICEF Executive Director Henry Labouisse and in accord with the UN's Decade of Development, UNICEF increased its focus on development, particularly on clean water and sanitation projects. Some of the projects required sophisticated feats of engineering—drilling in drought-prone, hard-rock regions of India, for instance.

But perhaps the greatest advance of the entire decade was also the simplest—the discovery that oral rehydration salts (ORS), a solution of sugar, salts and water, could reverse dehydration caused by diarrhea. Packets of ORS were produced for pennies each yet could save the lives of 5 million children who died of diarrheal dehydration each year. Millions more could be freed from persistent, debilitating sickness, allowing them to grow up healthy and strong.

Since its discovery in Dhaka, Bangladesh, oral rehydration therapy (ORT) has saved the lives of millions of children, though each year 3 million continue to die

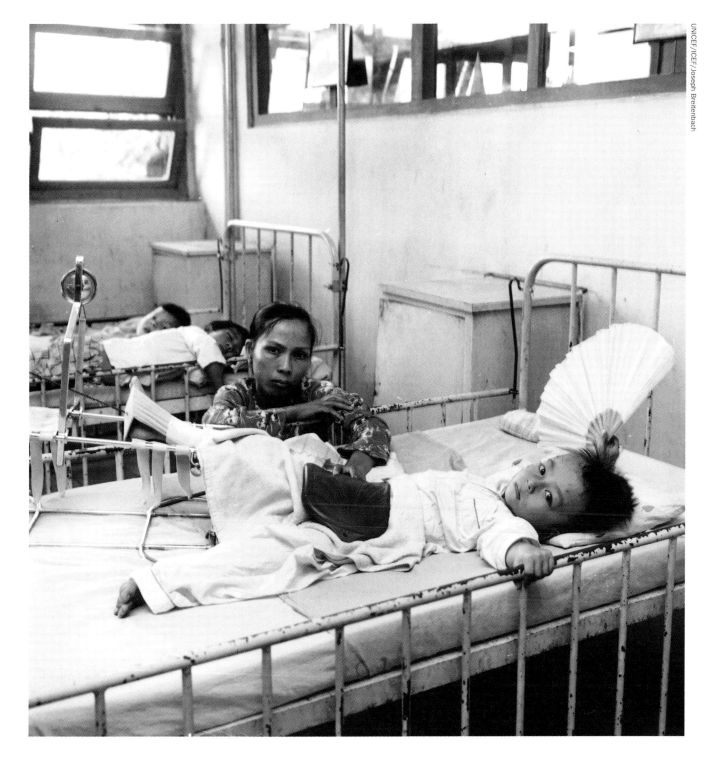

TOP LEFT *Henry Labouisse, executive director of UNICEF from 1965 to 1979, greets a Thai child in 1973. Mrs. Labouisse and UNICEF colleagues look on.*

MIDDLE LEFT *A young nomad gets a delousing in Pakistan in a 1962 UNICEF-sponsored typhus control program. Traveling herdsmen, constantly migrating with their livestock, were especially susceptible to the disease.*

LEFT *Six-year-old Malika hands over her medical record to a doctor in a Moroccan clinic in 1962. She was one of 1,100 children who received aid from the International Red Cross and UNICEF after being poisoned by adulterated cooking oil.*

ABOVE *Even with South Vietnam in political crisis in the early 1960s, a young child was getting modern medical attention at the Children's Hospital at Saigon University, where UNICEF and WHO were providing equipment and training.*

needlessly from diarrheal dehydration because, UNICEF says, "their parents are unaware of or unwilling to use ORT."

Educating parents about ORT and making the packets available in even the most remote regions of the world continues to be a UNICEF priority. It is part of UNICEF's campaign to build a wall of protection around children in their first years of life, a campaign that also encourages mothers to breast-feed babies and to make sure their children receive shots to immunize them against six common childhood diseases—diphtheria, measles, polio, tetanus, tuberculosis and whooping cough.

UNICEF has employed some of the same logistical methods to supply vaccines to poor communities that it uses to deliver ORS. But unlike ORT, which can be administered by a parent, vaccinations must be given by trained personnel. Some vaccinations require refrigeration and multiple doses over several months.

Despite all that's involved, many countries have made dramatic progress in vaccinating children within only a few years.

The rate of progress in meeting goals for immunization and other programs reveals that success depends more on national commitment than on national resources. "Why is it," asked James Grant, "that a country like Bhutan, with an average per capita income of 180 US dollars a year, manages to immunize 82 percent of its children against measles,

TOP LEFT *UNICEF's first ambassador-at-large, Danny Kaye, plays pied piper to a group of youngsters during a trip to Asia in 1954 to film* Assignment: Children, *a documentary film about UNICEF's work in that part of the world.*

LEFT *UNICEF Goodwill Ambassador Harry Belafonte gives a hand to Rwandan children being transported to a camp for orphans run by the nongovernmental organization Caritas in 1994.*

ABOVE *Audrey Hepburn cradles one of Somalia's smallest victims outside a feeding center run by Concern, a nongovernmental organization in Baidoa, Somalia, in 1992. Hepburn was an indefatigable ambassador for UNICEF right up to the time of her death a few months after this trip.*

His work with all the rushing from country to country has saved the lives of more than 25 million children, and prevented even more than that from growing up handicapped.

On those first travels with Jim, he would insist on continuing meetings into the night. Those evenings, more often than not, ended with a president or a minister or a health worker promising to incorporate Jim's ideas.

Coming back to the same countries years later, I would see strangers stand just like Jim and put their hands in their pockets like him. They'd take out their little packets of ORS and talk with his enthusiasm of the lives they had saved.

At the beginning of the horrible war in former Yugoslavia, the combatants agreed to a cease-fire—a week of no shooting. Jim phoned and asked me if I would join him on a peace march through Sniper's Alley—the most dangerous spot there—to show that peace was possible.

But what if the cease-fire is broken, I protested. "Well," Jim said, "We'll be there and find out."

You were so proud, Jim, when you showed-off your little carry-on bag packed for 14 days of travels to 10 different countries and almost as many climates. "There is no time to wait for luggage at airports" you would explain.

Last time I was with you, Jim, we discussed new travels, and you suggested we go to Bosnia together. "Let's do it in May," you said. "I'm not free before late autumn," I said. "No, I can't do it then," you said. "Let's say May."

You made me promise, Jim. And it was the first time you did not keep a promise, although I now think that you may have wished to convey that you are still with us at the scheduled dates. Just like the invisible boy from my childhood fairy tales, who is flying up there with the birds, you know that your message is a powerful one that has touched millions, inspiring them by your deeds.

So flying from Norway to New York today, Jim, I have the feeling that you are already sitting with God and you're holding up your package of oral rehydration salts just like you've done so many times before. And now it's God you are making very, very busy!

—**Liv Ullmann, remarks at memorial service for James P. Grant, February 2, 1995**

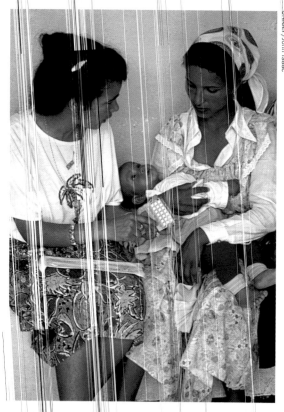

TOP A Mexican doctor instructs a mother on the proper use of oral rehydration salts.

ABOVE A Tunisian mother at a health center in 1986.

TOP RIGHT A Turkish toddler is immunized.

RIGHT A malnourished child gets some attention at a feeding center in Ayod, Sudan, in 1993.

Dear Jim,
Flying here, I was reminded of a story I learned as a child. A little boy magically became almost invisibly small, yet full of power. He spends the rest of his life on the back of a goose flying all over the world....Along the way, he listened to the dreams of the young and the old and worked to make them a reality. The longer he flew, the more birds with their passengers joined him, helping him with his goal of making the world a better place for the millions that followed.

Many years ago I went on my first trip with Jim, who at the time was new as UNICEF's executive director. We flew, and we walked, and he never tired....At the time, I thought I was much younger than Jim, but I was the one getting tired!

His goal was always clear—make the world a better place for children. It was there when he sat down with a mother and her sick baby. It was there when he stood before a president. He would reach into his pocket and take out a packet of oral rehydration salts. He would show the mother and he would show the president how to fill a spoon with water and salt and save the life of a child with diarrhea.

And once he had left, both of them would now be messengers, joining Jim in his battle against preventable disease.

Jim's work was a revolution—a fight for the survival of young boys and girls and for the dignity of life.

when countries with incomes ranging from $13,000 to $27,000 have coverage rates ranging from 42 to 77 percent?"

In recent years UNICEF has exerted political pressure on negligent nations. The 1989 Convention on the Rights of the Child, a codification of children's rights to survival, development and protection, has been ratified by more nations, more quickly, than any other human rights treaty in history. Ratification does not guarantee action, but having staked a degree of their prestige on agreeing to protect children's rights, ratifiers are more susceptible to pressure to live up to their word.

Similarly, UNICEF's annual "Progress of Nations" report spotlights the impressive commitment of nations like Sri Lanka and Vietnam to improving the lives of its children alongside the failure of much more prosperous countries, such as Britain and the US, to do the same. The report monitors the progress

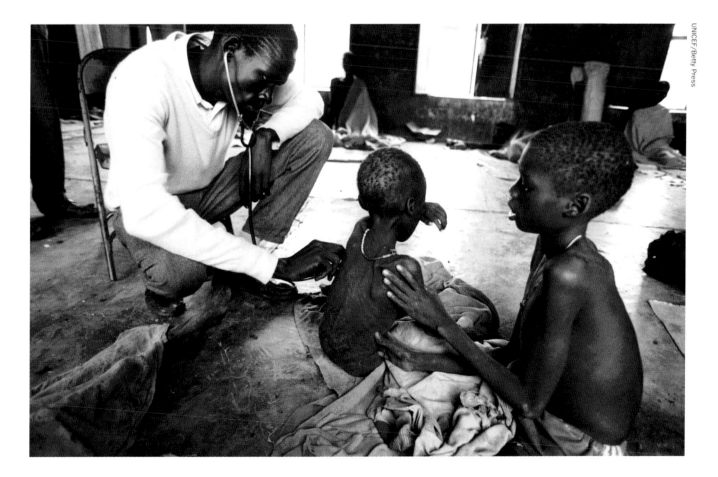

LEFT *One of Bogota's "kangaroo" mothers: To nurture premature babies, UNICEF supports a Colombian program that encourages mothers to swaddle the tiny infants close to their breast in a pouch with womb-like warmth, an alternative to high-cost incubators.*

BELOW *The anguish of it all: a young girl who had been separated from her parents during the Rwandan crisis, waits to be registered at an orphanage near Goma, Zaire.*

BOTTOM RIGHT *A young Bosnian mother draws support from her six-year-old son in 1992 at the Kosovo Hospital in Sarajevo. When a grenade exploded in her home, she lost the baby she was carrying, and nearly lost her leg.*

made by nations towards achieving 27 key goals agreed upon by world leaders (including 71 heads of state or government) who attended the World Summit for Children at UN headquarters in 1990.

WHILE UNICEF, LIKE MOST BUREAUCRACIES, HAS KNOWN SCANDAL AND inefficiency—in 1995 it is recovering from a well-publicized incident of theft by employees in its Kenya office—it has remained a source of pride to many of its 75,000 employees. "You get a huge sense of satisfaction going back to a village after having inaugurated a clean water supply system," says one UNICEF veteran. "The kids are clean, their hair is combed, they have a spark of life when, before, they just had diarrhea all the time. It's an incredible high."

Although UNICEF's annual budget—slightly less than the cost of a sophisticated bomber—has never matched its ambitions, the organization has attempted to influence indirectly what it cannot change directly. To mitigate the worst effects of the debt crisis and the international recession of the 1980s, which pummeled many poor countries, UNICEF called for "adjustment with a human face," encouraging the World Bank and the International Monetary Fund to cushion the poorest of the poor from the painful effects of government cuts in public services due to economic adjustment. It has encouraged special attention to the health and education of girls, knowing that investment in girls will ultimately lead to safer, more productive lives for women—and their families.

Through five decades, however, UNICEF has never

been able to abandon its first calling—emergency relief. Amid slaughter in Rwanda, starvation in Somalia and a genocidal war of "ethnic cleansing" in the former Yugoslavia, UNICEF has continued to respond to cataclysmic suffering. To ensure that life-saving care reaches children in the midst of conflict, UNICEF has helped engineer temporary cease-fires—"Days of Tranquillity"—that enable vaccination campaigns to proceed in El Salvador and Lebanon, and "Corridors of Peace" for humanitarian relief in the Sudan, Uganda and the former Yugoslavia. The work has grown more dangerous. Macharia Kamau, a UNICEF senior program officer from Kenya, supervised emergency food distribution in Operation Lifeline Sudan in 1989. "When we got there, the civil war and drought effects were at their peak," he says. "We were bombed a couple of times." In 1993 and 1994, 19 UNICEF workers were killed in the line of duty, more than in the previous two decades.

War in the former Yugoslavia and several other parts of the world in recent years has given UNICEF a new challenge—to help salve the psychological wounds inflicted on children in the midst of conflict. Psychologists and trained volunteers working with UNICEF's local offices in Croatia and Bosnia-Herzegovina, for example, have conducted art therapy classes in local schools and hospitals, encouraging children

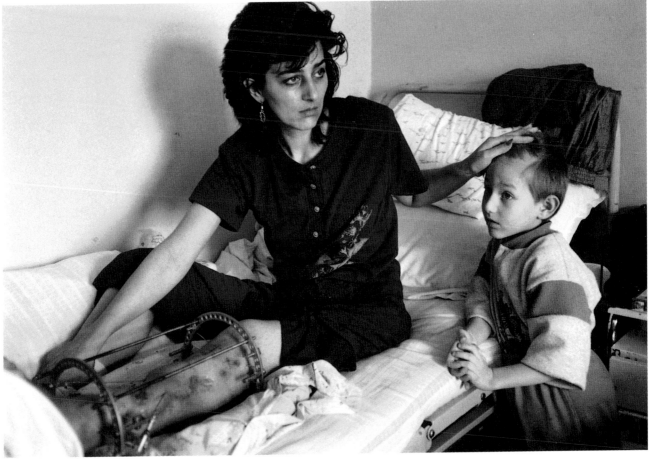

ABOVE *Dressed in their best, Chinese youngsters line up to register before being vaccinated at a UNICEF-supported health clinic in Shaanxi province.*

TOP RIGHT *Reading period at a UNICEF-supported school in Pakistan, 1983.*

RIGHT *A pump donated by UNICEF draws fresh water at the Damba Maria refugee camp in Benguele province, Angola.*

traumatized by war to communicate through art. The expression of fears and painful memories—as well as happy recollections and budding hopes—helps to alleviate the trauma. Stark drawings and poems by children punished by the war have been created in this psychological release process. "I swear to you, I do not kick the football like before, I do not sing the way I did," writes 11-year-old Nemanja from Sutomore in 1993. "I have locked up my bicycle, and I have locked up my smile. I have locked up my games and my childish jokes as well."

One of UNICEF's great strengths is its ability to prick the conscience, and move individuals and governments to action. But war in the former Yugoslavia—which has driven more than 600,000 children from their homes, killed perhaps 15,000 and injured many more—has demonstrated the limits of such a power. Like so many tools of peace, it makes a dull weapon against barbarism. And yet, who knows what other horrors it may have kept at bay?

The UN Spirit

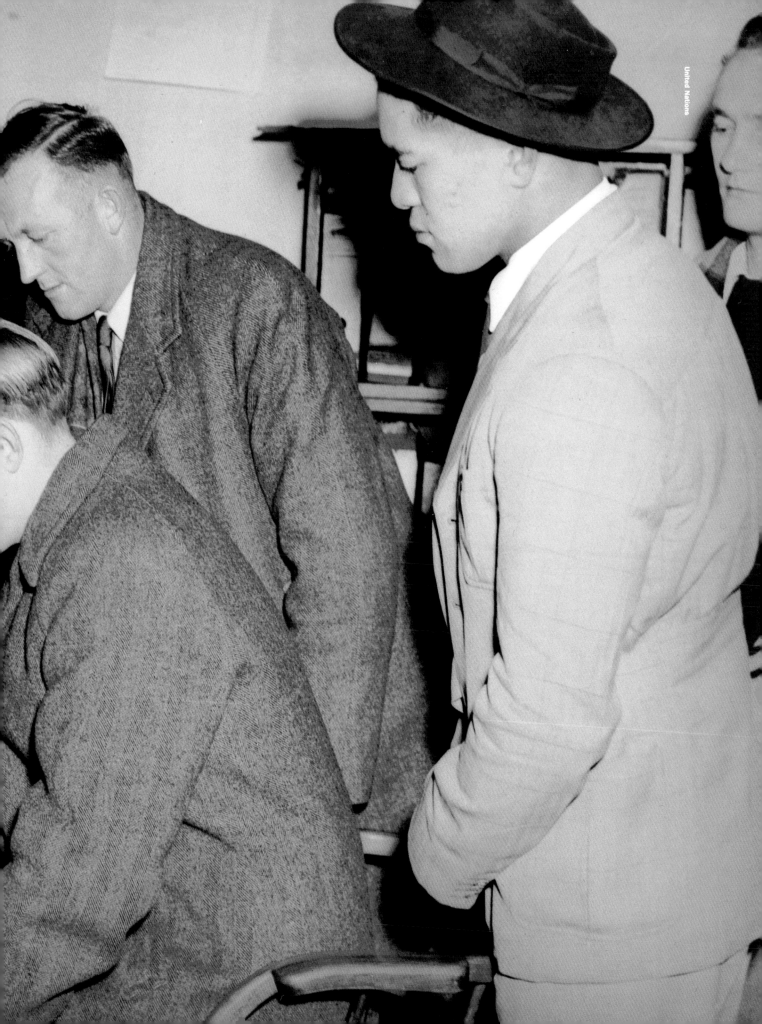

The UN Spirit

Michael Ryan

EMERSON HAD IT WRONG. AN INSTITUTION IS NOT, AS HE WROTE, simply the lengthened shadow of one person. In the half-century of its existence, the United Nations has been shaped and sustained by thousands of individuals from almost every nation on earth. Some have grown famous; a few are even household names worldwide. But many have labored in obscurity, their achievements known only to themselves and their friends and families—and to the millions of people whose lives are the better for their efforts.

BETTY TESLENKO'S CHANCE TO WORK FOR THE UN CAME OUT OF THE sky—literally. A former court reporter, she had taken a job as a United Airlines flight attendant during World War II. "I began talking to a man on one of my flights, and he told me he was on his way to San Francisco to help set up the United Nations conference," she recalls. "He told me they would be needing verbatim reporters. He took my address and number, and a short while later I heard from the organizers. This was 1945; it was the best year of my life."

"There was so much optimism," Teslenko remembers, growing excited at the memory even half a century later. "We had all these delegates who had just left war-devastated European countries, people who had been living for years without lights, without food. Some of them had come to San Francisco from prison camps. All you had to do was wear the little button that identified you as being from the United Nations conference, and people couldn't do enough for you."

The early years were demanding for Teslenko and her colleagues, as civil servants from all over the world held meetings and conferences to iron out the procedures that would allow them to work together. "They made speeches during the day, and we worked at night transcribing our stenotype notes," she remembers. "I stayed in a hotel in San Francisco for most of the time, even though I lived with my mother just

PREVIOUS SPREAD *Enlisting in the UN cause: New Zealanders, including one Maori (right), sign up for duty with the multination forces in Korea, 1950.*

ABOVE *In Yakima, Washington, citizens celebrated United Nations Day in 1950 by hand-sewing a UN flag in a program sponsored by the US Department of Agriculture.*

RIGHT *A toast to peace: Israeli soldiers stationed on the Cairo-Suez Road invited UN peacekeepers and even Egyptian officers to an impromptu party at their tent in 1973. The UN troops were there to supervise a cease-fire between Israel and Egypt.*

across the Bay. There was just no time to get home."

As Teslenko recalls, the early days were charged with excitement because, long before the advent of satellites and faxes and shuttle diplomacy, "delegates were authorized to make decisions on the spot and say, 'This is our position.' So you used to have great debates—real debates."

From the beginning, the United Nations became a focus of world attention—and Teslenko reveled in her aisle seat on history. As she followed the UN through various temporary homes until it came to rest in Turtle Bay, Teslenko witnessed the world's great events and the people who shaped them. In Paris she stenotyped speeches by John Foster Dulles. "I remember he was so sure that he was going to be the next secretary of state, under President Dewey," she recalls. (Dulles, of course, had to wait.) In 1950 she and her sister were sunbathing at Jones Beach on Long Island when she heard on a radio that the Korean War had broken out. "I just had time to drive back to New York and get some clothes, then went back to Lake Success for the Security Council meeting," she remembers.

ABOVE In the thick of things: A verbatim reporter at work during the San Francisco conference. Philippine delegate Francisco Delgado (left) and others observe the proceedings.

TOP RIGHT A pass to history: Betty Teslenko's ID card for the 1945 San Francisco conference.

We had the great difficulty getting interpreters, particularly simultaneous….because of the problem, we had decided, as the host government, that English would be the working language. This was contrary to all prior diplomatic conferences where French was always at least an equal official language. But we had just not been able to get enough interpreters….At the first meeting of the steering committee, Stettinius was greeting them as the host of the conference, "Ladies and gentlemen, we welcome," etc., when a voice right near him spoke in perfect French, repeating what he said. He stopped and then went on, and a person in the rear who also spoke in perfect French, repeated it. When this happened the third time, the audience began to chuckle. Stettinius turned to me and said, "What is going on?" and I said, "We've just been outsmarted!" He turned to me and said, "What shall we do?" and I said, "Let's accept gracefully, they've obviously picked up first-class interpreters whom we couldn't find."

—Alger Hiss, UN Oral History Collection

The most impressive figure of Teslenko's career was Dag Hammarskjöld, a courtly man who, she discovered, could be excruciatingly shy. One Saturday morning she was called in to transcribe a meeting in his private conference room; when she arrived, only the secretary-general was in the room. "After a while, he said, 'It's not so bad working on a Saturday if we can have a charming lady here,' " she remembers. "Because I was so in awe of this brilliant man, I foolishly said, 'Well, you know, I work on weekdays, too.' I meant it as a joke, but I think he took it seriously. He was not a person for small talk and so for the next five minutes, until some other people arrived, we sat in silence."

For all his personal reserve, Hammarskjöld was much loved by the UN staff, whom he entertained every year at his home; indeed, he had a picnic every year for the maintenance people. "When he was killed, everyone in my neighborhood just stood around crying," Teslenko says.

Even in the serious business of the Security Council, Teslenko has seen moments of great—if unintentional—humor. Former US Ambassador Jeanne Kirkpatrick was notorious for leaving the Council immediately after speaking. "She never waited to hear anybody's answers," Teslenko recalls. "Once, a very bright Soviet delegate, who had obviously been waiting for the chance, said, 'Point of order' when Kirkpatrick

finished speaking. The President called on him and he said, 'I want to speak in reply to what the ambassador has just said.' The President said, 'Replies come at the end of the meeting; you're out of order.' The Soviet said, 'But I can't wait for the end of the meeting; she'll be gone.' " A visibly blushing US ambassador stuck it out to the end.

The Cold War brought many mock-serious clashes like that. When the government of Taiwan held the Chinese seat on the Security Council, Soviet delegates refused to refer to their colleague from Taipei as "the delegate from China," according to protocol. Instead, they took to calling the Taiwanese representative simply "the gentleman." The US ambassador, Henry Cabot Lodge, decided to engage in some turnabout; when he took the chair and the Soviet delegate sought recognition, Lodge announced: "I call on the gentleman." Sputtering with anger, the Soviet retorted, "I am not a gentleman! I'm a representative of the Soviet Union."

"I didn't know the two were mutually exclusive," Lodge snapped before the Soviet delegate realized what he had said.

Fifty years after she arrived, Betty Teslenko is still at the United Nations. Although she has officially retired as chief of the English verbatim reporting unit and deputy head of the entire verbatim section, she can still be found in Turtle Bay when the Security Council or the General Assembly is in session. She met her husband, the late Nicolas Teslenko, a simultaneous interpreter, at the United Nations; her social life has revolved around it. But, most of all, it has given her hope for the

TOP LEFT *Betty Teslenko had a front row seat as history was made (right). A verbatim reporter during the San Francisco conference in 1945, she records Andrei Gromyko, Soviet ambassador to the United States, as he addresses the conference.*

ABOVE *At a steering committee meeting during the San Francisco conference, Betty Teslenko (facing camera, upper right) records the debate. Facing front, left to right: the Earl of Halifax, British*

ambassador to the US; T. V. Soong, foreign minister of China; Guillermo Belt Ramírez, Cuban ambassador to the US; US Secretary of State Edward Stettinius (standing); Conference Secretary-General Alger Hiss; Soviet Ambassador to the US Andrei Gromyko; an unidentified Soviet delegate; Francis Michael Ford, deputy prime minister of Australia; Herbert Vere Evatt (head turned), minister of external affairs of Australia; and Kuzma Kiselev, foreign minister of the Byelorussia Soviet Socialist Republic.

future of the world.

"I was at the UN during the Berlin airlift when Malik met the American ambassador in the delegates' lounge and said, 'Let's call this whole thing off,' " she remembers. "If they had not had a place where they could meet, the world would have done what it did in 1914, and gone to war.

"A lot of people don't understand how much the UN has accomplished," Teslenko reflects. "What it can do has been totally misunderstood. I don't know how many wars have been avoided because people could come here and talk to each other— even make terrible speeches at each other—rather than taking up arms. That's just what the UN was supposed to do."

"I'LL NEVER FORGET WHAT SECRETARY-GENERAL PÉREZ DE CUÉLLAR once told me: 'You have the best job in the entire United Nations,' " John Isaac says. "I asked him why, and he told me, 'Not only do you get out and see what's in the field and get involved in it, you come back and see the results of your work. A lot of us do not have that privilege.' " For Isaac, a native of Madras, India, and a UN photographer since 1978, that privilege has been bittersweet: It has brought him face to face with some great human moments, and delivered him into the presence of the greatest human misery of our age.

LEFT *Still at work: Betty Teslenko covers a press conference given by Secretary-General Boutros Boutros-Ghali at UN headquarters in 1995.*

BELOW *US Ambassador Henry Cabot Lodge, Jr. (center left) during a vote of the UN Political Committee in 1953. Other members include Enrique Fabregat of Uruguay (left), Selwyn Lloyd (center right) of Great Britain and Andrei Vyshinsky (right) of the Soviet Union. A French verbatim reporter, Marie-Hélène Quédiniac (front), records the outcome.*

RIGHT BOTTOM *A photographer stretches for the right angle while taking pictures of Secretary-General Trygve Lie (left) and US Ambassador to the UN Warren Austin in 1951.*

I knew this was going to be quite a night. Tension had mounted all day as the Middle East crisis deepened....I was seated within the horseshoe table of the UN Security Council adjusting my headphones and watching for the nod of the reporter I was relieving. He signaled, and I found myself taking down the simultaneously interpreted remarks of the permanent representative of the Soviet Union, Nikolai Federenko.

My shift was to last ten minutes. We were a six-man relay. I stole a glance at Ambassador Arthur Goldberg, who first scribbled furiously and then stared straight ahead at the SG, U Thant, who sat Sphinx-like. Arab and Israeli delegates at the council table pointedly ignored each other. The visitors' gallery was packed. TV cameras panned the tense scene. The world was agog at what was happening— and so was I.

The hands of the clock moved swiftly, and I was surprised to see my relief man beckoning. I rose a trifle self-consciously, headed out of the chamber....down a flight of stairs to the Verbatim Section ....Jones was my typist. I wrote page numbers 146–150 next to his name and inquired where he was....I tried to jog my memory about the house rules on style in the UN record....

I recalled that the main idea was to report and transcribe the words of the speaker, not necessarily as they were spoken but rather as they should have been spoken had Noah Webster, say, and H. W. Fowler had something to say about it. For the majority of the 122 permanent delegates, English was not the mother tongue, yet they were expected to manage its nuances in a manner suitable for public exhibition....

My dictation went in fits and starts. I finished with five minutes to spare before my next turn. What had taken 55 minutes to transcribe? I remembered the joshing that official court reporters were wont to give UN reporters. "Ten-minute takes and a whole hour to get each of them out? Hah! A cinch." If only they were here sweating it out, how they would topple off their high horses!....

Time for my next take. I bounded up the flight of stairs heading for the council chamber, walked double-time past the delegates' lounge....

At 8 p.m., as shadows lengthened in the well-manicured UN gardens, and neon lights began to blaze a trail up First Avenue, the Security Council called a halt to its deliberations and rose. Bone tired, I slumped into the seat of my car, and headed over the Queensboro Bridge....What a grueling day it had been!....

My hat was off to the veteran members of the verbatim staff who had survived two decades of war and peace since Hunter College and Lake Success....they had developed into the finest parliamentary team of shorthand reporters in the world. The verbatim record of the UN spoke eloquently for them.

At 9 p.m. I pulled into the driveway of my home, with visions of a soft bed. My wife was standing at the door smiling curiously. "They just called," she said. "The meeting has been reconvened. They want you back immediately."

—Arnold Cohen

"I stay here because I really believe in the UN," says Isaac, who started at the UN in 1968 as a messenger. "You'd understand if you'd seen what I've seen at the grassroots level. A lot of people think of the UN as Security Council meetings and the General Assembly building. Nobody realizes the little things that happen that make a difference in small villages around the world. They don't see an organization like UNIFEM, which sets up revolving loan programs and helps a widow buy a sewing machine that makes her self-sufficient. They don't see UNHCR, UNICEF, the World Food Programme, the World Health Organization, working together in the field, 24 hours a day, with a mass of refugees and a shoestring budget."

Isaac himself has been part of that grassroots action to help humanity, which is why he chooses to stay at the UN, after winning a portfolio of awards culminating in his selection as 1993's Photographer of the Year by a consortium of the world's camera and filmmakers. As he puts it, "This job gives me the satisfaction of being a human being first. That makes it all worthwhile."

In 1979 Isaac spent 10 weeks in Southeast Asia with the Vietnamese boat people. "At one point," he remembers, "I saw this little girl who had been raped by pirates in the South China Sea. Her father had been shot; her mother had committed suicide after seeing what had happened to her daughter. The girl had not been admitted into the refugee camp yet because she had to go through the paperwork.

"I brought the girl some chocolates," he says. "She just held my hand for about 15 minutes; then she smiled and she took the chocolates. Earlier I had met three nuns who I went and found. I asked them to take care of this girl. They took her. Today she lives in California."

If you ask John Isaac for a picture of this girl, he admits, "I didn't ever take a picture. Everybody commented on that. If I'd worked for a magazine with a short deadline, all they would have wanted was a dramatic picture. To me, it was worth it to be able to help."

For Isaac, the job of UN photographer is both a blessing and a burden. "It gives me a kind of involvement, and that's what we're all here for," he says. "But the toughest job is to hide my tears and focus the camera and shoot." During the Ethiopian famines, he was confronted with a situation of almost intolerable

Leo Rosenthal Collection/UN Archives

United Nations

LEFT: UN cameraman Grant McLean draws an inquisitive audience as he shoots a UN film in Inchon, Korea, in 1950.

BELOW: UN photographer John Isaac poses Jaime de Piníes, UN ambassador from Spain, for his official picture on becoming president of the 40th session of the General Assembly in 1985.

pathos. Entering a refugee camp, where a single doctor and two nurses were trying to minister to thousands of the starving, Isaac was stopped by a woman whose child lay dying in her arms. "The interpreter told me, 'She's begging you to relieve her from the agony of her last child dying,' " Isaac recalls. "She handed me the child, and left. She had lost two other children and this one died in my arms. I spent half the day finding out whether it was a Christian or a Muslim. They do the burials differently, and I wanted to get it right."

Still, anyone who has ever toured the United Nations knows that Isaac's job also brings him joy. The corridors at Turtle Bay are lined with hundreds of photographs, many of them by Isaac, showing Ethiopian farmers at their harvest, Bolivian women weaving cloth, Bedouin horsemen marking a holiday with a raucous discharge of gunfire into the sky. Most of the photographs show the possibility, the hope, the beauty of life, not just desolation and despair. Isaac's pictures are distributed around the world by the UN's Department of Public Information. They have been seen in every country, as part of multipage spreads in *Newsweek* and as individual photographs in Third World publications with no budget

Fred R. Conrad/The New York Times

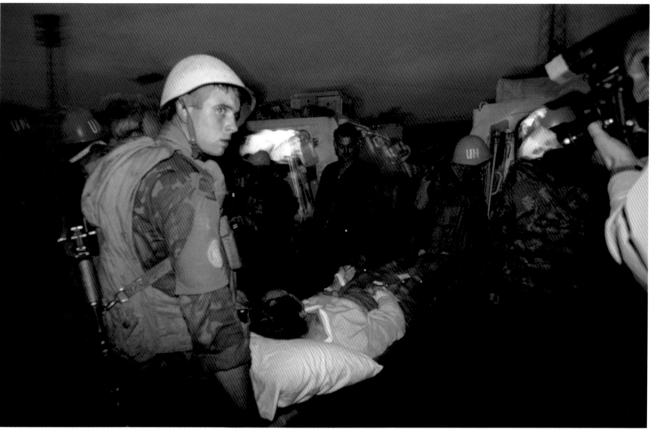

ABOVE *A photojournalist documents the 1994 UN evacuation of wounded residents from Gorazde, in Bosnia.*

to send their own staff abroad. He brings the UN's mission to life for millions of viewers around the world, and that is payment enough for him.

WHEN DONALD MILLS ARRIVED AT THE UN AS JAMAICA'S AMBASSADOR in 1973, he had already compiled an impressive record, first as director of economic planning in his own country, then as the founder of the ministry of development in the Bahamas, and ultimately as the first Jamaican to sit on the board of the International Monetary Fund. "I had not prepared for diplomacy in the formal sense of having training in international affairs," he recalls. "But my experience proved to be very, very helpful. I found out very quickly that if you come into the UN system with experience, it will be recognized."

Ambassador Mills came to New York at a time of crisis—and opportunity. "It was a watershed in international affairs," he recalls. "The crisis in the international monetary system resulting from the unilateral suspension of the convertibility of the US dollar to gold occurred in 1971 shortly after I went to the IMF. Then the OPEC action on oil prices took place. Coming on the heels of those events, in 1974, the proposition on the New International Economic Order was tabled."

The air was heady with talk of change, as smaller nations first felt the possibility that their concerns might receive a full airing in the world forum. The New International Economic Order, as its proponents saw it, was nothing less than an attempt to throw off 500 years of thinking shaped by the colonial era. As Tunisia's ambassador, Mahmoud Mestiri, warned his fellow delegates: "The global economy today is increasingly like the human body. It cannot be healthy in parts. If an arm or leg, even a finger or toe, is infected, the body as a whole is in danger of infection and ill health."

Mills tried to push his colleagues to recognize the changes in international economics he thought the post-colonial era would demand. "When the UN started in 1945, there were only 20 member countries in Latin America, and only four in Africa," he recalls. "In 1973 I was one of only four ambassadors from the Caribbean." The developing countries within the UN formed a caucus, known as the Group of 77 (membership has since risen to 131); as the Group's chair through much of the 1970s Mills took a leading role in debate. He warned his colleagues: "The failure to listen is the obituary of the industrialized world."

Along with other members of the Group, he hoped to convince industrialized nations to reconsider their trade policies toward developing nations. Ideally, the Group of 77 believed, a New International Economic Order would recognize the rights of developing nations to control their natural resources, and encourage the development of a mutually beneficial trade between nations of the North and South.

"The Sixth Special Session of the General Assembly in 1974 was a confrontation," Mills recalls. "When the OPEC nations took control of their own assets and raised oil prices, a panic had set in among the developed nations. We were accused of creating a confrontation, but in fact, the whole world was confronted with an issue that had to be faced. When the Special Session reconvened in 1975, Mills recalls, the atmosphere had changed. "We had spent a lot of time in between in informal discussions, seminars and contacts among people concerned about North–South issues," he recalls. "That is one of the great virtues of the UN system. By the time of the second session, the panic had gradually disappeared. The rhetoric was restrained, and it looked like we had crossed a philosophical bridge in that we had agreed to negotiate. There was a sense of hope."

The following year, the French government sponsored a conference on economic affairs in Paris. "It ended with better understanding of the issues, but no real progress," Mills says. "The lesson I took from that is that no real international economic issue can be handled outside the UN, which is able to find ways of balancing interest between competing groups."

Just prior to a 1979 UN Security Council meeting on Angola, delegates confer: left to right, Donald Mills of Jamaica, Paul John Firmino of Zambia, Leon N'Dong of Gabon, Elisio de Figueiredo of Angola and Abdalla Yaccoub Bishara of Kuwait.

In 1979, Jamaican UN Ambassador Donald Mills, who was then president of the UN Security Council, calls it to order.

Mills' expertise gained him high standing among his colleagues from North and South, East and West; he was president of the Security Council when Vietnam's invasion of Cambodia came before that body in 1979. "It was a major challenge to work together with seven non-aligned countries to reach a consensus," he recalls. "but, on the Security Council, if you can get nine votes, you can achieve a positive result."

Mills went on to serve as president of the UN's Economic and Social Council, and to serve as a prime mover in the North–South dialogue. Although he remains convinced that real change is possible, he looks back with regret at missed opportunities. "If you go to a meeting on the issue today, there's a hidden agenda; it's always there," he says. "It's not an issue created by the developing countries; it's leftover from the 500 years when a small group of countries dominated the world. That system is gone now, but the melody lingers on. You cannot create a system based on equity without addressing the fundamental issues raised by those years, in political, cultural and economic terms."

When he assesses the results of those heady days of the 1970s, Ambassador Mills quotes Chou En-Lai's famous verdict on the French Revolution: "It's too soon to tell." Still, he sees reason for hope. "I believe I can detect some of the things we were talking about in the

1970s in today's discourse," he says. "There is better understanding ... unsustainable production methods ... the developed countries, based on the use of fossil fuel, must be changed ... there is a feeling that the eradication of poverty is an extension of sustainable development. There is a better understanding of North--South ... "

Donald Mills left his position as ambassador in 1981, but he has remained active, performing special ... for the UN and serving as his nation's representative on environmental issues. "I still have a very strong feeling, a very strong sentiment, ... my contact with the UN," he says. "It's the highlight of my career ..."

FOR DAVID SCHAAD, WORKING FOR THE UNITED NATIONS HAS BEEN A homecoming—both physically and emotionally. "I was born and raised in Angola," he says. "The job has helped me get back to my roots."

In 1991 Schaad left a job with a multinational corporation to take a position that was at once demanding, occasionally dangerous, and infinitely rewarding. As manager of the World Food Programme's air operations in Angola, he was responsible for getting up to 3,000 tons of food each week to Angolans in areas occupied by both sides during the nation's internal struggle. "The food came from the WFP and other nongovernmental organizations," Schaad says. "We would sit down with them on Tuesday morning each week and make a distribution plan. We broke down the deliveries into two or three parts, and sent one to the local government for their approval and the other to UNITA (the opposition force). It took four or five days to get any positive reaction from either side.

"Generally speaking, there was always some political involvement, issues on both sides of where we could and couldn't fly. Generally, if we weren't allowed to fly to Malanje by one side, we wouldn't be allowed to fly to Huambo by the other. There was a lot of playing on both sides, but on average they were quite good in letting us go in."

Even so, Schaad and his staff risked their lives every time they flew. "Whenever you take to the air in Angola you're in physical danger," he admitted. "Before each plane left, it had to get a green light at the receiving end. On board each flight we had one of our own flight followers, people who talked to the ground within 10 minutes before to just before landing and got a second assurance that ground conditions were all right." Not even those precautions always worked: One of Schaad's planes was hit by hostile fire and was forced to make a crash landing. "The crew survived the impact of the crash," he reported, "but in leaving the crash site, mines were detonated, and six people were quite severely hurt. One died of the injuries."

Like most UN workers in the field, Schaad observes a strict

Although Dag Hammarskjöld always was reluctant to discuss publicly any aspects of his personal life or tastes, occasionally some details came to light—such as his devotion to poetry.

Leila Doss, a staff member from Egypt, had only a few encounters with the Swedish secretary-general but some remain fresh in her memory more than three decades later. And they involve a shared appreciation for poetry.

She first met the secretary-general while he was on a visit to East ... mission in 1954 and she was in Cairo on home leave from her UN job. Her own UN career began earlier in 1947 when, as a young radio broadcaster she was recruited to help set up the world organization's information services.

Enjoying a leisurely outdoor luncheon within sight of Egypt's pyramids, she was startled to see three familiar figures emerging from between the giant paws. She was spotted by two members of the party, George Ivan Smith, a close aide to the secretary-general, and Sivan Korle, a Turkish national who would become the UN's chief of protocol. The two grabbed and hugged her and then introduced the secretary-general, explaining they had used their few precious hours away from UN business to do some sightseeing.

She had another face-to-face meeting in Bangkok where she was stationed and found herself at a formal luncheon placed opposite the visiting secretary-general (an honor conferred to the only woman guest). Somehow the luncheon patter inspired her to quote but not to identify a line of poetry and the obviously pleased secretary-general completed the refrain.

Poetry next played a part a few years later when increasingly hostile East-West conflicts over the UN's role in the Congo led Moscow to make a blistering attack on Hammarskjöld. Still stationed in Bangkok, Leila Doss was moved to send the secretary-general a short poem, identifying herself only as an unnamed, admiring staff member. The poem was "The Price of

ABOVE *Rwandan refugees encamped around the airport in Goma, Zaire, watch a cargo plane bearing UN relief supplies arrive in 1994.*

Peace" and was written by Amelia Earhart, the American aviator who died while on a plane flight.

"I sent it because the secretary-general was under such tremendous attack and it was a poem about courage and loneliness and seemed to fit him to a T."

It was only a few months later that Hammarskjöld and his party perished when their plane crashed while he was on another Congo peace mission.

"I have been told by his close aides that he often carried that poem in his pocket. I can't help wonder if he was carrying it on his last mission as well."

—Kathleen Teltsch

impartiality; if he had sympathies for either side in the conflict, he keeps them to himself. "We tend to hope that we felt impartial, and operated in an impartial way," he says. "But often it was very hard to convince one side or the other that there was absolutely no partiality in any of this."

Both sides caused damage that threatened wholesale starvation in parts of the countryside; Schaad and his workers threw themselves wholeheartedly into repairing the devastation. The task began when they arrived at "a place that had been made totally incapable of feeding itself—whatever side might have stormed it—and finding just total misery." The reward came "six months later, after our food implementation program, when we saw the people starting to make a living again."

Even though keeping Angola fed was a full-time job, Schaad was called on during the Rwanda refugee crisis to organize airlifts to Goma and Kigali, as well. "We had an average of two flights a day, putting 1,000 tons of food in," he says. "From there, it was shipped out by truck to other locations." In Goma, Schaad's already hard-worked staff essentially created an international airfield out of a strip of bare ground. "Our personnel set up some spare vehicles and some generators to help get the operation off the ground," he recalls. "The day after they arrived, the skies around Goma were congested with airplanes. We had specific

A warehouse full of aid destined for Mogadishu's hungry in 1992: distribution had been stalled by clan fighting in the Somali capital.

allotted landing and takeoff times, and we had to stick to them quite rigidly. The off-loading was boom, boom, boom—quick so that the ramp could be cleared for the next aircraft. It was exciting to be able to help."

Schaad signed on for a short tour of duty, but even with a settlement between Angola's factions in late 1994, he realizes that he is now likely to stay at this "temporary" job for a long time. "Because of the condition of the roads and the needs of the people here, air support is going to be needed for many, many months, or even years," he says. "We're prepared to stay as long as we're needed."

LIKE MANY OTHER PEOPLE FROM AROUND THE WORLD, LENA DISSIN first came to the United Nations as a tourist. Her parents brought her along on a vacation to New York from their native Sweden, and one of the items on their itinerary was the UN tour. "That was in 1969," she recalls. "I was 11 years old. I was impressed by the building, and by the whole institution. It was a childhood dream of mine to work here; the dream came true."

Ten years later, Dissin returned to New York on her own as a tourist, and stopped at the UN to fill out a job application. "In Sweden, the UN is a very idealized institution," she says. "It sounds corny, but I wanted to do something for the betterment of the world, and the UN seemed the natural organization to go to." Shortly after she returned home, Dissin received a telegram from New York, offering her a job as a guide; she has worked at the UN ever since.

"I was in awe at first," she remembers. "I couldn't believe they would even let me in the gate."

She took to the job instantly, giving guided tours in Swedish, English, French and Portuguese. "It's physically exhausting work, giving up to five tours a day," she says. "But no matter how frustrated you are, you have to remember that, for most visitors, this will be their only time at the UN, and you can't let your mood affect their visit."

Dissin moved up through the ranks and is now chief of the UN's guided tours unit. "We average about 1,500 visitors a day, although it varies tremendously with the seasons," she reports. "On a busy day, we have as many as 3,000. The busiest months are May and August—May because it's near the end of the school year, and a lot of New York school groups come, and August because it's the heaviest tourism month."

In peak times about 50 guides are employed, about two-thirds of them women—men have been officially employed as guides only since 1977. Guides must be fluent in English and at least one other language. "We do tours in about 20 languages," Dissin says.

In hiring guides, Dissin looks not just for education but for an interest in world affairs. "You want them to be able to talk about the issues, but you don't want them to be too political," she says. Inevitably, some guides find themselves conducting tours for groups with which their own countries have been in conflict. "It's not at all unusual for an Israeli guide to lead an Arab tour group or a Greek to lead a Turkish group, for example," Dissin says. "They have to learn to be objective, and even to react calmly when tourists try to put them on the spot or antagonize them."

Every day, guides are briefed on current events at the United Nations; often, they receive special briefings from senior staff members on topics of particular interest. What guides say may change from day to day. "Right now, for instance," Dissin said in November 1994, "we are mentioning that the Security Council just terminated the trusteeship status of Palau, ending the job of decolonization. We try to get a little of the spice of the day into every tour."

For all their detailed briefing, guides are often hit with questions that have little to do with contemporary affairs. "The most frequently asked question is, 'Where did Khrushchev bang his shoe?' " Dissin says. "A lot of visitors ask the guides personal questions, like, 'Where do you come from?' or, 'How did you get this job?' One tourist even asked, 'How many hours of sleep does the secretary-general get?' The guide had a good answer: 'I don't know; I don't sleep with him.' "

By far the most amusing questions come from children. "Many of them have no concept of what a country is or what an international organization is," Dissin says. "Some are too young to have any frame of reference beyond New York. One boy asked a guide, 'Where are you from?' and she said, 'I'm from Holland.' He was shocked. He said, 'You mean you were born in the Holland Tunnel?' Another guide was showing a school group the General Assembly hall and told them it was the biggest room in the UN. One boy asked, 'How many dinosaurs would it hold?' I guess that was his measure of bigness. The guide thought for a minute, looked it over and answered, 'Four.' He was satisfied."

Major international crises usually see a sharp rise in the number of visitors. During the summer of 1990, before the Gulf War, the United Nations was in the news every day. "We had a dramatic increase in visitors," Dissin says, "although, when the war actually broke out, we saw a drop. I think people were afraid of terrorist attacks."

UN guides have gone on to a stunning variety of careers in diplomacy, law, medicine and other fields. The current Finnish ambassador to the UN is a former guide. So is Elizabeth Dole, president of the American Red Cross and a former US cabinet official. Few guides stay longer than two years before moving on, which makes Lena Dissin an exception. "I feel privileged to be in this organization," she says. "Whenever it starts feeling like just a job, I just have to look at the schoolchildren

Resting up between tours in 1955 are UN guides (left to right) K. Kwok of China, M. Mysyschyn of Austria, M. Kybal of Czechoslovakia, K. Crowe of the United States, E. Gustafsson of Denmark and I. Wewalka of Norway. Guides today give as many as five tours a day in as many languages.

...watch how excited...seeing the flags and the
...it reminds you...people place...
...to be a part of.

JAMES MURPHY IS ONE OF THOSE UN WORKERS WHO
played...indispensable part in building the United Nations...
...and living in his native city of Cork, Ireland...
...to carry out the UN peacekeeping mission—
...once, but six times... unusual, is it?"
...who he did it. "I mean, we all want peace. That's w...
...world wants, I think. We just believed in our mission."
...young private at the Collins Barracks in Cork in
...commanding officer came in asking for volunteers to...
...the Congo. Irish troops had never been overseas, and a lot of the
...looked at each other and said, "Where's the Congo?" " Murphy
...but Mr. Boland was president of the General Assembly
...and General Sean MacEoin was commanding the UN troops,
and Mr. Conor Cruise O'Brien was working in the Congo, so it made
sense for us to go. There was a terrible war going on, a civil war. It had
to be stopped.

They watched in horror...what should have been
a success story...of Africa's largest nations, just achieving freedom
from colonial rule—threatened to go up in smoke. The mineral-
rich province of Katanga attempted to secede from the new nation; if
the rebellion was not put down, the newborn state, starved of
resources, would probably not survive. Murphy's 33rd Irish Battalion
was airlifted by American planes to Kindu, in the Congo. "Our job was

Guides are important ambassadors in shaping the UN's image among visitors from throughout the world, [Maurice] Liu [chief of the Visitors Service] says. He and his staff agree that an indeterminate, but probably substantial, number of people start the tours indifferent or hostile to the UN but wind up convinced that the "parliament of man" has something to be said for it after all.

"We see a lot of grumbling husbands obviously dragged in, kicking, by their wives," one guide says. "But before the tour is over, they've perked up and joined in with a barrage of questions. At the end, they seem sorry to leave."

Liu recalls a California doctor, admittedly no friend of the UN, who took the tour under duress. A few days later, the US Mission to the UN received a laudatory letter from the medic, who concluded: "Please see that the enclosed is used to further the UN's good work." Attached was a check for $100.

—Ted Morello, *New York World-Telegram,* **1964**

to secure the airport and keep the peace in the town," he says. "We succeeded pretty well. The people were suspicious at first, but they grew to trust us and like us. The Congo was a lovely, green country. You could compare it to Ireland."

The 32nd Irish was assigned to eliminate the roadblocks that bands of rebels were setting up around the town. "They were killing their enemies, raping nuns and killing missionaries, and terrorizing the people," Murphy recalls. "Thank God, we were able to stop it." After a few months, the unit pulled out—and disaster struck. "Two Italian transports came into the Kindu airstrip with supplies shortly after we left," he says. "The moment they landed, they were massacred. Thirteen Italian air force men were killed. They weren't combat troops; they were just bringing in supplies."

The United Nations moved back into the area, and Murphy returned. He would eventually volunteer four times for the Congo, each time living through the horrors of war, each time believing that the mission of peace was worth the risk. But even he had moments of doubt.

"The 33rd Irish Battalion came in after us and went to Katanga," he recalls. "Nine of them were massacred in a place called Niemba. They were shot with bows and arrows, and their bodies were hacked up with machetes. It kind of killed our morale even though we were a thousand miles away from it. I spoke to a soldier who had to go out and collect the bodies. He told me they were putting the sergeant's head in with a trooper's body because they couldn't figure out which was which. It was heartbreaking."

Still, Murphy and his UN colleagues—from Nigeria, Austria and Sweden, as well as Ireland—soldiered on. "One night, we were sleeping in this big field in a place called Elizabethville," he says. "We were all told to get up and into our battle dress at 2:30 in the morning. We thought they were only testing us, but then a priest came out and gave us all the last rites."

Elizabethville, a major strategic city in Katanga, was reached by a main road that at one point passed through a short tunnel under a railroad. Mercenaries allied with the rebels had captured the tunnel. "We were told, You've got to take it over from them," Murphy remembers. "If they held the tunnel we'd be cut off from supplies. By 3:30 in the morning, there were tracers coming over our heads, guns banging and mortar bombs flying. We had to dig in right on the railway line."

The siege of the tunnel went on for two weeks, with the Irish troops and their Swahili-speaking Swedish liaison dug in under withering rebel fire. Although his own life was in danger the entire time, Murphy remembers most his sadness when the order came to unleash a mortar attack on the tunnel. "Not one of us wanted to kill anybody," he says. "That wasn't what we were there for. But it was our job."

After the Congo, Murphy served two tours of peacekeeping duty with the UN in Cyprus, then retired from the military as a corporal. As he sat in the lobby of the Cork Opera House one morning telling his story, he suddenly remembered something held long forgotten. "There was a company sergeant named O'Lachlan, a good man," he said. "He ordered the engineers to put this massive memorial cross on the spot where the lads were killed, with their names and all the information about them. Someday I'd like to find out if it's still there."

IN FIFTY YEARS, THE UNITED NATIONS HAS SURVIVED AND GROWN because of the people who believe in it. All have been willing to dedicate their lives to its aims; some have even given their lives for what the UN stands for. This is the UN spirit—a belief, strongly held and carefully nurtured, that it is possible to make a better world, and that the United Nations can help bring that world into being.

Irish peacekeepers in the Congo in 1960: They were part of a contingent of 15,700 UN peacekeepers from 11 countries sent to ease the transition to independence.

CHAPTER FIVE

Safeguarding the Environment

Safeguarding the Environment

David E. Pitt

H ISTORY'S BIGGEST DIPLOMATIC GATHERING ENDED MUCH AS IT
had begun: with talk of children, and of children to come.
"I'm at a stage of my life where probably none of this is going to affect
me personally," said Maurice F. Strong of Canada, the then 63-year-old
chief UN organizer of the Earth Summit. "But it will affect my children, and your children, and all of our grandchildren."

Eleven frenetic days earlier, on an earth-toned dais adorned with
gigantic Amazonian potted plants and twin video screens, Secretary-
General Boutros Boutros-Ghali had opened the summit on a similar
note. "Never in history will so much depend on what you do or not do,
for yourself, for others, for your children, for your grandchildren, for life
in all its varied forms," he told hundreds of ambassadors, who had filed
into the hangar-sized Plenary Hall in their pin-striped, dashikied and
sari-draped best. It was June 3, 1992.

The secretary-general, his address punctuated by the whir of
motor-driven cameras and the other-worldly chirp of cellular telephones, predicted that the Earth Summit would mark not only a turning point for the planet but "a new point of departure for the United
Nations system," one in which its specialized agencies would become
the organization's cutting edge in the new world emerging from the
rubble of the Cold War.

Officially, the meeting in Rio de Janeiro, Brazil, was called the
United Nations Conference on Environment and Development—
UNCED, in the alphabet soup of UN acronyms. Headline writers soon
dubbed it the Earth Summit. To the delight of Maurice Strong, who
had dreamed up the name long before, it stuck.

In keeping with its mandate, the summit was gargantuan: 178
governments and 30,000 participants, of whom 9,000 were accredited
journalists and 3,000 were citizens representing nearly 1,500 nongovernmental organizations accredited by the United Nations. Thou-

Bill Gentile/SIPA Press

Stephen Ferry/JB Pictures

WFP/Roodkonsky

PREVIOUS SPREAD *When retreating Iraqi troops set fire to Kuwaiti oil fields in early 1991, between 4 million and 8 million barrels of oil were destroyed, sending viscous black clouds over northern Kuwait for months. The scale of the destruction sent shock waves around the world, prompting the United Nations to establish a disaster fund to coordinate cleanup efforts.*

TOP *A river of waste courses through the backyards of a Haitian community in 1990.*

ABOVE *A Brazilian worker ignites forest land to clear it for development: Extensive destruction of the Amazon rain forests threatens a delicate ecological balance.*

ABOVE *Special nurturing for a seedling in an effort to turn a bit of Mali desert back to green. According to a UN report, 160 million acres of productive land in sub-Saharan Africa has turned to sand over the past 50 years.*

sands of others came to Rio without special credentials.

There were 108 national leaders—the largest such gathering until 1995 (when the World Summit for Social Development in Copenhagen drew 117). There were seven vice-presidents; two princes; an emir (of Kuwait); the Holy See's secretary of state; two ruling chairmen—of Lesotho and Belarus—and a governor-general, Sir Wiwa Korowi of Papua New Guinea.

Assembled on risers for a group photograph, implacable enemies like Presidents George Bush of the United States and Fidel Castro of Cuba rubbed elbows with counterparts they had rarely, if ever, seen—people like Prime Minister Tofilau Eti Alesana of Western Samoa and President Vigdis Finnbogandottir of Iceland. A bystander remarked later that it looked like a college graduation ceremony. As flash-bulbs popped, President François Mitter-rand of France, Prime Minister John Major of Britain and Premier Li Peng of China traded quips with President Suharto of Indonesia and Prime Minister P. V. Narasimha Rao of India. Chancellor Helmut Kohl of Germany exchanged pleasantries with President Jean-Bertrand

ABOVE *In a show of solidarity, UNCED Secretary-General Maurice Strong smokes a peace pipe with Brazilian and North American Indians at the World Conference of Indigenous Peoples on Territory, Environment and Development.*

Aristide of Haiti and Prime Minister Girija Prasad Koirala of Nepal.

A separate galaxy of famous people was also in Rio for the summit, many of them at Maurice Strong's invitation. A multimillionaire businessman as well as a diplomat, Strong had created his own private public-relations network to augment the UN's. The celebrities included Shirley Maclaine, Olivia Newton-John, Roger Moore, John Denver, the Beach Boys, Jane Fonda and Placido Domingo. Even the Dalai Lama showed up. The painter Robert Rauschenberg, deeply moved by the goals of the summit, contributed a poster, painted in bold greens and yellows, whose image was also used on T-shirts. At the top was an oath: "I pledge to make the earth a secure and hospitable home for present and future generations."

A HALF-HOUR'S DRIVE FROM THE SUMMIT SITE, PAST RIO DE JANEIRO'S most wretched favelas, another summit was opening its doors—a parallel conference of 7,892 registered citizens' groups that called itself the '92 Global Forum. Beset by last-minute money problems, it had gotten off to a wobbly start. But thanks to the frantic efforts of its coordinators, Warren Lindner of the US and Tony Gross of Brazil, and the propellent energy of thousands of activists from 167 countries, it soon steadied itself. It was a dizzyingly diverse gathering, including, for exam-

LEFT *One important performer at the opening of the Rio Earth Summit takes a beach break.*

BOTTOM RIGHT *Conferring at the 1972 UN Conference on the Human Environment in Stockholm are delegates Gordon J. F. Mac-Donald of the US, D. M. Kitching of the UK and A. Van Tilburg of the Netherlands. They were among the 1,200 UN delegates from 130 nations who attended the two-week conference.*

ple, a contingent of Esperanto proponents from Rotterdam, a sheet-metal and air-conditioning contractors' association from São Paulo and a guild representing filmmakers in Kazakhstan. But it was made up mostly of people representing causes close to the hearts of most non-governmental organizations: environmentalists, women, the young, businesspeople, scientists, industrialists, trade unionists, farm and plantation workers, religious and spiritual leaders.

The forum was also the sponsor of one of the first world conferences of indigenous peoples, whose highlight was a meeting of loin-clothed hunter-gatherers, which took place in a down-to-the-last-detail Amazonian village specially constructed for the occasion near the Earth Summit site. But the Global Forum's main business was conducted in Flamengo Park, a seaside expanse of green and white tents near Rio's business district, where seminars, debates, speakers' forums, séances, teach-ins, prayer services, parades and the like went on virtually round the clock for 12 days. For those who spent most of their time at the forum, it might as well have been Carnival time—a blur of marches, parties, concerts, demonstrations, revelation, inspiration, no sleep, bad food and good fun.

THE MAIN OBJECTIVE OF THE SUMMIT WAS TWOFOLD: TO FIND WAYS TO curb the industrial nations' appetite for natural resources and their contributions to global pollution, and to help the less developed countries pursue economic development in dramatically less destructive ways. It was an agenda that had grown out of a gradual but momentous shift in public understanding of the natural world.

They came by the hundreds that late summer of 1949—naturalists, diplomats, economists, ichthyologists, engineers, geologists, physicists, mammalogists, social scientists, even a renowned mathematician—thronging a cavernous former aircraft-stabilizer factory in Lake Success, Long Island, for the UN's first scientific conference on the environment.

Truman had proposed the 52-nation gathering in 1946, convinced that the postwar world had to find ways to preserve and properly exploit the natural resources that struggling countries needed to lift themselves out of poverty.

The goals of the UN Scientific Conference on the Conservation and Utilization of Resources were modest. No treaties or ringing declarations were contemplated. And beyond an opening address by Secretary-General Trygve Lie, there was little ceremony. In fact, it was less a conference than an outsized brainstorming session. And that was the beauty of it: 708 of the world's best minds free to indulge in three weeks of uninhibited debate.

"The conference was a way to get past the foreign offices of the world to involve people who really had something to say," recalled Arthur E. Goldschmidt, a US delegate and top adviser to the Secretary of the Interior.

The delegates' output was prodigious. By the end of the conference, they had produced 550 papers on everything from fuel, energy, minerals and water to land, forests, fish and wildlife.

The layout of the converted

Sperry Gyroscope plant seemed to help. "There was something about the horizontality of the place I always felt nostalgic about," he said. "It was a huge space in a single-story building, so you were always meeting new people.

"A lot of problems were discussed, but nobody brought up any specific solutions," Goldschmidt said. "That would have been difficult in those early days."

But with Truman's encouragement, the UN began shaping a role for itself as a catalyst for bold new programs of aid to the neediest.

"The conference was a wonderful beginning for the UN in terms of Third World development, especially the UN's technical assistance programs," said Goldschmidt, who went on to help design many of them himself. "It was part of an important educational process."

—David E. Pitt

In the traditional view, the planet was an infinite supermarket without the inconvenience of a checkout line, its resources freely available in any quantity. But beginning in the 1970s, a realization took root that the earth's carrying capacity was limited; and that environmental problems, once thought of as local matters, were beyond the capacity of any one nation to solve. With that came a more profound insight: that the earth is an interdependent, infinitely complex system of organisms and biochemical processes that can be abused only at our peril.

The seeds of the UN's involvement were sown soon after its founding, when the United Nations Educational, Scientific and Cultural Organization, UNESCO—established in 1945—began an effort to persuade governments to back collective environmental protection measures. The initiative, including a conference held at Fontainebleau in October 1948, led to the creation of a pioneering nongovernmental organization: the International Union for the Conservation of Nature and Natural Resources.

Other UN-sponsored conferences followed. Two were especially significant: the 1949 UN Scientific Conference on the Conservation and Utilization of Resources, said to have originated with a suggestion

Yutaka Nagata/UN

133

by President Franklin D. Roosevelt, held in Lake Success, New York; and the 1968 Biosphere Conference in Paris, which offered 20 recommendations for how to move toward cooperative action on the environment. But these and other early conferences came at a time when governments tended to view the protection or destruction of their environment as a purely internal matter.

By the late 1960s and early 1970s, transboundary threats to air, land, water and life itself were becoming more apparent to scientists. So, too, was the link between economic activity and a deteriorating global environment.

This link and the notion that humans, if prodded, are smart enough to alter self-destructive forms of behavior, became principal themes at the UN Conference on the Human Environment, held in Stockholm, Sweden, in 1972.

The Stockholm meeting helped put environmental concerns on national and international agendas as never before. It established the principle that the health of the environment was a matter of concern to all nations, and it led to the establishment of the United Nations Environment Programme. UNEP had a double mandate: to push for international action, and to establish a world-

134

TOP LEFT *Haitian school children make their way in Cité Soleil, Port-au-Prince in 1995: When poor nations must meet a daunting array of basic needs, environmental concerns are often the first to be put on the back burner.*

LEFT *A river of debris from a Bangkok construction site becomes a swimming hole for youngsters in 1992—a graphic reminder of the environmental down-side of some modern-day development.*

ABOVE *Life in the shadow of a Calcutta power station in 1990. Pressed to supply ever-growing populations with inexpensive energy, developing nations often turn to coal-power, which can contribute to global warming. If current trends continue, carbon dioxide emissions from developing countries will eventually exceed those of the developed world.*

Josef Polleross/JB Pictures

Smudged faces and filthy clothes—as well as respiratory infections for 96 percent of the children—are the norm in Copsa Mica, Romania, in 1990. The problems result from the toxic emissions of nearby ink and tire factories that are so thick on some days the town is shrouded in black clouds.

wide scientific monitoring system to identify problems early.

The agency operated on a virtual shoestring. But under Maurice Strong, its first executive director, and later Dr. Mostafa K. Tolba, an Egyptian scientist who served tirelessly as UNEP's chief for nearly two decades, it encouraged the spread of thousands of nongovernmental organizations whose members helped prod governments into action. The results were dramatic. In the 10 years after the Stockholm conference, more than 40 separate international conventions or treaties on the environment were concluded, almost as many as in the preceding 40 years.

But the Stockholm gathering failed to come to grips with the issue that was to overshadow international debate two decades later: how to close the gulf between rich and poor countries. The industrialized nations represented only 20 percent of the world's population, yet they controlled 80 percent of its income, 75 percent of its energy, 85 percent of its wood products and 72 percent of its steel production—and they had shown little inclination to alter the situation.

Fifteen years after the Stockholm meeting, a blue-ribbon UN panel, the World Commission on Environment and Development, declared that the need for cooperation between rich and poor was essential to human survival. The commission, headed by Prime Minister Gro Harlem Brundtland of Norway, said it was no longer realistic to consider issues of environment, development, poverty and uncontrolled population growth in isolation from each other. "These are not separate crises," the Brundtland Commission told the General Assembly in its book-length report, *Our Common Future*, "They are all one."

Two months before the Earth Summit, the Brundtland Commission reconvened in London to reaffirm the urgency of putting the world economy on a path toward sustainable development.

"We know what we have to do; it is time to do it," said the commission, whose members included William D. Ruckelshaus, the US Environmental Protection Agency administrator in the early 1970s; Shridath S. Ramphal of Guyana, former secretary-general of the Commonwealth of Nations; and Bukar Shaib, Nigeria's minister of agriculture, water resources and rural development.

"Unsustainable forms of development have destroyed previous civilizations," the commissioners said, "but we have now endangered life on a planetary scale. Sustainable development, with its concern for the needs of people today and tomorrow, is ultimately a moral and ethical issue. Yet it unites virtually all human concerns: for security, a nourishing environment, economic progress, democracy, international cooperation and a safe future for our children."

Asserting that sustainable development was good for what ailed the world was one thing; mustering support for a coherent program of action was another. The obstacles were both demographic and attitudinal: a bred-in-the-bone yearning for affluence, and all that money can

Refuse pickers sift through Smokey Mountain, Manila's largest dump, in 1986. It is thick with the haze of smoldering fires caused by spontaneous combustion deep within the mounds of garbage.

buy, in the industrial countries; a likely doubling of world population to perhaps 10 billion people by the middle of the next century; deepening disparities between rich and poor that had left more than a billion people, mainly in Africa and Asia, struggling just to feed themselves; and a globalized economic system that had taken no account of ecological costs or damage, touting unfettered growth as progress.

Meanwhile the whole concept of sustainable development—defined by Maurice Strong as "development that does not destroy or undermine the ecological, economic or social basis on which continued development depends"—came under flanking fire from a couple of formidable critics.

Edward Goldsmith, founder of *The Ecologist* magazine, dismissed sustainable development as a contradiction in terms. Economic development, Goldsmith declared, had long been civilization's foremost organizing principle. The difficulty, he argued, is that development is also "a process which by its very nature must increase systematically the impact of our economic activities on an environment ever less capable of sustaining them, and ever more deeply degraded by them."

José Lutzenberger, a Brazilian ecologist who was briefly his country's environment secretary, was similarly blunt. If sustainable development meant more schemes of the sort the World Bank had traditionally financed, like dams and coal-fired generating plants, the human race was doomed, he said. Moreover, Lutzenberger insisted, there was no evidence that the 20 percent of humanity who control nearly all of the world's wealth was prepared to cut back on its wasteful consumption of natural resources—or to stop promoting its

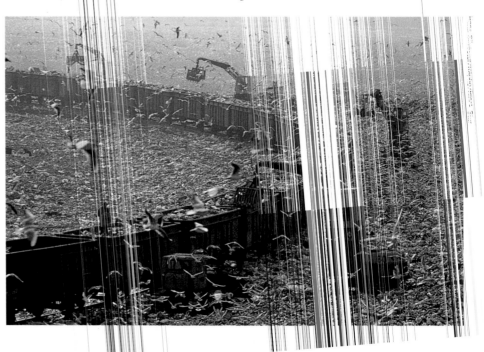

LEFT Waste from Spolchemie, a Czech chemical plant, in 1990. The parting of the Iron Curtain revealed widespread destruction of the environment in former communist countries.

BELOW At the Entressen dump in Marseilles, the largest in France, 130 train cars unload a thousand tons of refuse every day. In 199_, studies suggest that ground water in surrounding areas has been contaminated by the huge mountain of garbage.

ABOVE *The Fresh Kills landfill in Staten Island, New York, rivals the Great Wall of China as the largest man-made construct in the world.*

consumer-driven lifestyle as something to which the rest of humanity should aspire.

"If the whole world had the consumption patterns of the US, Germany, Holland and so on, we'd all be dead," Lutzenberger said at a UN seminar in New York shortly before the Rio summit. He blamed business and political interests in his own country for laying waste to Brazil's rain forests. He also advised industrial nations to withhold environmental aid from developing countries unless they wanted to see it siphoned off by corrupt politicians.

His candor did not go unnoticed in Brazil. Word of his remarks soon reached President Fernando Collor de Mello, and less than three months before the Earth Summit, Lutzenberger was booted from the cabinet.

BY THE TIME THE SUMMIT CONVENED, IT WAS CLEAR THAT THE TRANSI-tion to sustainable development, if it ever came, would not come easily or cheaply.

Two and a half months before Rio, at a stormy conference in New York, Strong had shocked the seven major industrial governments with his estimate of how much the developing Southern countries would need in assistance from the North. It came to $125 billion a year, a $70 billion increase over existing annual aid flows.

Eventually the developing countries would be expected to cover the bulk of that bill—but "first and foremost," Strong said, they would need "financial support to strengthen their own scientific, technological, professional, educational and related institutional capacities." Where to get the money? For starters, Strong listed debt reduction, improved terms of trade and new sources of revenue, such as global taxes on polluters.

Compared with the trillions spent worldwide on military budgets—at a rate the UN put at nearly $800 billion a year in 1991 dollars—the money Strong mentioned was modest. But in an era of recession and economic retrenchment, the reaction of the industrialized North was one of sour skepticism.

"Unrealistic," grumbled Michael Hazeltine, Britain's secretary of state for the environment. Besides, Hazeltine said, "You can't just say, 'Here's the money' without knowing what you're getting for it."

Britain and other Northern governments were also insisting that any new money would have to go through channels that they then effectively controlled, such as the Global Environment Facility, a fund administered jointly by the World Bank, the United Nations Environment Programme and the United Nations Development Programme. This attitude reflected increasing skepticism about the use to which development funds had been put over the years. With industrial nations under growing pressure to cut back on public spending of all kinds, many questioned whether developing countries could be trusted to put the money to proper use—or, indeed, whether the transfer of aid from rich to poor countries—an estimated $1.4 trillion since 1960 (in 1988 dollars)—had made any difference at all.

The developing countries were outraged. The burden of responsibility for the environmental crisis rested with the North, they argued, and if the rich countries weren't prepared to finance environmentally benign development in the South, there was little more to be said. "We'll do what we please with our environmental resources," the refrain went, "and we're not going to become conservationists unless you pay for it."

"The moment of truth has arrived," said Ambassador Chandrashekar Dasgupta of India, whose eloquence and deep baritone made him a star spokesman for the so-called Group of 77, the then-129-member bloc of developing countries. "All of us will be watching," he said. "And when I say all of us, I don't just mean the countries of the South. I mean everybody who is concerned about the environment, every serious NGO, every citizen of this planet who has a genuine concern about the

Children plunge through layers of garbage to cool off in the waters around Naples, Italy, in August 1979.

141

environment will now be watching to see whether rhetoric is matched with finances."

Some Western leaders counseled understanding. "We should not be surprised that the developing nations are approaching the Rio Summit with open economic demands," said Norway's Brundtland. "For them it is essentially a conference about development and justice."

DESPITE ALL THE TALK ABOUT SUSTAINABLE DEVELOPMENT, THERE WAS nothing particularly sustainable about the pre-summit preparations in Rio. The government of President Collor—who months later would be driven from office in a corruption scandal—spent what many Brazilians thought were obscenely large sums to spruce up the city, inspiring endless comments about how the money might have been better spent in a country of desperate poverty and vanishing rain forests.

Officials laid out millions just to upgrade the summit site, a modernistic convention center in an exclusive beach suburb west of the city. They also built an expensive blacktop highway to whisk dignitaries from the airport—and to spare them any views of Rio's ubiquitous street urchins and favelas.

The security was imposing, to say the least. The government stationed so many tanks and gun-packing soldiers on the streets that ordi-

Ray Witlin/UN

BELOW *A dust storm whips through the countryside near Lake Baringo, Kenya, in 1984. Poor agricultural practices, combined with sustained droughts, have made such dust storms and the specter of famine common throughout much of Africa.*

Up in smoke: Ten percent of the forest cover of Brazil's rain-forest has been burned off.

BOTTOM RIGHT *Enrique Iglesias, sec-retary-general of the 1981 UN Conference on New and Renew-able Sources of Energy in Nairobi, wields a load of firewood, an energy source that can be replen-ished, during a demonstration over the energy crisis. On his left is Kenyan Minister for Energy John Okwanyo.*

nary Brazilians began to wonder whether the military had quietly seized power again.

The bristling show of force was also a reminder of the refusal of most governments at the summit to acknowledge war and militarism as a factor in social and environmental destruction. The conflagration in the Kuwaiti oil fields after the Gulf War erupted in 1991 was only the most recent example. Other controversial subjects were either finessed or completely avoided in the summit documents. The Vatican and its allies succeeded in keeping the texts free of any specific references to family planning and contraception, while France, whose electricity is produced largely by nuclear generators, led a drive against any language relating to the production and use of atomic energy. In yet another conference room, Saudi Arabia and its oil-exporting allies repeatedly blocked debate on the use of fossil fuels, a major factor in air pollution and global warming. And the United States and most Northern governments closed ranks against any extended debate about their own wasteful patterns of production and con-sumption.

The conference man-aged nonetheless to address a multitude of pressing issues: It focused attention on the consequences of cli-mate change; on the deci-mation of wildlife occur-ring in tandem with the

destruction of the world's remaining forests; on transboundary pollution, global poverty, clean water, the degradation of the world's drylands and the special environmental vulnerability of small island nations. It affirmed the vital importance of women's rights, the prerogatives of indigenous peoples, the rights of children, youth and students. Negotiators talked about equity, about rich and poor, North and South, life and death. But ultimately the summit was about money—lots of it.

MORE THAN TWO YEARS LATER, ON THE EVE OF THE UN's 50TH anniversary, the legacy of the Earth Summit remained hard to define.

"The millennium it ain't," Bella Abzug, the former American congresswoman and women's advocate, had said on the last day of the conference. "But it's a great beginning."

By 1994 many wondered about even that.

Friends of the Earth, an international citizens' group, said the summit agreements represented little more than "business as usual."

They and other nongovernmental critics saw the Rio conference as simply a reaffirmation of the very developmental values that had helped create the environmental crisis in the first place.

"At school you teach us to behave in the world," 12-year-old Severn Cullis-Suzuki, the daughter of an outspoken Canadian environmentalist, said in a UNICEF-sponsored speech to the delegates in Rio. "You teach us not to fight with others, to work things out, to respect others, to clean up our mess, not to hurt other creatures, to share and not be greedy. Then why do you go out and do those things you teach us not to do?"

Maurice Strong had said in his keynote address that nations must remain ever-conscious that "we are all in this together." But by 1994 there was little evidence that governments had taken his warning to heart. The financial commitments Strong and others sought not only never materialized; the overall level of development assistance from the 24 industrialized rich countries actually plummeted 10 percent between 1992 and 1993, from $60.8 billion to $54.8 billion—a result partly of a long-running global recession. "Even the rich are feeling poor," he said.

The collapse of communism had yielded nothing resembling a hoped-for "peace dividend." Indeed, with the end of the competition among superpowers for influence over the developing nations, there was less overseas development money than before. Extreme poverty continued to spread, even in the developed nations, while unemployment and signs of social distress deepened on a global scale.

The UN Commission on Sustainable Development, set up to monitor implementation of Agenda 21, the summit's 800-page "blueprint" for sustainable development, bemoaned the lack of money for

Pilot whales are slaughtered for meat in the Faro Islands in 1992. When such traditional hunting methods fly in the face of efforts to protect whales, they often become the focus of international attention.

development and what seemed to be an overall lack of momentum—but offered little hope it could do much to improve matters.

"Development is in crisis," Secretary-General Boutros-Ghali declared gloomily in May 1994.

Little was done to redress the summit's most singular failure—the collapse of efforts to save the world's forests. Two years later the developing countries were still accusing the industrial nations of hypocrisy and obstructionism, and the timber continued to fall, at a rate estimated at close to 200 square miles a day.

The Framework Convention on Climate Change, negotiated separately and signed in Rio, remained essentially toothless thanks to the efforts of US President George Bush. He had opposed "targets and timetables" for reducing carbon dioxide emissions, calling them a threat to jobs and free enterprise.

The Framework Convention on Biological Diversity, an agreement to conserve the world's plant, animal and microbial species, fared better. Bush had disavowed it as unfair to American companies, but his successor, Bill Clinton, agreed to sign a version with the understanding that businesses would be offered more patent protection for products made from genetic material found in the rain forests of developing nations.

By late 1995, ratification efforts remained stalled in Congress.

Late in 1994 Under Secretary-General Nitin Desai, an Indian economist who had worked for years alongside Strong and Brundtland, told the General Assembly that, while the momentum had ebbed somewhat, progress had been made. He cited, among other things, the October 1994 signing of a treaty to combat land degradation and desertification, especially in Africa; a 1994 global conference on how to promote sustainable development in environmentally fragile small-island nations; and advances in talks on controlling marine pollution, the export of hazardous waste and coastal-zone management.

For many people, including numerous diplomats, the summit's most palpable single accomplishment was to legitimize the role of non-governmental organizations as players in the negotiating process—an unprecedented development in the history of a famously insular organization. By 1994, with the UN in the midst of a series of major follow-up conferences on various aspects of development, the presence of NGOs in the inner sanctums of government negotiators had become routine.

Desai—chief of the UN's newly created Department for Policy Coordination and Sustainable Development—told the General Assembly that the high level of citizen involvement in the Commission on Sustainable Development was already one of Rio's most enduring accomplishments.

Strong, who had startled some supporters by returning to Canada to head up a giant utility known as Ontario Hydro, commented that, while there had been "a natural tendency to lapse back to business as usual, there are encouraging signs that Rio has given rise to an explosion of interest and initiatives at the grassroots level."

Despite the mixed results and dashed hopes, many believe that the Earth Summit will come to be seen as the UN's first step toward fulfilling the promise of its 1945 charter: to be "a center for harmonizing the actions of nations" in solving international problems, building the economic, social, cultural and humanitarian conditions for a peaceful world.

"We now have a framework for global environmental cooperation and a set of principles for global environmental action," said Dr. Noel Brown, the former North American regional director of the United Nations Environment Programme. "The common ground has been found."

John Nordell/JB Pictures

LEFT *A field of windmills in California harnesses the wind: According to the UN, achieving sustainable development means increasing the use of renewable sources of energy, like wind and solar power.*

ABOVE *Indian women hand-water a small grove of trees in 1989.*

CHAPTER SIX

The Population Challenge

The Population Challenge

Vivienne Walt

THIS IS HOW THE WORLD LOOKED FROM THE SAN FRANCISCO conference in 1945: Little more than 2 billion people lived on the planet, of whom about two-thirds lived in what was known as the Third World. One-quarter lived in big cities. New York was the biggest, with 12 million people. Only one developing world city, Shanghai, had as many as 5 million people. By the turn of the century, the thinking went, there would be a bulging world population of 3.8 billion.

Five years short of the new millennium, there were in fact 5.7 billion people living on earth, about 80 percent of whom were living in the less developed countries of the world. And although the rate of increase has slowed, according to some projections, by the year 2015, there will probably be about 7.47 billion people with most in the developing world. Of those, 450 million will live in 27 cities of 10 million or more people each. Shanghai is now dwarfed by other developing world mega-lopolises (a word that came into use only in the 1960s) like Mexico City, São Paulo, Lagos and Bangkok.

Whole communities unimaginable in 1945 have sprung up amid the mausoleums of Cairo and atop the garbage dumps of Port-au-Prince. Cities have split their seams, sprawling in a jumble of high-rise housing projects and shanties and swallowing up the countryside.

It took several thousand years for the world's population to reach 1 billion; more than one century for it to reach 2 billion; and just 30 years---from 1930 to 1960—to reach 3 billion. Until very recently, "most of mankind subsisted in a uniform state of natural propagation, with a fertility close to the maximum level, passively responding to the changing toll of death," said an early UN report, attempting to come to grips with the new circumstances.

By the time the UN was founded, the nature of how people lived and died had begun changing fundamentally and forever. As better health pushed lifespans far beyond the limits to which people had lived

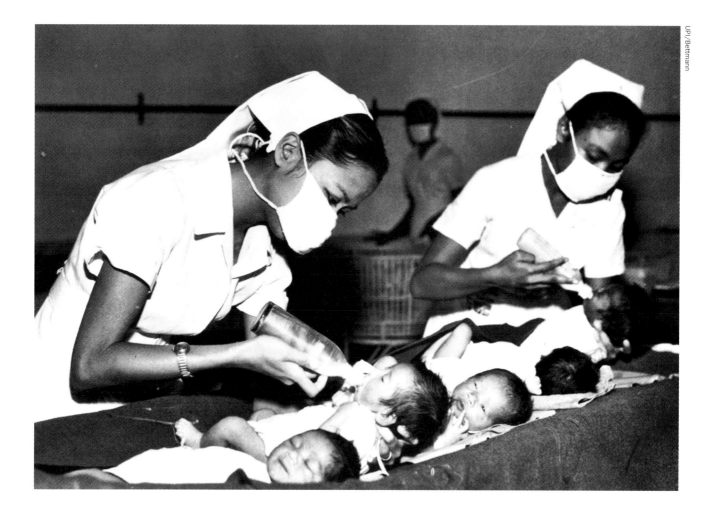

PREVIOUS SPREAD *Time for breastfeeding in a busy Philippine maternity ward.*

TOP *Newborns at Surabaya General Hospital in Indonesia line up for feeding in 1961.*

ABOVE LEFT *UN Secretary-General Javier Pérez de Cuéllar visits newly-born Matija Gaspar in 1987 at a Zagreb, Yugoslavia, hospital. The United Nations Population Fund chose the boy, born July 11 of that year, to symbolize the 5-billionth baby to enter the world.*

ABOVE *Listening for the heartbeat of a baby in utero, a nurse at a health center outside Phnom Penh, Cambodia, attends to a mother-in-waiting in 1992.*

United Nations

for centuries, human beings were finally defeating their natural enemies, and multiplying at a much more rapid rate.

The finer details of population growth were sketchy in 1945. Yet the UN's founders understood that an essential first step in developing the world's poorest nations was knowing how many people lived within their borders. The founders also realized that, before the UN could address the problem of how many people the planet could support, it would need a reliable head count of its present population.

At the time, however, few reliable censuses existed outside Europe and North America. "Census and vital statistics, were so incomplete that it was hardly possible to speak of world population trends or of world population problems," said Richard N. Gardner, a key US official pushing population action during the 1950s.

In 1947, the United Nations formed the Population Commission, a group made up largely of scientists, which set out to train demographers and conduct studies in different parts of the world. Early on, the UN's Population Division, which served the Commission, its more technical body, established three demographic centers---in Bombay, Cairo and Santiago. For at least the first decade of the UN's existence, the Division was the primary interpreter of demographic statistics, for use in planning economic programs.

One of the earliest, and most enduring initiatives, was the Population Council, which John D. Rockefeller III founded in New York in 1952. Like the UN at the time, it began by researching population rather than trying to affect its growth. Still a major population research organization, the Council now works closely with UN agencies. "When we started, there was no demographic study, so we didn't know the extent of population problems," said Sandra Waldman the Council's spokesperson. "It was also a very controversial subject." The Council helped organize the Population Division's regional research centers, which provided some of the first close-up studies of the developing world urban population growth.

In 1966, Rockefeller drafted and circulated a statement to some 30 heads of state in the first public endorsement of international family planning programs. Three years later, the United Nations Fund for Population Activities (UNFPA) began to coordinate those efforts.

"The big issue was, what was too many people?" recalled Rosalind

Delegates chat during the 10th session of the UN Population Commission at the Palais des Nations in Geneva in 1959. Left to right, standing: Pao-Yi Tsao of the Republic of China; Emile de Curton of France; Jacques Mertens de Willmars of Belgium, the chairman of the Commission; and C.E. Bourbonniere of Canada. In the foreground is Germano Jardim of Brazil.

A Peruvian military cadet interviews a Lima family as part of a government-organized national census in 1961. The effort was part of a UN-sponsored world population census.

Harris, a longtime population consultant to the United Nations who later headed CONGO (a coalition of nongovernmental organizations). "And if you had development, would you get an automatic drop in population growth, like the United States?" It would take almost 17 years—until UNFPA was created in 1969—for officials to stop arguing over that question and actually do something.

The UN first ventured into the highly charged area of family planning in 1952, when the World Health Organization (WHO) sent Dr. Abraham Stone to India, at the Indian government's request, to begin a program promoting the "rhythm" method of contraception. The issue was so controversial that Stone's experimental mission was the last such initiative for several years.

"The usual ploy at the UN was to ask for studies when you didn't want action," said Julia Henderson, who headed the International Planned Parenthood Federation for decades and who worked on population issues as a senior UN official during the 1950s and 1960s. "They asked for studies expecting there would be so little interest in following up on them that we'd all be discouraged."

Family planning advocates like Henderson suspected UN officials

LEFT *Kids in Bihar, India, get a meal prepared by mothers who took a nutrition class in 1975. The classes were offered to help overcome the anemia that afflicted nearly half of India's children under five.*

BELOW *A Haitian woman heads for home with food and clean water—basics for a healthy family.*

BOTTOM RIGHT *Baking corn tortillas at a refugee camp in El Salvador during the height of the civil war in 1981. Poverty and crisis have often strained the capacity of many developing countries to meet the nutritional needs of their people.*

of dodging the issue to avoid a confrontation with the Vatican, whose supporters included member nations and UN officials. The Roman Catholic Church was the only religious organization to have permanent observer status at the United Nations, though no vote. And long before UNFPA was founded, Rome drew up the battle lines. "Your task is to ensure that there is enough bread on the table of mankind," Pope Paul VI told the General Assembly in his first address to the UN in October 1965, "and not to favor an artificial control of births, which would be irrational, in order to lessen the number of guests at the banquet of life."

Henderson recalls that after Secretary-General Dag Hammarskjöld asked her to take over the Population Commission in 1954, she faced bitter arguments among officials over whether the UN should start any family planning initiatives at all.

The World Health Organization had won some significant battles against disease and early death in the developing world. Yet Henderson notes that when its first director, Dr. Brock Chisholm, suggested family planning programs as a means of controlling the population explosion, "his board not only refused to take any action, he was severely rebuked for having brought the subject up." WHO's board included several Catholics, and like many UN delegates from the developing world, they preferred to keep governments out of the world's bedrooms.

Under FAO's Freedom from Hunger Campaign, NGOs and others were invited into the development dialogue and together with the Campaign's national committees raised monies to go for development projects in cooperation with governments and the UN.

One project brought the government of India, UNICEF, FAO and the Joint UN/FAO/WFP together to help increase milk production and improve nutrition in Gujarat State. There was to be a feed mixing mill, a center to improve the breeding and care of buffalo and a dairy plant to process and dry milk. UNICEF and FAO were involved in advice on milk plants and buffalo breeding, the UN/FAO/WFP was to supply feed grains for two years until local supplies could meet the mill's capacity and the Campaign's UK committee the money to equip the feed mixing mill—a seven-story complex to house all its machinery.

So its dedication was a political event of national importance with the prime minister of India, Sri Lal Bahadur Shastri, A. H. Boerma, the first executive director of WFP, and, on behalf of the UK Freedom from Hunger Committee, myself as coordinator of the Campaign.

It was a great day with tours of the buffalo center, mixing mill and villages in the surrounding area. Its culmination was the dedication ceremony with thousands upon thousands of peasants on the ground under the vast white tenting. Boerma spoke his short piece and I spoke my few words. Both little speeches to deathly silence of tens of thousands who hadn't a clue as to who we were or what we had said in a foreign tongue. Then the prime minister went forward and there was an awkward delay while the microphones were brought down from the height needed by Boerma and I, both nearly two meters tall, to Shastri's height just about a meter and a half! He began quietly and with a notable change in audience attention—one could feel the concentration. Then there was an uproar of laughter, which went through the throng and turned solid stares into broad grins and rocking body motions.

Boerma and I pressed the prime minister's aide who was seated between us to let us in on the joke. And with some embarrassment he translated that the prime minister had said that this was an important gathering, important for each person there and their children too. The great building which was next to them would provide better food for their buffalo and their buffalo would give more milk and this would mean better health for them and their children and more money for them too. But they had to work hard, they had to grow more grain and care for their buffalo. Maybe, he said, if they did work hard and were serious, they could see their children grow up and become giants—like these two gentlemen who have brought you the feed mill and grain to feed your buffalo.

—Charles H. Weitz

By the 1960s, however, food providers—including the UN's own Food and Agricultural Organization (FAO)—were not at all sure that the banquet table could seat all the world's people. In 1964 B. R. Sen, an Indian who served as the FAO's director-general between 1956 and 1967, offered a stark challenge to delegates attending a religious conference in Bombay: "Can we any more turn our faces away from the concept of family planning when the alternative is starvation and death?"

A question around which many discussions had centered for years now became a matter of intense global debate: Would economic development—simply a rise in living standards—by itself lead people to opt for smaller families? Or would aggressive population programs be needed? Some voices argued that waiting for development to take an evolutionary course was cruelly unrealistic. In the developing world, the efforts of Western groups like the International Planned Parenthood Federation were often viewed as a kind of demographic imperialism, a means of preventing billions of developing world citizens from overrunning the industrialized West.

By the end of the 1960s, some powerful Western figures were pushing the United Nations to take more action. Among the most influential was World Bank President Robert S. McNamara, who believed

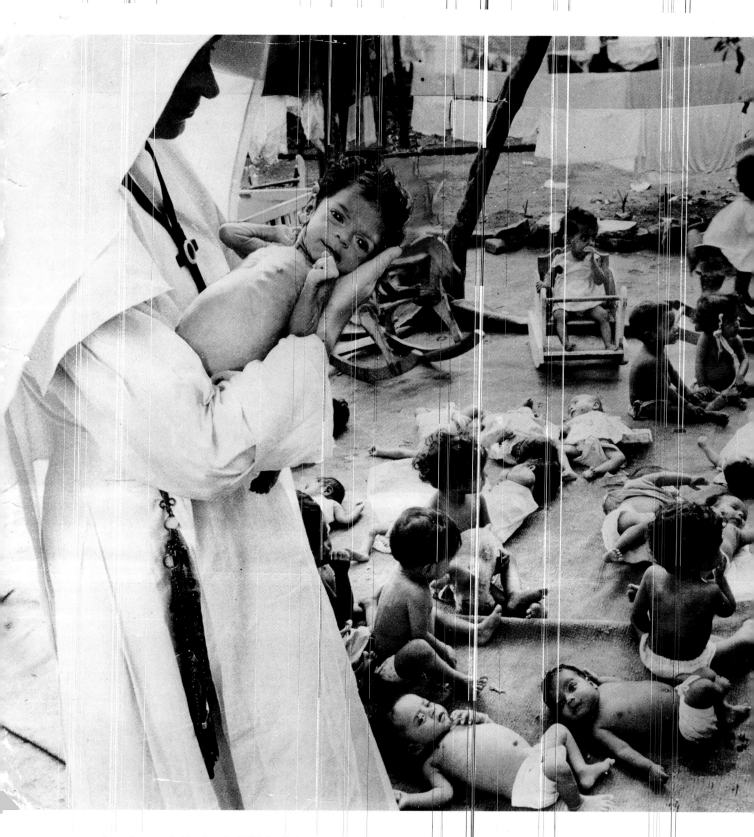

ABOVE *An orphanage in Bombay in 1961 is filled to capacity—living evidence of India's population surge.*

RIGHT *A matched pair: Twins born at the Maternity Hospital in Ankara, Turkey, in 1973.*

the institution's loans to developing world countries were being undermined by rapidly expanding populations whose demands were outstripping whatever economic growth was achieved. In 1968 McNamara told his board of governors that "more than anything else it is the population explosion which…is blowing apart the rich and the poor."

"It had to be a worldwide movement; it couldn't be the US telling the developing world how to control its population," recalls William H. Draper III, who later became administrator of the UN Development Programme. His father, General William H. Draper, Jr., founded the Population Crisis Committee, one of the central advocacy groups that helped implement UNFPA's mission. After returning from service in World War II, the general went to work for an electrical company in Mexico, where, his son says, the overwhelming poverty shook him so profoundly that he devoted the rest of his working life to population policy. The younger Draper recalls his father's badgering of President John F. Kennedy. "My father convinced Kennedy—Kennedy the Catholic!—that this was really an important issue for the government to sign on to."

In the Cold War era, however, statements like McNamara's and Draper's inevitably sparked hostility from socialist countries, whose leaders argued that their economies could provide enough for everybody and that the West's overconsumption of resources was a greater cause of poverty than the world's numbers.

Chairman Mao Zedong, for example, believed that his style of communism would be best served by having many millions of peasants. It was only during the mid-1960s that China's leadership embraced the idea of population control as a key to its modernization program; in 1979 China announced a one-child-per-couple target, with a goal of 1.2 billion people by 2000.

In fact, by 1994 China had already surpassed its goal for the end of the century, but the rate of growth had slowed dramatically. By the second millennium, projections

suggested, India could well overtake China as the world's most populous nation.

For many years it was the nations of Southeast Asia, particularly India, that provided the impetus for direct UN action. In the words of Rafael M. Salas, a Philippine politician who became the first executive director of UNFPA, "It was the Asian countries which kept population issues alive in international forums and which began an international laboratory for the formulation and implementation of strategies...."

ABOVE *Bath day on the streets of Phnom Penh in 1992: Years of civil war in Cambodia have taken their toll on basic services, making everyday tasks a challenge.*

BELOW *Within sight of the modern downtown high-rises of Lima, a Peruvian child grows up in poverty. By the year 2000 more than half the people on earth will live in cities.*

THE WORLD POPULATION CONFERENCE, HELD IN BUCHAREST IN 1974, began a once-a-decade political evaluation of the world's progress. At each of these get-togethers, the era's political schisms have been played out in debates that have touched on some of the most personal and politically charged decisions in people's lives.

Thus in 1974 the gathering of more than a thousand delegates from 136 countries became an occasion for heated sniping between socialist countries of the East and capitalist countries of the West. It was also a stage upon which to battle over the ideological schisms dividing the impoverished South and the rich North.

The chief delegate of Algeria, who chaired a working group at the conference involved with drafting a World Population Plan of Action, led the developing nations' attack on the document, demanding that the plan should include redistributing the world's wealth in a so-called New International Economic Order and blaming much of the world's poverty not on overpopulation but on the West's overconsumption of resources.

ABOVE *Children play in a garbage-strewn puddle in a suburb of Port-au-Prince, Haiti, in 1994. Poverty and the political crisis of the early 1990s aggravated Haiti's health and sanitation problems, triggering an increase in infant and maternal mortality.*

China's chief delegate similarly argued that "the primary way of solving the population problem lies in combating the aggression and plunder of the imperialists...."

After days of often acrimonious debate, a compromise was delicately negotiated in which Western governments accepted that controlling population and reordering the world economy were not mutually contradictory. The plan included guarantees that no program would be imposed globally on individual nations—a principle adhered to during the following decades.

While the conference helped to spread the message that for countries to thrive economically they must stabilize their population, the plan of action drawn up in Bucharest was woefully lacking in specific programs. A disappointed Julia Henderson, still head of the International Planned Parenthood Federation in 1974, complained that the document "virtually amounts to no plan, no action."

The mid-1970s saw a growing realization that population programs were doomed to fail if women were not actively involved in formulating them. Yet most delegates to Bucharest were men, and Rafael Salas, while grasping the critical need to strengthen the right of women to determine family size, focused heavily on building the political

consensus and less on building women's capacity to decide family size.

In the years following the Bucharest conference, it was clear that family planning successes depended heavily on the religious and political peculiarities of each country. At this time, too, Africa emerged as the continent most likely to present severe population problems. In some countries, women—particularly in rural areas—saw having numerous children as a way to ease their workload and enhance their social standing. Where the infant mortality rate was still high, having more children increased the chance that some offspring would survive into adulthood. And in Nigeria, Africa's most populous country, the constitution tied federal representation to the number of people living in each area. "Each community regarded as suicidal absurdity any effort to reduce its fertility rate," says Omari Kokole, a Ugandan academic now teaching at the State University of New York in Binghamton.

So far, only a few African countries have been able to check their birth rates. Although more and more Africans have access to birth-control methods, the continent now is the fastest-growing region in the world. By the United Nations' 50th anniversary in 1995, UN demographers were warning that within a century, Africa—though least able to afford it— could have about double the population of the industrialized countries.

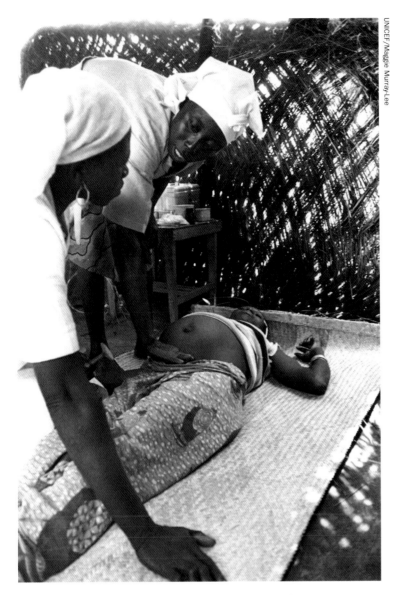

ABOVE *A traditional birth attendant instructs a young trainee while examining a pregnant woman in rural Chad in 1990.*

BY THE TIME OF THE SECOND GLOBAL population conference, held in Mexico City in 1984, there was almost universal agreement that world population growth had to be brought under control, with or without dramatic economic reforms.

"In Bucharest, there was a sense that, if we just developed everyone, you didn't need family planning programs," recalls Joseph Speidel. Speidel spent 14 years setting up population programs in the developing world for the US Agency for International Development. "By the time of the Mexico conference, that thinking had vanished," said Speidel, who had since become the head of Population Action International, an advocacy organization based in Washington, D.C. "It was amazing to me. It seemed there had been substantial change."

That change left the American delegates isolated. Under the guidance of President Ronald Reagan, delegation head James L. Buckley announced that the US would freeze millions of dollars to UN and private population programs, which the Americans claimed indirectly financed abortions and subsidized coercive family planning policies. Sensitive to their powerful anti-abortion supporters a few hundred miles north of the conference hall, US delegates argued strongly for programs driven by economic development.

The Americans, said a delegate from the conservative British government "will be totally alone on this."

Jason L. Finkle, a University of Michigan professor who has written widely about UN population policies, noted that the US's hard-line approach had an unintended effect: "Donor countries and developing countries alike departed with a renewed commitment to strengthening population policies and programs."

In retrospect, this was the real news from Mexico City.

SINCE ITS FOUNDING, UNFPA HAS USED ITS SMALL FIELD STAFF AND ITS political clout at headquarters to build consensus, to encourage policymakers to pay attention to population and push for action. When Nafis

Sadik assumed control of UNFPA in 1987—the same year the organization changed its name to the United Nations Population Fund—the emphasis shifted from consensus-building to action with women as the focus of attention. The shift came at a time when donor nations began demanding that the UN use their money for more nuts-and-bolts activities.

Sadik was uniquely qualified for the job. She had begun her career as a doctor and family planning educator in her native Pakistan, making a name for herself as someone who could win over both peasant women and their husbands, and be politically savvy as well.

As she prepared for the third global population conference, the International Conference on Population and Development, held in Cairo in 1994, Sadik decided to make women's rights—largely sidestepped at Bucharest 20 years before—the centerpiece of the plan. Sadik's strategy was to give grassroots organizations a direct say in the Cairo document, thus addressing a problem that had dogged governments for all of UNFPA's 25 years: By trying to impose policy from the top, population programs often created resistance at the bottom.

Thus, in April 1994, as delegates gathered at UN headquarters to draft the conference documents, more than 4,000 representatives of nongovernmental organizations—overwhelmingly dominated by women's groups—were registering to attend their own conference, the NGO Forum. In earlier deliberations, in New York, they started pushing for freedom of choice in reproduction and child-rearing, and for a far stronger emphasis on educating and improving the skills of women in the developing world. Their presence in Cairo in September 19__ ensured that the decision-making delegates at the summit across the street would be held accountable for years to come by a well-organized network of determined women.

"Governments are losing authority," observed Steven W. Sinding, director of population sciences at The Rockefeller Foundation. "That vacuum is being filled by NGOs, which are now defining the agenda. I don't think any future UN conference will be controlled by governments as past UN conferences were."

The 20-year plan that resulted from the Cairo conference was hugely ambitious, demanding primary education and literacy for every-

Early in my medical career, I worked as a doctor in a Pakistani army clinic on a base where my husband was posted. I noticed that the wives of the soldiers were constantly ill, some very seriously, mostly due to complications from too frequent pregnancies. I counseled the women to space their pregnancies and, in some cases where there was a grave risk to their health, not to have any more children.

Their response shocked me. It was their husbands and families, the women said, that insisted they keep on having children, preferably boys. They had no say in the matter.

I realized that in order for family planning to be effective, something had to be done to help women who were powerless to control their own destinies.

I decided to bring family planning to the clinic. I knew I had to create an atmosphere that would make family planning less of a taboo subject. Although it caused a bit of a scandal in those days, not only did I speak to the women about family planning but I also lectured the men about not getting their wives pregnant all the time, even purchased condoms with the clinic funds and started to distribute them.

Because of my interest in the subject, I eventually began to work directly in the fledgling family planning movement, rising to head the Pakistan National Population Office before joining UNFPA in 19__ shortly after its formation in Pakistan, and later in many countries I visited as a UNFPA official, I found that women were in much the same position as the women who visited the army clinic—they had little power to make decisions for themselves. What good was establishing family planning clinics if women had no say in how many children they were going to have? How could we have development that neglects the health and well being of women?

— Dr. Nafis Sadik, executive director, UNFPA

one, better employment opportunities for women and universal access to basic health services. In all, it would take billions annually to implement. More than that, in many countries it would require a virtual revolution in thinking.

Although thousands of women flew to Cairo as delegates, most returned to countries, and homes, where almost all decisions are made by men. "We are in the minority of those making the laws," said Bene Madunagu, a family planning advocate from Lagos, at the NGO meeting in Cairo. "Men will have to have the will to change those laws."

OVER THE 26 YEARS OF ITS EXISTENCE, UNFPA HAS MADE SOME REAL gains in spreading a family planning culture and the message that uncontrolled population growth can drain a nation's resources and devastate its environment. The UN may still be seen by some as a Western-dominated institution intruding on developing world sensitivities. Yet in many countries UN funding has resulted in new national population policies and action plans, marking a break from past reluctance to tackle the issue at all.

Looking back over UNFPA's life, Sinding summed up: "The old argument that characterized the issue since 1974—development versus family planning—is over. Today we know we have to work on both."

Securing Relief and Refuge

Securing Relief and Refuge

Sheila Rule

THE SPRING OF 1992 WITNESSED THE BEGINNING OF ONE OF THE greatest migrations of the century—the hopeful return of more than 6 million Afghan refugees who had fled their homeland during a 14-year-long war that ended in April 1992, when a coalition of Islamic guerrilla armies toppled the Soviet-backed government in Kabul.

They had lived for years in the sprawling encampments set up to house them in Pakistan and Iran. Now, they thought it would be safe to return.

At the time, Robert Breen was the senior repatriation officer for the United Nations High Commissioner for Refugees in Peshawar, Pakistan. He recalls rising at 4:00 AM to watch the surge of humanity moving out of the city and up toward the dust-colored peaks of the Khyber Pass: "I'd go to the camps around Peshawar to watch people loading up their belongings. It was overwhelming to be able to go along the road through the Khyber Pass and watch lines of trucks loaded with animals, bedding and children on top and bikes tied to the back. People were festive; there was such optimism."

The refugees were impatient to return. Their numbers were staggering. Breen and other UNHCR staff members decided that, given the immensity of the problem, it would be best to let the refugees themselves arrange for their return. Meanwhile, UNHCR would provide each family with about $130 in cash to help family members get back on their feet once they had returned to their home village or city, and a three-month ration of 300 kilograms—roughly 660 pounds—of wheat.

The decision to assist in their return was immediately challenged. It was wrong, the critics said, to encourage people to return to a countryside littered with mines. For Breen and others, this missed the point: The Afghans had formed a human flood that could not be held back. For UNHCR staff, the whole issue boiled down to a single question: How can we help these people?

Reuters/Bettmann

PREVIOUS SPREAD *Landscape of despair: Rwandan refugees set up camp in Tanzania in 1994 to avoid the bloodshed of civil war in their own country.*

ABOVE *In 1991 a million Kurds fled northern Iraq for Turkish tent camps when Saddam Hussein's military declared war on them. Relief workers often had to protect children from being crushed by starving adults in the scramble for food.*

RIGHT *Having fled the fighting in the country-side, Afghan refugees cram a UNICEF food distribution center in Kabul in February 1989.*

Alain Keler/Gamma Liaison

At the height of the Soviet-Afghan war, as a photojournalist, I spent a few months with the Afghans and their leader, Commander Massoud.

In 1990, the United Nations asked me to be a consultant in opening a grain supply road between Termez in the former Soviet Union and the northern part of Afghanistan, controlled by Massoud. The pro-Soviet government was in control of the cities in Afghanistan. The rest of the country, broken up into many political, ethnic or religious parts, was challenging the government's authority. Due to the danger, Massoud was refusing to allow the negotiators to pass through his territory.

So the UN asked my help in persuading Massoud to change his mind. Why me, a photojournalist? It's a thin line between humanitarian work and journalism. I view the humanitarian world as a field army with the nongovernmental organizations acting as reconnaissance troops and the United Nations as the heavy artillery. I agreed to carry out this mission because I wanted to help the Afghans and to learn more about this army.

In nine months, we were able to knock down political barriers, open some roads, help to hold elections, establish a food-for-work program for 10,000 workers, as well as clinics, schools and other programs.

I view the United Nations as a modern, bureaucratic Tower of Babel. Indeed, this is the way it was described by a "wise man" I met in the Pamir Mountains. Before he gave me permission to let the grain go through, he asked me many questions. And then he said: "Now I understand: the United Nations is the pioneer for world government of the future."

Having completed my mission, I resumed my career as a photojournalist.

—Reza

LEFT *Near the frontier dividing the Soviet Union and Afghanistan, road conditions were often so treacherous that food arrived one bag at a time.*

RIGHT *In northern Afghanistan, a road construction crew gets a meal in a UN-supported food-for-work program at the height of the Soviet–Afghan war in 1990.*

BELOW *Afghan refugees-turned-road-builders set out for work in northern Afghanistan near the Soviet border in 1990. Part of a 10,000-man crew in a UN-supported food-for-work program, they constructed passages through the mountainous terrain to get food and relief to remote regions of the war-torn country.*

ABOVE When Seoul fell to the Communists in the winter of 1950, 1 million of the city's 1.2 million citizens fled the city for safer zones in the south. Retreating UN troops frequently stopped to rescue babies strapped to the backs of mothers who had fallen dead from disease or starvation.

TOP RIGHT Polish refugees traveled in boxcars to return home at the end of World War II. They were among the more than 6 million European refugees assisted by the United Nations Relief and Rehabilitation Administration in the aftermath of the war.

RIGHT Emergency facilities at the Municipal Hospital in Athens were so crowded during the Greek civil war in 1947 that the wounded were treated wherever there was room.

Throughout the summer of 1992, the flood surged over the borders. Then, in August, came "the stab in the heart," as Breen puts it. Fighting erupted among the guerrillas, this time in and around Kabul, the capital, which had survived intact throughout the previous years of war.

When the renewed fighting began, Breen recalls, "100,000 people a week were crossing the border. The fighting in Kabul meant that a new population was fleeing. So our people positioned at the border crossings started counting both ways. In the period through the winter of 1992–93, we had 90,000 leaving Afghanistan and 1.2 million on their way back into their homeland."

EVER SINCE THE END OF WORLD WAR II, THE EBB AND FLOW OF refugees has posed a vast and complicated problem for the United Nations. The UN founded the agency known as the United Nations High Commissioner for Refugees in 1951. (High Commissioner is both the name of the agency and the title of its chief officer, who is nominated by the secretary-general and elected by the General Assembly.) At the

ABOVE *At least 200,000 Algerian women and children fled to Morocco and Tunisia during liberation struggles in the 1950s. With no hope of asylum, the United Nations High Commissioner for Refugees provided enough aid to keep them alive until they could return home.*

TOP RIGHT *Refugees of Greek ethnic origin from the Soviet Union are settled in Greece with the help of UNHCR in 1959. Then, as*

now, *the UN's policy was that voluntary repatriation is preferable to resettlement in other countries.*

RIGHT *Refugees fleeing the bloody Soviet crackdown against Hungary's democracy movement clogged the roads leading to Yugoslavia in 1957. Many who found refuge in empty hotels along the way had to leave when the tourist season began.*

time, almost all of the refugees were Eastern Europeans, impelled to flee their homelands by the chaos after World War II. Because the problem seemed temporary, UNHCR was given only a three-year mandate.

When UNHCR came into being, "refugee" was defined in essentially Cold War terms. The 1951 Convention Relating to the Status of Refugees stated that a refugee was a person who, "owing to well-founded fear of persecution for reasons of race, religion, nationality, membership of a particular social group or political opinion, is outside the country of his nationality and is unable, or owing to such fear, is unwilling to avail himself of the protection of that country."

Over time, however, as floods and famine and other calamities uprooted hundreds of thousands of people throughout the world, it became apparent that this definition was cruelly limited. Thus, in recent years, the UN's secretary-general and General Assembly have asked UNHCR to assist people like those in the former Yugoslavia who are living like refugees within their own country.

Larry Burrows/Life

Over the years, too, the responsibilities of the office of the high commissioner have been redefined. Originally, its role was limited to helping to coordinate the work of private organizations. The hands-on work of delivering aid was the responsibility of host countries and nongovernmental organizations, with UNHCR providing supervision, technical advice and a limited amount of money. Now, the agency has been pressed into service as a take-charge group that helps to arrange temporary asylum for refugees and to provide food, water and shelter to encampments the size of cities. As a minor concession to the magnitude of UNHCR's never-ending task, its mandate is now renewed every five years instead of every three.

The agency has always operated on a slender budget. Its first high commissioner, Dutch lawyer Gerrit Jan van Heuven Goedhart, faced with a refugee emergency and finding donors slow to contribute, raised a quick $14,000 by selling a bar of gold left by a League of Nations predecessor organization. It was during Goedhart's term of office, in 1955, that UNHCR won the first of two Nobel Peace Prizes.

In 1956, just as it seemed that Europe's postwar refugee problem

Nearly half a million people were killed when a monstrous tidal wave swept over the coastal regions of East Pakistan in 1970, literally washing away everything in its path. The only way food relief could reach the starving survivors was by helicopter.

An East Pakistani family flees civil strife for a refugee camp in India's northeastern region in March 1971. More than 9.5 million such refugees fled to camps within India where UNICEF and UNHCR provided food and assistance.

had been settled, another wave of refugees spilled over European borders. This time the refugees were hundreds of thousands of Hungarians fleeing their homeland during and after the brutal suppression of a popular uprising against their Soviet masters. In less than three weeks, 35,000 people crossed the border into Austria, whose government promptly turned to the High Commissioner for help. The agency dug into its shallow pockets, came up with $25,000 in emergency funds and then—forcefully and with considerable success—called on UN member nations to contribute real money and provide asylum.

In the 1960s, UNHCR was often called upon to help in Africa, as ethnic hatred forced large numbers of Tutsis in Rwanda to flee to neighboring Burundi and, a few years later, caused Hutus from Burundi to seek refuge in Rwanda. Mozambique, during its protracted war of independence, was the source of another stream of refugees.

During the next decade, the focus was on Southeast Asia. In 1971 nearly 10 million Bengalis fled from what is now Bangladesh to escape fighting between Pakistan and India. They flowed back the following year to the newly established nation of Bangladesh. Later in the 1970s, UNHCR did what it could to ameliorate the condition of hundreds of thousands of Indochinese refugees who fled from Vietnam and Laos into neighboring countries or, with whole families crowded into small fishing boats, ventured into the South China Sea to seek asylum.

"The flood of boat people reached such proportions that, at a certain point, the countries they first came to—the so-called countries of first asylum—didn't want to receive any more of them," recalls Pierre Jambor, who was UNHCR's deputy representative in Thailand from 1977 to 1980 and its representative there from 1988 to 1990. "There were episodes in which people were not being admitted to the shores. There was piracy, a lot of people killed at sea.

This led in 1979 to the first international conference on Indo-

UNICEF/Jonathan Weinberger

chinese refugees, mainly boat people. The agreement reached at that conference was that countries of first asylum would continue providing asylum on the understanding that other countries—through UNHCR and other agencies—would then financially support these people and give a guarantee that they would eventually be accepted for resettlement elsewhere."

In 1981 UNHCR was honored with a second Nobel Peace Prize, for providing assistance to the "tremendous and

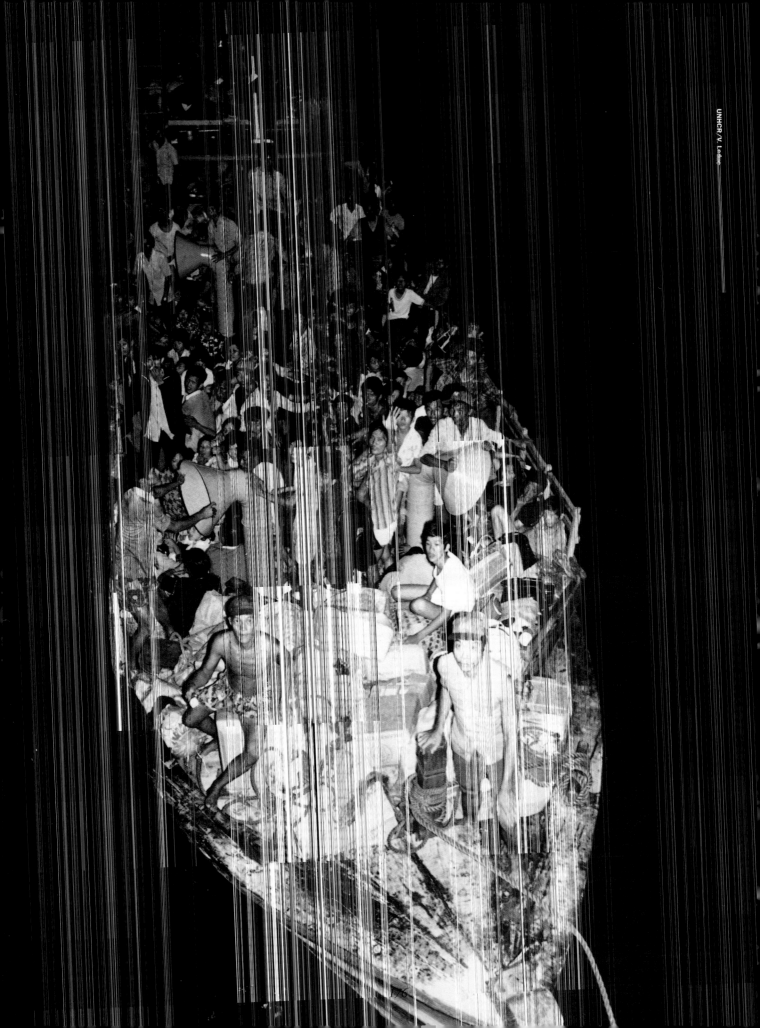

LEFT *In the mid-1970s, over a million Vietnamese boat people set out in search of safe haven, but four in six never reached their destination. Lost on the South China Sea near Indonesia, 326 refugees find rescue.*

ABOVE *Commercial and naval craft frequently intercepted dilapidated Vietnamese boats to retrieve a sad cargo of dead and dying refugees. In high seas, 55 refugees make a precarious climb to the safety of a US naval vessel.*

increasing number of refugees" and for trying to cope with "a veritable flood of human catastrophe and suffering." The agency's chief officer at the time, Poul Hartling, former prime minister of Denmark, characterized the award as a message to the world's refugees that "you are not forgotten."

Throughout the decade, UNHCR continued to answer calls for help—assisting Afghan refugees, Sri Lankans, Ethiopians and Sudanese, all driven from their homelands by civil war.

IN THE 1950S THE WORLD'S REFUGEES NUMBERED AROUND ONE MILLION. By 1974 their number had grown to 2.4 million. By 1984 the figure had swelled to 10.5 million. Ten years later the number had more than doubled, to exceed 23 million.

"It's a very bad sign when our business is booming," observes Pierre Jambor.

There was reason to hope that UNHCR could consider closing up shop when the last decade of the 20th century began. Cold War enemies were now friends. East and West were no longer walled off from one another. People spoke of a peace dividend.

And then, incredibly, war broke out again in Europe as Yugoslavia split apart in 1991. A year later, ethnic hatred fanned by demagogues led to a conflagration that has yet to be put out. Once again, civilians

were massacred and prisoners starved and tortured; once again, the dead were buried in mass graves.

The conflict in the former Yugoslavia caused the largest mass movement of refugees and displaced people in Europe since World War II. In April 1993 High Commissioner Sadako Ogata noted with alarm that nearly 3 million people in Bosnia and Herzegovina depended on the United Nations for rations. In an appeal to the leaders of the aid-giving countries, she spoke of her "deep alarm" at the shortage of food supplies, adding that there had been no response to her appeal a month earlier for $817 million to fund relief efforts in the former Yugoslavia for the rest of the year.

For months the staff of UNHCR, nongovernmental organizations and others had been risking their lives to deliver humanitarian aid. But the rival armies failed to honor their commitment to let convoys of food and medicine go through to those for whom the aid meant survival. In February 1993, in an attempt to pressure the opposing political leaders into letting the convoys pass, Ogata suspended most relief operations.

After several days, UN Secretary-General Boutros Boutros-Ghali rescinded her order. For many, the act seemed to symbolize the world body's confusion over how to deal with a maddeningly complex problem.

UNHCR's special

TOP LEFT *Water distribution for Rwandan refugees in Zaire in 1994. Supplying clean, potable water is essential to avoiding disease in crowded refugee camps, and one of the first chores of UN relief workers.*

LEFT *Rwandan refugees have their wounds treated at a first aid tent in the Benako Camp on the Tanzanian border in May 1994.*

ABOVE *A fearsome combination of war and drought in the mid-1980s forced hundreds of thousands of Ethiopians to search for food and security. Weakened by hunger and leaning on walking sticks, many traveled for weeks to reach relief camps in neighboring countries.*

In just one 24-hour period, when civil war erupted in April 1994, a quarter-million Rwandans swept into Tanzania. It was the largest and most rapid exodus UNHCR had ever witnessed. In the months that followed, more than a third of Rwanda's 7.3 million people fled their homes.

ABOVE *A Saudi soldier hands out food supplies to some of the 18,000 refugees in the town of Safwan in southern Iraq. They had fled Saddam's vengeance when Shiite rebels tried to take advantage of his vulnerable Sunni-dominated government in the wake of the Gulf War.*

TOP RIGHT *Hungry Kurdish refugees rush a UN relief helicopter as peacekeepers struggle to maintain order at a camp in Turkey in 1991.*

RIGHT *German planes air-drop supplies from the United Nations in 1991 to a Kurdish refugee camp run by the Red Crescent along the mountainous Turkish–Iraq border.*

envoy to the former Yugoslavia, Jose Maria Mendiluce of Spain, directed relief operations in Bosnia-Herzegovina from the beginning of the war, in April 1992, until his departure, in May 1993. Mendiluce viewed the war from a different perspective. He witnessed and endured the shelling of Sarajevo.

"It was a nightmare," Mendiluce recalls. "We didn't believe that sort of massive shelling against a civilian town, the capital of an independent country, would last long. But things got worse and worse, and some days we were totally under siege. Many times they were shooting at us. We witnessed people killed in the streets. We would try to bring wounded children into our car. We would take someone by the arms. We would end up only with the arms, which were separated from the body because the people were already destroyed.

"It was difficult to accept the fact that the siege and the shelling aroused no significant reaction from the international community. Like the people of Sarajevo, we felt abandoned. We felt this killing, this atrocity, was not going to be accepted, but it was accepted by the international community, by the UN, with only resolutions and declarations being issued to cover our conscience and convince public opinion that we were doing something.

"We realized from the beginning that the only argument criminals under-

stand is force, and the criminals knew the Western world was not ready to use force against them."

While Secretary-General Boutros-Ghali and High Commissioner Ogata differed on how to make the rival armies honor their commitment to let humanitarian supplies reach suffering civilians, and while European countries balked at providing asylum to those fleeing from the war, Mendiluce strove to honor UNHCR's mandate.

In April 1992, shortly after the start of the war, Mendiluce was traveling by car from Belgrade to Sarajevo. The only way open led through the town of Zvornik, where a Serbian offensive was under way to "ethnically cleanse" the town of Muslims.

"I found myself in the middle of Zvornik, where I saw the shooting, the way they were putting bodies of children and elderly people in trucks," he recalled. "There was so much blood that our car was slipping in blood. I was stopped by a group of nervous and drunk

Enrique Martí/Impact Visuals

RIGHT *The weight of the moment bears down on a woman from the Croatian town of Vukovar as she prepares to leave her embattled home. The town fell to the Serbs in November 1991 after a three-month siege.*

BOTTOM RIGHT *Muslim children peer from a refugee bus in Bosnia in 1993. By 1994 the war in the former Yugoslavia had created nearly 4 million refugees of whom more than 600,000 were children. An estimated 15,000 children had died.*

militiamen who had realized what I had just witnessed."

Fearing that he and his driver would be killed, Mendiluce tried to contact the nearest UNHCR office by car radio. But the radio wasn't working, so he pretended to make contact, first with UNHCR, then with Serbian leaders in Belgrade. He is convinced that the ploy saved his life and that of his driver.

"They moved barricades and allowed us to leave," he says. "For the first 500 meters I was concerned about my future. There was an enormous number of Serbians behind me, and it would have been easy for them to shoot me and accuse the Muslims."

But no shots rang out. Eventually, out in the countryside, Mendiluce came upon a group of Muslims. They told him that, up ahead, he would find thousands of survivors of the Zvornik massacre who were trying to escape through the mountains. They pleaded with him to help them.

"So," Mendiluce says, "instead of continuing on to Sarajevo, I decided to go and see what I could do. I found 6,000 survivors, many of them wounded, desperate, terrified. Finally, I succeeded in establishing contact with Sarajevo. I declared all these people under my protection and asked my people to evacuate these survivors to a

ABOVE *UN High Commissioner for Refugees Sadako Ogata briefs the press along the Thai-Cambodian border in 1992 as UNHCR's repatriation of 350,000 Cambodian refugees gets under way.*

TOP RIGHT *Having fled the Vietnamese occupation of their country, a group of 14 anxious Cambodian teenagers arrive in Zurich in 1984 from a UNHCR-run camp in Thailand for resettlement in eastern Switzerland.*

RIGHT *At the Otaki Reception Center in Battambang province in 1992, a helicopter transports former Cambodian refugees in one of the largest repatriation operations ever undertaken by UNHCR. A thousand refugees a day returned to Cambodia between 1992 and 1993.*

town under the control of Bosnia.

"At that moment, UNHCR's involvement was decided. It proved that sometimes, if you are there and if you make the decision to do something, you can save many, many lives."

Catalyst for Trade
and Development

Catalyst for Trade and Development

Bhaskar Menon

THE WELL-DRESSED MEN AND WOMEN WERE HUSHED AS THE FIGHT-ing cocks were brought into the ring. A nervous laugh rippled through the group as the handlers checked the razor-sharp spurs on the birds and set them at each other. The action was swift. The birds lunged and thrust in quick, short flurries. Specks of crimson soon flecked the ground; then the iridescent feathers became damp and dull with blood. Finally, the birds were too weak to fight. They stood in the winter sun, necks touching, their lives dribbling into the dirt, still jabbing wearily at each other. The crowd was mesmerized, silent. Then someone said, "Consensus. They've reached consensus," and the tension was broken. The onlookers laughed. They had all come to the country to attend a United Nations conference on development that, like many others during the 1970s, reached "consensus" the same way the birds had—through exhaustion.

TWO DECADES LATER, IN 1995, THE GOVERNMENTS OF RICH AND POOR countries reached a real consensus and created a new World Trade Organization. Their decision to do so and to lower trade barriers around the world faced stiff opposition based on legitimate concerns about how millions of workers worldwide would be affected by vigorous new competition, but governments realized there was no alternative. International trade had made obsolete the rules and regulations created to protect a host of old parochial interests.

A half-century ago, when the United Nations first took up the issue of economic and social development, it was entering uncharted territory. The concept of international cooperation for development was itself new, for most of the poorer parts of the world had been incorporated in European empires. Imperial governments attended to the economic and social development of colonial territories to both ensure a controlled flow of low-priced raw materials, supplied by a docile

PREVIOUS SPREAD *Harvesting the tomato crop in Mozambique: The United Nations Development Programme (UNDP) provided technical assistance to that country's farmers in the 1980s to increase crop yields and income.*

TOP *Otavalo Indians in Ecuador's Cotama Cooperative plow their fields in record time with a tractor and multiblade plow, acquired with the help of UNDP and the Food and Agriculture Organization (FAO).*

ABOVE LEFT *In Zimbabwe, a health worker shows off a new community water pump, one of many built throughout the country in the 1980s with UNDP support.*

ABOVE *Turkish engineers-in-training examine the components of an electric power plant in Geneva, Switzerland.*

work force, and to create a ready market for manufactured goods.

To colonial administrators and propagandists, the exploited populations were "backward peoples"—the "lesser breed without the law," in Rudyard Kipling's famous phrase. Their condition was attributed to various factors, ranging from climate (the enervating Tropics discouraged development) to skin color and religion. Development itself was conceived of in simplistic terms, as no more than industrialization.

The collapse of that whole structure of colonial power and thought after World War II provided the backdrop to the story of the UN's involvement in trade and development. Within two decades of the war's end, the empires of the British, French, Dutch, Belgians, Spanish and Portuguese were dismantled. The independent countries that emerged were uniformly poor and industrially undeveloped but were anxious to "catch up" with their erstwhile rulers. They had a long way to go, for colonial rule had left them lacking the skilled people needed to run a modern economy. In 1958, for instance, there were only 10,000 university students in all of sub-Saharan Africa, and 65 percent of them were from two countries—Ghana and Nigeria. In 1960, when 17 territories in Africa were decolonized, there was not a single university in the French African territories, and there were only two embryonic institutions in what used to be the Belgian Congo (now Zaire). Asia and Latin America were better off in terms of education, but capital and technology were in short supply. All poor countries suffered from such debilitating problems as poverty, mass malnutrition and a host of preventable diseases. A remedy to all those problems—development—quickly became a priority for the United Nations.

OVER THE LAST FIVE DECADES, THE UNITED NATIONS HAS BEEN THE world's main "talk shop" on economic and social development. Every level of its hierarchy of forums has been involved, from small groups of experts to the General Assembly. With an interdisciplinary Secretariat servicing this structure, the UN has been able to identify major problems as they've evolved, analyze how the problems should be dealt with, negotiate overall agreements and coordinate action. Critics tend to emphasize all the talk and overlook or willfully ignore the fact that talk has led to a great deal of useful action.

TOP LEFT *Polish delegates Roman Brudzuinski and M. Blusztein attend the 1947 UN Conference on Trade and Employment in Havana, Cuba.*

ABOVE *The latest in agricultural technology arrives in Shanghai, China, in 1947, part of a major United Nations Relief and Rehabilitation Administration undertaking to get China's rural economy back on its feet.*

TOP *On the Indian training ship Dufferin, seamen get a lesson in rope splicing, part of an ILO program to impart better maritime skills to the nearly 90,000 Asian seamen who crew on international ships.*

ABOVE LEFT *Students in the National Apprenticeship Service in Bogotá, Colombia, take classes at a hotel training school.*

ABOVE RIGHT *Learning a trade: Students study the mechanics of the combustion engine at an ILO-supported vocational training center in Senegal.*

TOP LEFT *On-the-job training for student nurses at a hospital in Quito, Ecuador.*

TOP RIGHT *Tanzanian students get hands-on training in auto mechanics—part of a 1984 National Vocational Training Program. It was established with the help of UNDP and trained both men and women in basic mechanics.*

ABOVE *Aspiring plumbers test their skills in 1970 at a UNDP/ILO supported Vocational Training Institute in Seoul, South Korea.*

LEFT *Young Cypriot chefs get a pastry lesson at the Hotel and Catering Institute in Nicosia.*

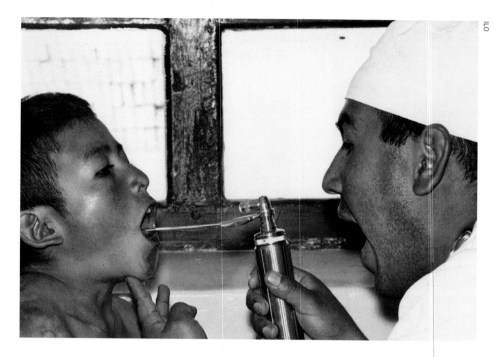

Take the UN Commission on International Trade Law. Its meetings are known among journalists as some of the dullest at the UN, and beyond its own circle of expert participants, almost no one pays any attention to them. Yet the commission's dogged work since its creation by the General Assembly in 1966 has had a real impact on the way the world does business. Mandated to remove obstacles to international trade arising from differences in national laws, the commission has produced major conventions setting uniform rules on the international sale and transport of goods, commercial arbitration and conciliation and international payments. Among other projects in 1995, it was currently working on standards to govern the booming computer-driven world of international electronic transfers.

Over the years, UN deliberations have also led to the creation of a wide range of technical-assistance programs. The lives of millions have been touched by projects under such little-known initiatives of the General Assembly as the UN Development Programme and the World Food Programme. Each has disbursed billions of dollars in aid to developing countries annually. (The developed countries that donate most of the money have gained expanded business opportunities and eased their acute problem with farm surpluses.) Programs that focus on the study and analysis of international trade and on the role of multinational corporations have also been influential. That work is done in the Geneva-based UN Conference on Trade and Development (UNCTAD). The creation of UNCTAD coincided with the opening of the so-called North–South rift between developed and developing countries, and to understand the controversies that swirl around it one must look at how

By a wonderful series of accidents, I was sent to China in 1947, at the age of 29, to take over the final year's leadership of the China office of the UN Relief and Rehabilitation Administration—a mission of 4,000 people, scattered around China in 15 regional offices, stuffing $650 million (that's 1947 dollars) into a country torn up by a decade of war, trying (because we were the UN and by definition impartial) to deliver relief supplies to people on both sides of a raging civil war. UNRRA's biggest single project was to rebuild the dikes of the great Yellow River in the northern part of the country. A decade earlier, the river had been diverted by the Chinese as a defense mechanism against the Japanese invaders; it had since been depositing its heavy silt all over the North China landscape. Our task was to put it back in its old riverbed—a huge earth-moving operation comparable to building the Panama Canal.

But the Yellow River valley was also the scene of the sharpest clashes between Chiang Kai-shek's demoralized troops and the well-led communist guerillas. The dike work was behind schedule because the workers (paid with food imported by our mission and supervised by our multinational engineering team) were understandably reluctant to work in a military no-man's-land. We appealed to both sides to arrange a cease-fire, but the mutual suspicions precluded any real communication, even through the UN. I volunteered to fly to Yenan, an offer that was greeted by objections from the nationalists in Nanking and a stony silence from the communists in Yenan.

In desperation, we conceived the risky idea of using the UN's prestige, then very high, to declare a cease-fire on behalf of the world community—which was, after all, spending a lot of taxpayers' money to help the Chinese people. I could imagine the weeks of diplomatic pussyfooting such a proposal would engender if I asked for permission from UNRRA headquarters in Washington, 10,000 miles away.

So one day, without advance notice, I announced an "UNRRA cease-fire" in the Yellow River valley, to enable UNRRA to finish getting the river back where it belonged. The announcement, wrapped in eloquent rhetoric both global and humanitarian, caught both sides by surprise. Not knowing whether they were supposed to take us seriously, they both did—at first.

To our astonishment and delight the fighting suddenly stopped, the troops drew back a little and we were able to redouble the great dike-building effort. Neither nationalists nor communists wanted to be the first to break the "cease-fire." Foreign offices around the world, which would have branded this a harebrained scheme if they had known about it ahead of time, were professionally cautious when confronted with a fait accompli that actually seemed to be working. From my immediate superior in Washington—UNRRA's number-two man, Commander Robert G. A. Jackson, a notable risk taker himself—came confidential words of support.

I no longer remember just how many weeks my unenforceable edict lasted. One night, a skirmish between local patrols escalated into a major firefight, and the spell was broken.

—Harlan Cleveland, president, World Academy of Art and Science

the world economy has worked.

The expansion of international trade after the Second World War was rapid. It was a major factor in the growth of the world economy, which in the space of two decades doubled in size, then doubled again. But the growth was unbalanced: The industrialized countries had the lion's share. Poorer countries were not only cut out of much of the action, they were actually losing ground. Most developing countries depended heavily on the export of agricultural or mineral raw materials, which brought in less and less money even as the manufactured goods of their trading partners, the industrialized countries, kept getting more expensive. As a result, poor countries were constantly facing crises in their balance-of-payments.

According to the "equilibrium theories" then in vogue, the appropriate response to such imbalances was for the country in crisis to devalue its currency, making its exports cheaper in world markets and thus increasing demand. The operation of market forces was then supposed to bring exports and imports into equilibrium. This theory, propounded by economists from developed countries, failed to recognize that it did not apply to developing countries. A brilliant Argentine economist, Raúl Prebisch, rose to international prominence by explaining why.

Prebisch was living in Mexico as a refugee from the Perónist dictatorship in 1950, when the United Nations offered him the top job at its

David Seymour/UNESCO

Bernard Pierre Wolff/UNDP

AP/Wide World Photos

regional Economic Commission for Latin America. He came to the commission primed to question the nature of the relationship between rich and poor countries, for he had, in his formative years, witnessed Argentina's demotion from the world of affluent countries. Argentine prosperity had been built on exports of meat, wool and other commodities. After World War I, and again with the Great Depression, demand for its exports collapsed, bursting the bubble of domestic prosperity and relegating Argentina swiftly to the ranks of the developing countries. "The world depression had a tremendous intellectual impact on me," Prebisch later recalled. "I had to abandon my belief in free trade as well as in the positive results of the international division of labor."

Prebisch contended that developing countries on the "periphery" of the world economy did not benefit equitably from their trade with the countries at the industrialized "center." He argued that entirely different forces were at work in setting the prices of the raw-material exports of developing countries and the manufactured products of developed countries. The prices of raw materials were set by international markets on the basis of supply and demand, which meant that prices fell when exports increased. This law did not apply to the manufactured goods of developed countries; their prices were much more firmly under the control of producers. To level the playing field, Prebisch recommended that developing countries join in controlling supplies and mod-

United Nations

LEFT *Raúl Prebisch (standing), executive secretary of the UN's Economic Commission for Latin America, opens a 1961 meeting of the commission. With him, from left to right, are: Jorge Alessandri, president of Chile; Burrke Knapp, vice-president of the International Development Bank; and Enrique Ortuzar Escobar, Chilean foreign minister.*

BELOW *Developing country delegates gather at the founding UN Conference on Trade and Development in 1964 to plan strategy. It was the beginning of several decades of at times contentious negotiations with the developed nations over fair terms of trade.*

TOP RIGHT *US Ambassador to the UN Andrew Young addresses UNCTAD in Manila in 1979.*

For most of my career I served as the resident representative of the UN Development Programme or its predecessors in Third World countries. We tended to be transferred just as we were beginning to understand our environment, and it is sometimes hard to know how we survived the consequences of our ignorance.

In Yugoslavia in the 1950s I commenced by saying blandly in public that I was privileged to be present at this great experiment in socialism. I was sternly told by my hosts never to use the offensive word "experiment" again, for theirs was the *real* socialism. I recovered and eventually, only with difficulty, avoided the dubious honor of Order of Labor, third class.

In Burundi the King asked my advice about the education of the Crown Prince. When I warmly recommended St. Antony's College, Oxford, he abruptly terminated the conversation and I learned that the only person from Burundi ever to study at Oxford had been at St. Antony's and on his return had immediately shot the prime minister.

When I was responsible for our work in Botswana, Swaziland and

Lesotho I used to visit Pretoria to try to persuade a hostile South African foreign ministry to allow our experts transit through the Republic. On the third occasion the Afrikaaner official suddenly asked, "Have you brought your golf clubs?" Over 18 holes—or perhaps at the 19th hole—the breakthrough might have been achieved, I sadly felt, had the UNDP been farsighted enough to send not a rabbit but an athlete.

We had our ups and downs. In Tunisia I thought that the government had got my initials wrong until I was gratified to learn that SE stood for "Son Excellence." I was rapidly brought to earth a little later however when I was telexed from New York to address an itinerant group of American ladies on world poverty. I underestimated their earnestness and heard a loud and puzzled voice inquire, "Say, do we pay for this joker or does he come free with the tour?"

It was a challenging but satisfying profession, for one was fully extended, always trying to understand new kinds of people and problems.

—Richard Symonds

erating the volatility of international commodity markets.

This analysis had several effects. For one thing, it helped to shift the UN's focus in the field of development from aid to trade. There was general acknowledgment that "foreign aid"—the transfer of money from rich countries to poor, to finance development projects—would be entirely inadequate if the trade situation was not remedied. Work began in earnest to promote the formation of producer associations and the negotiation of agreements with groups of consumer countries.

As developing countries realized the potential for joint action, their collaboration increased within all UN organizations and on virtually every topic. At the first UN Conference on Trade and Development, held in Geneva in 1964, African, Asian and Latin American countries issued a far-reaching declaration of common purpose. "The developing countries regard their own unity…as the outstanding feature of this Conference," it stated. "This unity has sprung out of the fact that facing the basic problems of development they have a common interest in a new policy for international trade and development." They saw the need "for securing the adoption of new attitudes and new approaches in the international economic field."

Signed by all 77 developing countries that belonged to the United Nations, the declaration became the basis for the Group of 77, their main caucus on all economic and social issues. By 1995, the group had 131 members (with China as observer and active partner).

UNCTAD itself, with a permanent secretariat in Geneva, continued to meet every four years. It became the part of the UN system to which developing countries turned for support in substantiating their case that the international economy was rigged against them. By 1995

ABOVE *A coconut plantation near Paramaribo, Suriname, received UNDP and FAO assistance in 1970. The goal: to improve crop production and the processing of coconut oil and of coir, the fiber made from the outer husk of the shell and used to make ropes and matting.*

TOP RIGHT *A sugar worker harvests cane in Bacolod, the Philippines, in 1979. A world supplier of cheap sugar, the Philip-*

pines, like many countries that rely on such raw commodities for export earnings, has sought through UNCTAD and other UN negotiations, to increase the price of its commodity exports and to diversify into higher priced manufactured goods.

RIGHT *Logs float downriver on a five-week journey to the mill at Sapele, Nigeria. Once the ILO introduced diesel-engined tugs, the trip took less than a week.*

Greg Girard/Contact Press Images

TOP LEFT *A corned-beef canning factory in Kano, Nigeria, where women are a visible component of the labor force. UN agencies have supported such jobs by creating industries that process a nation's raw materials into consumer products for domestic and foreign consumption. Those products can garner a higher price than raw materials could.*

LEFT *The only woman in the Faridpur district of Bangladesh trained to use the modern power tiller, 40-year-old Rabaya attracts some attention. She was taught to till by Saptagram, a nongovernmental organization for women that offers education and skills training.*

ABOVE *Manning the controls at the Baoshan steel mill in Shanghai in 1989: To compete in the global marketplace, this and other state-owned enterprises in China must meet international standards, something they are working on with the help of UNDP.*

world has seen two antithetical trends. On the one hand, states have used armed force to gain and preserve advantageous forms of exchange. The trade-driven spread of European colonialism around the world from the 17th through the 20th centuries was a process of never ending conflict. During the 17th century, for instance, Europe was free of war for only four years; and the 20th century saw the competition for colonies and "trade wars" set the scene for the two most devastating conflicts in human history. This experience led governments to give formal expression to the other great trend of modern civilization: international cooperation. After the First World War, they created the League of Nations; in the wake of the Second World War, they created the United Nations system. That system now faces mounting challenges of population growth, environmental degradation and globalizing markets. Given these realities, the United Nations, now, even more than in its first five decades must, in the words of its founding charter, "employ international machinery for the promotion of economic and social advancement of all peoples."

Confronting the Nuclear Threat

Confronting the Nuclear Threat

William D. Hartung

ONLY SIX WEEKS AFTER THE UN CHARTER WAS SIGNED IN SAN Francisco—a charter whose ambitious goal was "to save succeeding generations from the scourge of war"—the United States dropped the first atomic bombs on Hiroshima and Nagasaki, killing or injuring nearly 200,000 people. Between the June 1945 signing and the August 1945 bombings, the nature of warfare had changed forever.

The UN General Assembly recognized the threat posed by the weapon, and feared the potential arms race that would inevitably be triggered should even a single nation acquire the atomic bomb. At its first meeting in London in January 1946, the Assembly voted unanimously to establish an Atomic Energy Commission. Its purpose was to work toward the "elimination from national armaments of atomic weapons."

The commission quickly became one of the first major diplomatic battlegrounds of the Cold War. On June 14, 1946, American elder statesman Bernard Baruch—described by one reporter as "looking like everyone's grandfather"—presented the US plan for ending the nuclear threat. He proposed the creation of an international atomic development agency that would control all the world's nuclear materials and production facilities. Its powers of inspection and punishment would not be subject to the veto power that had recently been vested in the permanent members of the UN Security Council. The US would give up its nuclear weapons only after the agency was fully established.

The Soviet representative, a self-confident young man named Andrei Gromyko, who would for the next four decades play a key role in every major US-Soviet arms control discussion came back with a counterproposal. He called for the elimination of all nuclear weapons within three months, and the development of arrangements for verification and enforcement under the auspices of the Security Council. *The New York Times* dryly observed that "the fact that Mr. Gromyko, besides

PREVIOUS SPREAD *Partial Test Ban Treaty signing at the Kremlin, 1963.*

TOP *Bernard Baruch (center), US representative to the UN's Atomic Energy Commission, at the opening meeting of the commission in June 1946, presents his country's plan to eliminate nuclear weapons. UN Secretary-General Trygve Lie (left) and Under Secretary-General for Political Affairs Arkady Sobolev (right) read along.*

ABOVE *Soviet Ambassador to the US Andrei Gromyko (left) and British disarmament advocate Philip Noel-Baker at a UN conference in London in September 1945, one month after the US dropped atomic bombs on Hiroshima and Nagasaki.*

ABOVE *The ominous mushroom cloud over Hiroshima in 1945: Repercussions from the explosion were felt around the world and for generations to come—keeping the issue of disarmament high on the UN agenda.*

UPI/Bettmann

insisting on rethinking the veto, had ignored the United States proposal was not considered an overfavorable sign."

That evening the diplomatic tension was broken for a few brief hours when Baruch took Gromyko and a group of UN delegates out to dinner at the Stork Club, followed by a trip to Yankee Stadium to watch the Joe Louis–Billy Conn heavyweight fight. The *New York Journal-American* ran a photo of Baruch and Gromyko arm in arm, with a caption that read "Presumably far apart in their views for sharing the secret of the atom bomb, Bernard Baruch and Andrei Gromyko are in a comradely mood as they watch the human replica of atomic energy explode on Billy Conn."

Unfortunately, it was going to take more than a night on the town to bridge the gap between the US and Soviet positions. The Soviets viewed the Baruch plan as a scheme to preserve the US monopoly on the bomb. The US dismissed the Soviet proposal as a tactic to buy time until the Soviets could develop their own bomb, which they did.

In September 1949, the Soviets tested their first atomic weapon. The pursuit of ever-bigger bombs began in earnest; the pursuit of international control was allowed to languish.

LEFT *During a deadlock in UN disarmament negotiations in 1946, Bernard Baruch (left) took Andrei Gromyko (center) and other delegates to witness more conventional weaponry at a boxing match held at Yankee Stadium.*

BELOW *Two longtime disarmament advocates, Bernard Baruch, batting, and Adlai Stevenson, catching, in a 1954 celebrity baseball game to raise money for the World Veteran's Fund. The umpire is Harold Russell, vice-president of the fund and best known for playing the disabled veteran in the 1946 film* The Best Years of Our Lives.

UPI/Bettmann

ABOVE *The US delegation listens gravely during a 1948 General Assembly meeting in Paris as Soviet delegate Andrei Vyshinsky accuses the United States of preparing for an atomic war against the Soviet Union. From left to right are US delegates Eleanor Roosevelt, John Foster Dulles, Warren Austin and George Marshall.*

During the early 1950s, the Cold War—exemplified by the consolidation of Soviet control over Eastern Europe and by the outbreak of the Korean War—spurred the development of new, more powerful hydrogen bombs by both the United States and the Soviet Union. At the same time, however, both superpowers felt obliged to seek an end to the arms race—or at least to play the role of serious seekers.

On May 10, 1955—described by British diplomat and disarmament advocate Philip Noel-Baker as "the moment of hope"—the Soviet Union put forward a proposal that mirrored a French and British plan for the abolition of stocks of nuclear and other weapons of mass destruction. The sincerity of the Soviet proposal was never tested; the Eisenhower administration abruptly shifted gears, countering in the fall of 1955 with a totally new proposal, the "Open Skies" plan for aerial monitoring of potential nuclear sites. Previous US support for the French and British plan was put on hold, and the negotiations stalled.

Noel-Baker, far from being discouraged by this missed opportunity, redoubled his own efforts and produced a landmark study, *The Arms*

UPI/Bettmann

Race—A Programme for World Disarmament, which distilled his 40 years of experience working in international forums to promote security and peace. A pacifist who won medals for bravery for his service in a Quaker ambulance corps during World War I and an accomplished athlete who captained the British Olympic team and won a silver medal in the 1,500 meter run in 1920, Noel-Baker embodied the tough-minded determination that was to sustain the quest for nuclear disarmament through the chills and thaws of the Cold War.

Noel-Baker was one among a growing global multitude of voices calling for an end to the arms race. Beginning in the mid-1950s, the non-nuclear nations, impatient with the US–Soviet practice of lobbing proposals and counterproposals at each other and changing course at the first sign of any real breakthrough, began to use the United Nations as a forum for promoting ideas that might break the superpower deadlock. It was in this spirit that Indian Prime Minister Jawaharlal Nehru called for a "standstill agreement" to stop nuclear testing. Nehru's initiative was

LEFT *US Ambassador to the United Nations Warren Austin reacts to the news in September 1949 that the Soviets have the bomb.*

BELOW *Testing a nuclear device: US military personnel are illuminated by the light of an atomic explosion in 1951 at the US Atomic Energy Commission's Pacific Proving Grounds.*

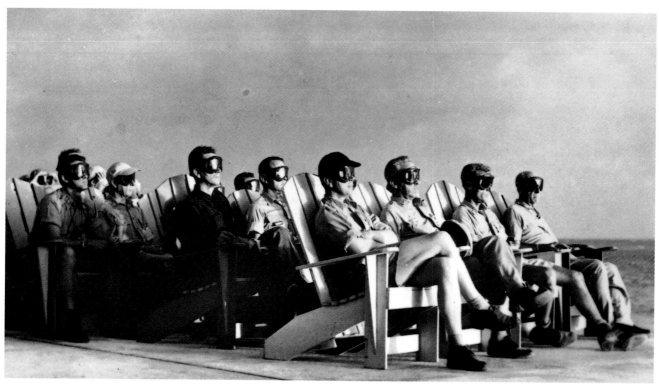

Owen D.B./Black Star

RIGHT *Soviet delegates Yakov Malik (center) and Andrei Vyshinsky (right) at the opening meeting of the General Assembly in 1950. Disarmament negotiations were overshadowed in the early 1950s by the weapons build-up of the Cold War.*

We midwives who went to San Francisco to help in the UN's birth were sent by a tired and weary world, yet the thought of peace—real, lasting peace—gave us new strength. Millions were dead; other millions were maimed and wounded; our fields were torn by alien plows. But our hands were eager to ring down the curtain on man's greatest tragedy. We saw in the UN that we were fashioning the final act of the drama.

I had left the battlefront but a few weeks before. As a member of General MacArthur's staff, I had participated in the campaign to free my country. I knew war. I hated it. I wanted no more of it.

To all of us, the drafting and signing of the United Nations Charter was the culmination of our struggle. It was the hope and determination of all the nations of the world that World War II should be World War Last. In letters of blood we wrote our hope that weapons of war would never again be turned by man against man. Mankind, after thousands of years, would be guaranteed those fundamental human rights: justice, social progress and a better life.

Maybe the UN we created wasn't the best organization that mankind could create. Trygve Lie expressed it: We built "as strong an organization as all of them could agree upon, and as, in their judgment, could in practice be effective at this stage in the history of the world."

—Carlos P. Romulo, *Saturday Review*, 1965

endorsed by the delegates to the historic 1955 Bandung meeting of non-aligned nations.

It was further reinforced by the emergence of a worldwide "Ban the Bomb" movement, fueled by the realization that nuclear test explosions posed a serious threat to public health by infecting the food chain with radioactive isotopes like Strontium-90. In January 1958, Linus Pauling, a Nobel Prize-winning chemist and tireless political activist, presented Secretary-General Dag Hammarskjöld with a petition from 9,000 scientists from 43 countries calling for an immediate international agreement to end nuclear testing. Responding to this campaign, the Soviet Union, the United States and the United Kingdom began a moratorium on nuclear weapons testing that lasted from late 1958 into the latter half of 1961. By that time, France had enlarged the membership of the nuclear club to four, conducting its first nuclear test in 1960.

Despite the resumption of testing, Pauling and his allies in the Ban the Bomb movement persevered in their fight to reverse the policies of the major powers. *The New York Times* noted that in 1962 Pauling "achieved a first in both social and social protest circles" by joining an anti-nuclear-testing picket line outside the White House one afternoon and dining there with a group of Nobel laureates that evening.

AT THE DAWN OF THE 1960S, INTERNATIONAL PRESSURE TO HALT THE arms race was disrupted as a series of events—the downing of a US U-2 spy plane over the Soviet Union in 1960, the abortive US-sponsored

Leo Rosenthal Collection/UN Archives

Bay of Pigs invasion of Cuba and Soviet moves to wall off East Berlin—created an atmosphere of crisis and confrontation. Despite these tensions, over the summer of 1961, the United States and the Soviet Union met under UN auspices in Washington, Moscow and New York. Together they hammered out a detailed joint statement of principles on general and complete disarmament (known informally as the McCloy-Zorin principles). Building on themes sounded by Soviet Premier Nikita S. Khrushchev in an address to the world body two years earlier, President John F. Kennedy argued before the General Assembly on September 25, 1961, that nuclear disarmament must be pursued regardless of short-term political obstacles. "The risks inherent in disarmament," he said, "pale in comparison to the risks inherent in an unlimited arms race."

The following spring both nations issued their own versions of a draft treaty on general and complete disarmament. Once again, real agreement seemed within reach. But differences arose over phasing and

AP/Wide World Photos

LEFT *Across the street from UN headquarters in the 1950s, demonstrators rally against nuclear weapons testing. Some of the protesters had marched from Philadelphia and other cities.*

BELOW *Indian Prime Minister Jawaharlal Nehru confers with Indian Ambassador to the UN Krishna Menon during the 1955 conference at Bandung, Indonesia, where 29 non-aligned nations endorsed an early proposal to stop nuclear testing.*

ABOVE *Nobel Peace Prize winner and lifelong disarmament advocate Dr. Linus Pauling marches with actress Julie Harris at a "Women Strike for Peace" demonstration in Dag Hammarskjöld Plaza, near UN headquarters, in May 1966.*

verification of the rival plans. After the Cuban missile crisis of October 1962 brought the world to the brink of a nuclear conflict, the negotiations were allowed to lapse.

The missile crisis did have one positive result: It struck enough fear into the hearts of the two nuclear superpowers to convince them that progress on arms control was imperative. The US-Soviet nuclear hotline agreement of 1963 was designed to reduce the danger of war by miscalculation. On August 5, 1963, the Partial Test Ban Treaty was signed, putting an end to all nuclear testing in the atmosphere and providing a first, partial victory for the worldwide citizens' disarmament movement. In subsequent negotiations, both sides promised to ban underground testing, but the world found itself still waiting for that critical next step.

Throughout this period, representatives of the non-nuclear powers continued to press for a stronger voice in developing the disarmament agenda. Among the most notable of these were Alva Myrdal, an accomplished social scientist who served as Sweden's UN disarmament repre-

sentative, and Alfonso García Robles, a Mexican diplomat who had been involved with the United Nations since its founding. Myrdal helped to craft a proposal that gave non-aligned nations a permanent role in UN disarmament negotiations in Geneva; García Robles was the prime mover in efforts to gain adherence to the 1967 Treaty for the Prohibition of Nuclear Weapons in Latin America (the Treaty of Tlatelolco) and a coauthor of the 1968 Nuclear Non-Proliferation Treaty. Myrdal, a distinguished educator and social reformer who took up the disarmament issue in 1961 at the age of 59, was a formidable presence in the UN's disarmament councils, and she spent the rest of her life working to influence government policies on the nuclear issue. García Robles, a

ABOVE *Soviet Premier Nikita S. Khrushchev addresses the press shortly after the signing of the 1963 Partial Test Ban Treaty. UN Secretary-General U Thant stands behind him.*

BELOW *Alva Myrdal, Sweden's minister for disarmament and its ambassador to the UN, confers with US delegate James F. Leonard during a disarmament debate at the United Nations in 1969.*

low-key, unassuming official who chose government service after an early interest in the priesthood, demonstrated the virtues of patient negotiation in winning support for two of the UN's most enduring achievements in controlling the spread of nuclear weapons. The two diplomats went on to share the 1982 Nobel Peace Prize, conferred in recognition of their years of effort on behalf of disarmament.

The Non-Proliferation Treaty (NPT) remains one of the most important potential building blocks of a nuclear disarma-

ment regime, with 178 signatories as of spring 1995. The treaty has helped to fend off the nightmare scenario that existed at the time of its signing—the fear that dozens of nations would acquire nuclear weapons, a fear that was rekindled in 1994 when North Korea balked at allowing international inspectors into several key nuclear facilities and threatened to pull out of the agreement. Since that episode, North Korea has tacitly agreed to abide by the terms of the treaty by entering into a bilateral understanding with the United States. Prospects for extending the treaty into the 21st century may hinge on whether the United States, Russia and the other states with nuclear weapons live up to their commitment under Article VI of the treaty to "pursue negotiations in good faith on effective measures relating to the cessation of the nuclear arms race at an early date and to nuclear disarmament."

DESPITE THESE FIRST STEPS TOWARD LIMITING THE SPREAD OF NUCLEAR weapons, the nuclear arms race was still going at full tilt at the beginning of the 1970s. The world stockpile of strategic and tactical nuclear weapons had reached the astonishing total of nearly 40,000. The vast majority of those weapons were in the hands of the United States and the Soviet Union.

Hoping to re-energize efforts to reduce the burgeoning nuclear threat, Secretary-General U Thant declared the 1970s the "Disarmament Decade." In 1978 the General Assembly held a nearly month-long special session on disarmament and produced the UN's most comprehensive statement to date of the priorities and processes for pursuing disarmament. Priorities set out in the final document, which Alfonso García Robles later described as "the bible for disarmament," include the adoption of a comprehensive nuclear test ban; an end to production of all nuclear weapons, including the fissionable materials that serve as the active ingredients in nuclear bombs; continued reductions in the nuclear arsenals of the superpowers; and reductions in conventional armaments and military spending.

Both the United States and the Soviet Union endorsed the terms of the 1978 disarmament plan, but their own energies during the 1970s were focused on the bilateral Strategic Arms Limitation Talks. SALT I, signed in 1972, and SALT II, signed in 1979, placed ceilings on each

side's nuclear weapons and delivery vehicles and put strict limits on the deployment of antiballistic missile systems. Critics of the treaties argued that they allowed such high levels of armaments that they represented at best an effort to "manage the arms race"; supporters asserted that the SALT process had a stabilizing effect on superpower relations and set the foundation for future agreements.

Secretary-General U Thant shares a joke at UN headquarters with US President Lyndon Johnson (left) and Arthur Goldberg, US ambassador to the UN (right), in 1968.

THEN, ONCE AGAIN, THE MOOD CHANGED. IN 1980 US OFFICIALS started talking about the possibility of "winning a nuclear war" and NATO accelerated plans to put extremely accurate cruise and Pershing missiles in Western Europe. As pressure on the nuclear trigger seemed to be getting tighter, citizens' movements in Europe, the United States and around the world stood up to demand an end to the nuclear arms race. This surge of citizen activity, beginning with the European Nuclear Disarmament movement, soon spread to encompass the Nuclear Weapons Freeze campaign in the United States, and culminated with the UN's Second Special Session on Disarmament in 1982. At the time of the session, more than half a million people marched from UN headquarters to New York's Central Park to dramatize their demands for real progress on disarmament. Among the most active participants in the events of

June 1982 was Philip Noel-Baker, who at the age of 92 was still fighting for disarmament; he was to die a few months later, comforted by the belief that millions of people around the world would carry on his life's work.

The change in public opinion brought on by nongovernmental organizations worked in concert with the sweeping changes in the international political landscape—among others, the ascension to power of Mikhail Gorbachev in the Soviet Union—to pave the path for the first agreements of the nuclear age to reduce the rival nuclear arsenals and eliminate entire classes of weaponry. The Intermediate Nuclear Forces Agreement of 1987 was followed by the Strategic Arms Reduction Treaty of 1988, and the START II Treaty, signed in January 1993. By mid-1993, the number of deployed nuclear warheads worldwide had been cut to less than half the levels of a decade earlier, and more nuclear weapons were being dismantled and retired than were being produced. After nearly 50 years, a disarmament process that had been sidetracked, frustrated and delayed by the overriding dynamic of Cold War confrontation was finally beginning to bear fruit.

AS SECRETARY-GENERAL BOUTROS BOUTROS-GHALI HAS OBSERVED, with the end of the Cold War "the world has become a little safer, but considerably more complicated." As a result, the UN's disarmament mission is at once more urgent and more achievable. The organization has been at the center of the multilateral disarmament efforts of the 1990s—through its effort to destroy Iraq's capabilities for building weapons of mass destruction; through the implementation of the Chemical Weapons Convention, a treaty to eliminate all production, stockpil-

Listening to US Vice President Walter Mondale address a special General Assembly session on disarmament in 1978 are actor Paul Newman (left), US Ambassador to the UN Andrew Young and Allard Lowenstein. The US delegation members are seated in front. Left to right, they are Secretary of State Cyrus Vance, Averell Harriman and Senator George McGovern.

221

ing and use of chemical weapons; through the May 1995 decision to extend the Nuclear Non-Proliferation Treaty; and through negotiations at the Conference on Disarmament in Geneva aimed at securing a comprehensive nuclear test ban. Meanwhile, there are new challenges. A short list would include the expansion of the United Nations Register of Conventional Arms, a system for reporting major transfers of conventional weaponry, into a system to monitor and eventually reduce the trade in weapons of war; the development of strategies for limiting the spread of ethnic and territorial conflicts; the elaboration of plans for investment of the post-Cold War "peace dividend" in projects to promote economic conversion and sustainable development; and further steps toward the abolition of nuclear weapons.

As former Secretary-General Javier Pérez de Cuéllar has noted, the ultimate fulfillment of the UN's disarmament mission will depend heavily on the actions of citizens throughout the world. "Every person on this earth has a stake in disarmament," he said in a 1984 address to the General Assembly. "In the nuclear age, decisions affecting war and peace cannot be left to military strategists or even to governments. They are indeed the responsibility of every man and woman."

TOP LEFT *Catching the world's attention: In 1982 a half-million-strong rally for disarmament got its start at the Olympic torch of peace in front of UN headquarters. Seated in wheelchairs are 100-year-old David Monongye of the Sacred Council of Hopi Elders Opposed to Nuclear War, 92-year-old Philip Noel-Baker and Nichidatsu Fujii of Nipponzan Miyohoji, one of the organizers of the march.*

LEFT *Soviet mothers and their children in Khabarovsk, at a 1984 march against the threat of nuclear war.*

ABOVE *US B-52 bombers have their wings clipped in the Arizona desert in 1995—visible evidence that cuts in strategic arms are moving ahead.*

CHAPTER TEN

Fostering Independence

Fostering Independence

Claude Robinson

As a boy growing up in Jamaica, I used to listen to the BBC to find out what was going on in the world. That was back in the 1950s, and many of the stories I heard were about how the newly created United Nations was helping to bring independence to this or that country. Other stories were about men who had made the long journey to the UN to plead for international help in expelling European settlers from their lands.

To a young West Indian living in a region still largely under British colonial rule, these stories seemed very important. My generation was greatly influenced by this older generation of nationalist intellectuals who were preaching the heady gospel of independence.

One name that came up time and again in those UN stories was Alex Quaison-Sackey, the Ghanaian representative to the United Nations. Ghana has special significance for Jamaicans. In 1957, under the leadership of Kwame Nkrumah, the British colony formerly known as the Gold Coast became the first African colony to win independence from Britain.

As schoolboys we had learned that Ghana's struggle for independence had been inspired by several black intellectuals from our region—Trinidadians George Padmore and C.L.R. James, for example, and Jamaica's own Marcus Garvey. So when Quaison-Sackey told the United Nations in 1960 that "it is morally indefensible and utterly unjustifiable for any group of people to claim that they have an inherent right to impose their rule…over others," his words struck a responsive chord.

The occasion was the General Assembly's historic 1960 debate on colonialism—a debate that culminated in the Assembly's adoption of Resolution 1514, titled "Declaration on the Granting of Independence to Colonial Countries and Peoples."

By the year the resolution was passed, colonialism had held sway over huge portions of the globe for roughly four centuries. A system of

PREVIOUS SPREAD *A day of celebration: Fireworks light the sky over the Windhoek Athletic Stadium in 1990, following the inaugural speech by President Sam Nujoma of the new nation of Namibia.*

TOP *Prime Minister Kwame Nkrumah at Ghana's 1957 independence celebration when British rule ceased and the country's name changed from the Gold Coast.*

ABOVE *At a special session of the UN General Assembly, Alex Quaison-Sackey, delegate from Ghana (right) and Diallo Telli, delegate from Guinea (left) confer.*

ABOVE *When Ghana gained its independence in 1957, members of Philadelphia's All African Students Union celebrated by unfurling the Ghanaian flag at Independence Hall, home of the Liberty Bell. Philadelphia Councilman Raymond Pace Alexander (second from right) joined the celebration with students, left to right, Esther Nimely, Ola Aina and Rudolf Ballmoos.*

LEFT *Lord and Lady Mountbatten are greeted in New Delhi, India in 1947. As viceroy of India, Lord Mountbatten had just concluded the negotiations for India's independence from Great Britain.*

BOTTOM LEFT *The flag of a newly independent India is raised by Indian delegate P. P. Pillai at UN headquarters at Lake Success in 1947. Sir Alexander Cadogan (hat in hand), UN delegate from the United Kingdom, looks on.*

total and often exceedingly brutal exploitation of those colonized, it was presented as a sometimes rather rough but essentially benign means of bringing civilization and Christianity to benighted Asians, Africans and Latin Americans. Over the centuries priests, preachers and plain people attacked the hypocrisy and inhumanity of the enterprise, with one of the most brilliant attacks appearing at the beginning of the twentieth century, Mark Twain's scathing essay "To the Person Sitting in Darkness." Aimé Césaire, the Caribbean poet and political leader from Martinique, put the matter succinctly: "There is an infinite distance between colonization and civilization."

But neither savage humor nor impassioned sermons nor any other attempts to appeal to the conscience of the Christian colonizers persuad-

ed them to grant independence to those whose resources they exploited and whose lives they largely controlled.

Where words failed, armed resistance and insurrection worked— sometimes. For example, although colonialism remained basically intact at the beginning of this

Negotiations between the Netherlands and Indonesia over independence get underway in 1947 aboard the US Army transport ship Renville in the harbor of Batavia (later renamed Jakarta). Justice Richard Kirby, Australian member of the UN Good Offices Committee (standing) addresses the group.

century, a liberation movement spearheaded by Símon Bolivár had already brought an end to Spanish colonial rule in South America. (Previously, of course, an armed uprising known as the American Revolution had proved an effective means of throwing off the colonizing power.)

As late as 1942, British Prime Minister Winston Churchill—though by then engaged in a war waged in the name of freedom and democracy—was unable to conceive that colonized peoples might deserve the freedom that many Asians, Africans and Indians were fighting alongside the British to preserve, for the British if not for themselves. Asked whether he considered granting independence to British possessions, Churchill replied, "We mean to hold our own. I have not become the King's First Minister in order to preside over the liquidation of the British Empire."

At the same time, however, another opinion was being voiced on the other side of the Atlantic. In a conversation with Soviet Foreign Minister Vyacheslav Molotov about Southeast Asia, US President Franklin Roosevelt said that "the white nations…could not hope to hold these areas as colonies in the long run," because there was a "palpable surge toward independence" throughout the area. Roosevelt believed there would probably be a "time lapse" before the colonies would be ready for full independence and during that time there could be "some form of international trusteeship" or training for self-government.

It was the view of the new world power, the United States of America, that ultimately prevailed and, after World War II, helped to speed decolonization. America's motives were a mixture of idealism and self-interest. As long as Britain, France, the Netherlands, Belgium and Portugal controlled the trade with their sundry colonies, American industry would have a hard time getting a foot in the door, much less do a brisk business. At the same time, it would be very difficult to justify the violent suppression of various Asian and African nationalist movements whose leaders and followers were ready to fight and die for their independence.

The United Nations played a significant role in decolonization, but it is doubtful that the process would have moved forward at the pace it did without the sacrifices of thousands of men and women—both militant and pacifist, like Gandhi of India—who could not wait for the colonizing powers or for a distant world body to put an end to a system that profited one group of humans, universally white, at the expense of another group, universally people of color.

WHEN THE DELEGATES GATHERED IN SAN FRANCISCO IN 1945, ALMOST all the so-called administering powers—those possessing colonies and/or territories—rejected a proposal to place their foreign holdings under some form of international trusteeship. They also rejected proposals from the Soviet Union and pre-communist China calling for stringent international supervision of colonies. The Soviets did succeed, however, in getting an important principle into the charter—that "friendly relations among nations should be based on the equal rights and self-determination of peoples." Innocuous as the wording may sound, the principle was to prove crucial in later decolonization struggles.

The delegates also agreed on two sets of UN guidelines for dealing with dependent territories. The first dealt with trusteeship. Eleven territories, mostly taken from Germany and the Ottoman Empire after World War II and given to several of the Allies as "mandates" by the League of Nations, were reassigned as "trust" territories. The administering powers were to promote the welfare of the people under their control and help them move toward self-government and independence.

The second set of guidelines took the form of a general statement of principles in Articles 73 and 74 of the UN Charter. Titled the "Declaration regarding non-self-governing territories," it advocated, in a gen-

On October 12, 1960, Soviet Prime Minister Nikita S. Khrushchev, head of his delegation in the General Assembly Hall, removed his right shoe, brandished it in the air and banged his desk with it.

The object of his ire was Filipino delegate Lorenzo Sumulong. Sumulong had just told the Assembly that a Soviet-proposed declaration on decolonization should also cover the right to independence of the "peoples of Eastern Europe and elsewhere which have been deprived of the free exercise of their civil and political rights and which have been swallowed up, so to speak, by the Soviet Union."

Bedlam erupted as Romanian Deputy Foreign Minister Eduard Mezincescu berated Assembly President Frederick Boland of Ireland for allowing "slanderous charges" to be made from the UN rostrum.

Boland replied that "We must be prepared...to hear stated views with which we strongly disagree."

Khrushchev marched to the rostrum to demand that Boland call Sumulong, "this toady of American imperialism," to order.

Back in his seat, Khrushchev removed his shoe, waved it menacingly in the direction of the Philippines delegate and then began banging his desk with this makeshift gavel. He also drummed his fists as the hapless Sumulong struggled through the rest of his speech, cautioned by the president to "avoid wandering out into an argument which is certain to provoke further interventions and which is bound to be very prejudicial to the decorum of this debate."

Khrushchev later raised another point of order, describing Sumulong as "not a bad man" and inviting him to visit the Soviet Union.

There was further uproar when a US delegate, Assistant Secretary of State Francis Wilcox, said that "Everyone here in the Assembly is fully aware of the sad fact that there are a number of states in Eastern Europe which do not have their complete independence."

When the president failed to intervene, Mezincescu, the

Romanian, popped up again to upbraid Boland, telling him: "You are free to sympathize with the colonial countries, that is your right, but I hope that the Irish people and all the peoples represented here...."

At that point, Boland had had enough, banging the gavel so hard that it broke in two, he said, "I am sure the Assembly will feel that, in view of the scene we have just witnessed, the appropriate step is that the assembly should be adjourned at once and it is hereby adjourned...."

It is the shoe-banging incident that has entered UN folklore [and] to this day visitors taking guided tours want to know just where in the hall it occurred.

The 1960 session of the General Assembly, attended by virtually all the prominent leaders of the time including Presidents Eisenhower, Nasser, Tito, Sukarno and Nkrumah, was a major media event watched by millions of Americans on TV.

Boland became a star. After he broke his gavel, admirers sent him scores of replacements, including one said to have been cast from molten Guinness bottles. He used several of the gift gavels later in the UN proceedings.

—Anthony Goodman, Reuters

TOP LEFT *The future prime minister of Tanganyika, Julius Nyerere, is lifted on the shoulders of elated supporters at the close of a two-day constitutional conference in Dar es Salaam in March 1961. Tanganyika became independent later that year and changed its name to Tanzania in 1964.*

RIGHT *A ritual for every new UN member state: delegates from Sierra Leone, including Prime Minister Milton Margai, at center with child, pose in front of their nation's flag, just raised for the first time in October 1961. The West African country gained its independence in April of that year.*

eral way, respect for human rights including the right to self-determination without regard to race, language, religion or gender. The declaration did not bind the administering powers to hasten the day when the territories became independent, but merely asked them to take steps to "promote the well-being" of the people.

This seemed to leave the old colonial system pretty much intact, except under different flags and using different names. Commenting on the Western powers' confidence that they could continue to do colonial business as usual, Ghana's Quaison-Sackey said, "Some people felt at San Francisco that they were dealing with a semi-permanent state of affairs in which millions of people in Africa, Asia, the Pacific and the Caribbean have to resign themselves to an indefinite period of tutelage exercised by other countries."

The misplaced confidence of the Western powers reflected the early imbalance of the UN's membership. In 1946 the United Nations had only 51 members, and power resided in the hands of a select few— the victorious allies of World War II, and China.

Their strength was repeatedly challenged, however. From the late 1940s through the 1950s, a generation of nationalist leaders rose up throughout the colonial world until all the major colonial powers faced either armed insurrection or civil disobedience. The British, for exam-

Leo Rosenthal Collection/UN Archives

231

ple, were forced to yield India, the "jewel in the crown" of their vast empire, in 1947. Two years later, the Netherlands was compelled to grant independence to Indonesia. In 1952 the Kikuyu ethnic majority in Kenya launched an armed campaign to drive out the British—a campaign that ended in 1956, but set the stage for the day the colony finally won its independence in 1963.

Bloodier by far than all these wars of liberation were those the French waged to hold on to Vietnam and Algeria. France suffered a major military defeat in Vietnam, pulling out in the mid-1950s—at which point the United States took up the fight with much the same result by 1975. The right to self-determination spelled out in the UN Charter was not to be denied to the Vietnamese or to the Algerians, who won their independence in 1962.

In October of that year, Ahmed Ben Bella, free Algeria's first prime minister, described his countrymen's eight-year struggle as "the supreme and most expressive manifestation of the great liberation movement which, after the Second World War, spread among the countries under foreign rule."

In 1958 another French colony in Africa, French Guinea, had won its independence. After its liberation, Guinea's delegate to the UN proposed that the colonial powers come to the 1960 session of the General Assembly with concrete plans—including a timetable—for granting independence to the territories under their control. By the time the Assembly convened, 25 African and Asian nations had signed a formal resolution to that effect. This African-Asian solidarity reflects the energizing influence of the non-aligned nations following the 1955 Bandung Conference hosted by Indonesia's leader, President Sukarno. The member nations, reluctant to take sides in the superpowers' Cold War games, came to play a major role in articulating the development priorities of the newly emergent nations both within and outside the UN.

It took 19 meetings, 72 speeches and 18 more sponsors to bring about the adoption of the resolution. Although not a single nation voted against it, the European colonial powers abstained, as did the United States.

As might be expected, debate over Resolution 1514 provided an opportunity for the superpowers to bash each other and to appeal to those nations that defined themselves as non-aligned. Soviet delegate

Now I recall more than one member saying of our independence that it is something we must demand...I am not sure the word "demand" is not too colonial a word for October 1960...Our independence is no longer [a question] of demanding but of planning. And the planning is really a question of decolonization...But I venture to suggest that one of the most difficult things to decolonize is going to be the minds of some Honorable Members here.

—Julius Nyerere, October 1960

TOP LEFT Kenneth Kaunda (center), president of Northern Rhodesia's United National Independence Party, in a 1962 address before a special committee of the UN General Assembly on ending colonialism. With him, from left to right, are T. L. Desai, Lieutenant Colonel Sir Stuart Gore-Brown and A.N.L. Wina. In 1964 Kaunda became the first president of his country when it gained independence and became Zambia.

AP/Wide World Photos

AP/Wide World Photos

UPI/Bettmann

TOP *Freedom fighters of the Mozambique Liberation Front (Frelimo) train in Tanzania in 1965.*

ABOVE *Algerian President Ahmed Ben Bella arrives in New York City from Algiers to attend ceremonies marking his country's admission to the UN in 1962.*

ABOVE *Jomo Kenyatta (in hat) celebrates his election as President of Kenya in 1963. Leader of the Mau Mau uprising against British rule in 1952, he was Kenya's president until his death in 1978.*

United Nations

Valerian Zorin cataloged the atrocities linked with colonial rule and charged the United States and the nations of Western Europe with trying to maintain their system of exploitation "by new means." British delegate Ormsby-Gore blasted back, accusing the Soviet Union of practicing a new kind of colonialism by exploiting its Eastern European satellites. Between 1939 and 1960, he said, some 500 million people lived in former British colonies that were now independent, while in the same period the Soviet Union "forcibly incorporated" 22 million people, including the world's "newest colonies" of Latvia, Lithuania, and Estonia.

Despite the rhetoric, an important shift in attitude had occurred. For the first time in the history of UN debates on the subject, the colonial powers expressed support for the principle of independence. And finally, on December 14, 1960, the General Assembly adopted the African-Asian resolution, whose key principles stated that all peoples have an inalienable right to complete freedom, that colonialism in all its forms must be brought to a speedy and unconditional end and that lack of political, economic, social or educational preparedness must never serve as a pretext for postponing independence.

In many ways, 1960 had been a watershed year with the declaration being adopted and 17 newly independent nations being admitted as members. But it was also a year in which the UN became polarized over a decolonization issue: independence for the Congo.

ON JULY 12, 1960, PRESIDENT JOSEPH KASAVUBU AND PRIME MINISTER Patrice Lumumba sent a telegram to UN Secretary-General Dag Hammarskjöld seeking help in protecting their nation's newly acquired independence achieved less than two weeks earlier. They urged that UN troops be sent to put down a secessionist rebellion in Katanga Province and to remove Belgians and other Westerners caught up in the chaos

One cardinal fact of our time is the momentous impact of Africa's awakening upon the modern world. The flowing tide of African nationalism sweeps everything before it and constitutes a challenge to the colonial powers to make a just restitution for the years of injustice and crime committed against our continent.

But Africa does not seek vengeance. It is against her very nature to harbor malice. Over 200,000,000 of our people cry out with one voice of tremendous power—and what do we say?

We do not ask for death for our oppressors; we do not pronounce wishes of ill-fate for our slave-masters; we make an assertion of a just and positive demand; our voice booms across the oceans and mountains, over the hills and valleys, in the desert places and through the vast expanse of mankind's habitation, and it calls out for the freedom of Africa...

For years and years Africa has been the footstool of colonialism and imperialism, exploitation and degradation. From the North to the South, from the East to the West, her sons languished in the chains of slavery and humiliation, and Africa's exploiters and self-appointed controllers of her destiny strode across our land with incredible inhumanity without mercy, without shame, and without honor.

Those days are gone and gone forever, and now I, an African, stand before this august assembly of the United Nations and speak with a voice of peace and freedom, proclaiming to the world the dawn of a new era.

I look upon the United Nations as the only organization that holds out any hope for the future of mankind. Mr. President, distinguished delegates, cast your eyes across Africa: The colonialists and imperialists are still there. In this twentieth century of enlightenment, some nations still extol the vainglories of colonialism and imperialism. As long as a single foot of African soil remains under foreign domination, the world shall know no peace.

The United Nations must therefore face up to its responsibilities and ask those who would bury their heads like the proverbial ostrich in their imperialist sands to pull their heads out and look at the blazing African sun now traveling across the sky of Africa's redemption.

The United Nations must call upon all nations that have colonies in Africa to grant complete independence to the territories still under their control. In my view possession of colonies is now quite incompatible with membership of the United Nations.

—President Kwame Nkrumah of Ghana, excerpt from General Assembly address, September 1960

and Belgian troops that had been earlier dispatched to protect them.

Much of that chaos was attributed to the nature of Belgian colonial rule. Critics pointed out that at the time of the hastily arranged granting of independence, there was no professional cadre trained to operate social and governmental institutions. President Kwame Nkrumah used stronger language during the September 1960 General Assembly debate on the "situation in the Republic of Congo." He described Belgium's colonial system as "calculated political castration in the hope that it would be completely impossible for African nationalists to fight for their emancipation."

The Belgian delegate conceded the lack of trained manpower but asserted that his country had agreed to leave 10,000 technocrats to work under Congolese control: "No one can deprive us of the honor of having created the Congo, which, before we arrived, was a mere conglomeration of warring racial groups and tribes. It is we who created it."

Understandably, the Belgian diplomat did not dwell on the early years of Belgium's "stewardship" of the vast African land. Yet the chaos of the 1960s was in a sense a replay of the chaos of the 1890s, when the whole Congo was essentially the private possession of Belgium's King Leopold II. He looked the other way as adventurer-entrepreneurs from various lands plundered the Congo, utterly disrupted traditional ways of living and, whether by introducing diseases or outright slaughter, caused the death of several million indigenous people. In her classic work *The*

United Nations

Origins of Totalitarianism, Hanna Arendt suggests that 20 to 40 million native people died in the Congo between 1899 and 1902. A nation that had been raped and brutalized in its earliest years was now primed to self-destruct. The international community could not condone the prospect of a return in force of Belgian troops.

Some of the most intractable decolonization issues faced by the United Nations involved countries in Southern Africa: Rhodesia, Namibia and South Africa. Back in the late 1880s, the British South Africa Company received the royal charter to administer what was then called the territory of Southern Rhodesia. In 1961, the year before their neighboring Congo blew up, the white settlers of Rhodesia adopted a constitution that disenfranchised the black majority and was duly approved by a complacent British government. In 1962, however, the UN General Assembly declared Rhodesia a non-self-governing territory and asked the British government to suspend the new constitution. Britain refused, saying that they had granted the territory internal self-government in the 1920s. In 1965, Prime Minister Ian Smith, leader of the minority regime, issued his defiant "Unilateral Declaration of Independence."

ABOVE A UN reception in the early 1960s in New York.

TOP RIGHT While on a fact-finding mission in West Africa in 1972, Salim A. Salim (right), UN delegate from Tanzania and Chairman of the UN's Special Committee of 24 on Decolonization, is presented with a battered Portuguese flag captured in Guinea by a member of the Partido Africano Independencia da Guine e Cabo Verde.

RIGHT Marcelino dos Santos, vice president of the Liberation Front of Mozambique (FRELIMO), addresses the UN Security Council in 1972. Dos Santos was responding to a resolution calling for an end to colonial aggression in Portuguese territories.

I believe that what is happening day by day at the United Nations represents the most challenging, the most original, even the most exhilarating work being done by man today...

As something of an expert in rebuffs and disappointments, I may be permitted to emphasize that our actions in the United Nations must not be based upon passing gains or setbacks, but rather upon the basic concepts of our faith in democracy. We should remember that the United Nations offers not a formula for "stability" but a framework for change. All the world's tensions are not bad; drives for self-expression and self-government form the dynamics of democracy.

I would say to our own people: Support the United Nations with your sympathetic attention and your prayers. To the smaller powers, especially the emergent states of Africa, I would repeat that the United Nations is of first importance above all to weaker states, since, without it, they have no ultimate protection against the force of more powerful and predatory governments.

—Adlai Stevenson, *National Geographic*, September 1961

The General Assembly's bold and sensible request that a sovereign government should reconsider a decision that would clearly do nothing but buy time for a racist regime was an indication that the Assembly was serious about decolonizing the world. It went on to approve sanctions against Rhodesia in an attempt to compel the minority regime to share power with the black majority. However, while the activist Assembly could impose sanctions, the Western nations and South Africa could—and did—ignore them. Thanks to the prevalent Cold War mentality, all liberation movements could be viewed as communist-inspired, while all those who resisted such movements, like Ian Smith, could be viewed as plucky allies in the fight for freedom.

As a guerrilla war that had begun in 1968 gained in intensity, so did diplomatic pressure. A negotiated settlement, reached in 1979, resulted in an agreement to hold free elections—one man, one vote—which were held in March 1980. Robert Mugabe, the winner, became the first prime minister of the independent nation of Zimbabwe.

Namibia, formerly under German rule and known as South West Africa, was the scene of the most protracted decolonization story in UN history. It began to unfold in the early years of the UN's predecessor, the League of Nations. Neighboring South African forces had seized the German colony at the outset of World War I—indeed, the Namibia campaign was the Allies' first victory. Following the war, the former British colony of South Africa inherited the territory under a

237

mandate from the League. Nearly half a century later, in 1966, the General Assembly terminated the mandate, asserting that the indigenous people were not benefiting from South Africa's administration.

Again, while the Assembly acted, the Western powers who alone could press South Africa to begin relinquishing its mandate, did nothing. South Africa was an ally, a bulwark against communism on the African continent. The struggle for independence then took place on two tracks—as an armed struggle waged by the South West Africa People's Organization (SWAPO) and as a diplomatic campaign. SWAPO brought off a diplomatic coup in 1973, when the General Assembly recognized it as the sole authentic representative of the Namibian people. At the beginning of 1976, the Assembly went further, endorsing SWAPO's fight as a legitimate means of achieving self-determination and granting SWAPO observer status at the world body. Finally, on January 30, 1976 the Security Council unanimously adopted Resolution 385, calling for free elections under UN control. It set an August 1976 deadline for the Council to review South Africa's compliance with the resolution.

At that point, a struggle that seemed to be moving toward resolution came to a grinding halt. Civil war had broken out in neighboring Angola, formerly a Portuguese colony. Both superpowers quickly took sides, and Cuban President Fidel Castro dispatched troops to fight on the side of Angolan President Augustinho Neto.

In the early 1980s, US President Ronald Reagan adopted a policy of "linkage." Progress on Namibian independence was henceforth linked to the withdrawal of Cuban troops from Angola. Finally, on December 22, 1988, the war-weary parties signed agreements: Cuban troops would withdraw once Angolan independence was respected and security guaranteed.

With the war in Angola winding down, the way was cleared for final implementation of the Security Council's Resolution on Namibia. In April 1989 a UN Transitional Assistance Group was quickly put in place: people who had lived in exile for years returned home, and with blue-helmeted UN troops keeping watch on the proceedings, free elections were held. SWAPO won and formed a national government whose first president was SWAPO leader Sam Nujoma.

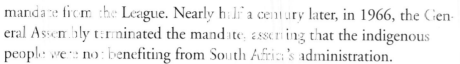

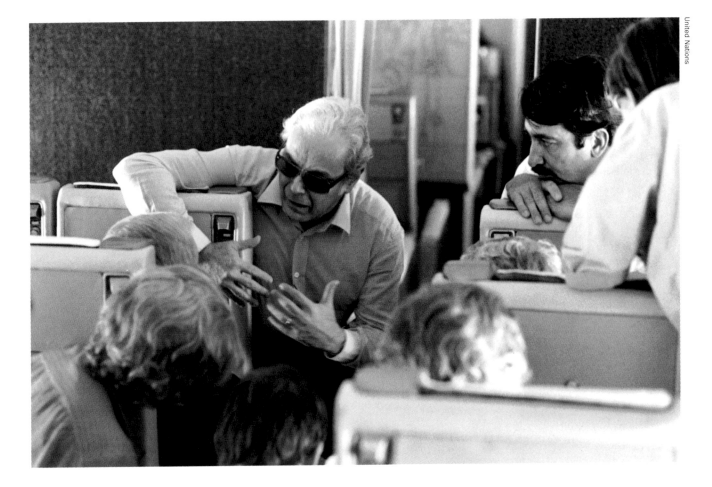

Another chapter in the decolonization process had come to an end—nearly a quarter of a century after it began.

WITH NAMIBIA'S INDEPENDENCE ACHIEVED, THE UNITED NATIONS could claim to have resolved the world's long list of decolonization issues. That the process had taken a long time could hardly be blamed on the United Nations. It was the member nations, acting in their own perceived self-interests, that had applied brakes whenever the General Assembly pressed the accelerator. The sovereign nations had exercised their sovereign right to ignore the will of the world body.

Meanwhile, though the major issues of decolonization have been dealt with, the UN still has some unfinished business—the business of helping a number of trust territories and non-self-governing territories achieve independence. As of the spring of 1995, there are 17 such territories, one of which poses a serious problem. This is East Timor, which Indonesia "annexed" in

ABOVE *A group of rural Namibians are glued to the TV watching election returns in their country's 1989 independence vote.*

TOP RIGHT *Young Namibians celebrate their nation's independence in Windhoek in 1990.*

RIGHT *Nelson Mandela makes a campaign stop during the 1994 elections in South Africa.*

Stern/T. Hegenbart/Black Star

Reuters/Bettmann

1975, the same year Portugal abruptly left its former colony to fend for itself. Ironically, it was Indonesia that hosted, in Bandung, the 1955 founding conference of the Non-Aligned Nations—a bloc which has long been committed to improving social and economic conditions in the developing world and to ending colonialism.

Until the 1990s the international community seemed content to let Indonesia have its way with East Timor where thousands were killed in the 1970s and where, nearly 20 years later, the pro-independence movement, Frente Revolucionaria de Timor Leste Independente (FRETILIN) wages its independence struggle. In May 1994 Secretary-General Boutros-Ghali said he had been meeting with the foreign ministers of Indonesia and Portugal since 1992, but could report no progress.

To resolve such a stalemate, a lesson might be borrowed from the decolonization struggles of the past three decades. Over time, western nations were compelled to heed the insistent calls for independence coming from Asia and Africa. In his own efforts to foster independence where it is desired, in remaining trust territories and non-self-governing territories, the UN secretary-general's voice would be considerably strengthened if it were joined more often by those of member states with experience—former colonies and former colonial powers included.

Peter Turnley/Black Star

CHAPTER ELEVEN

Defending Human Rights

Maggie Steber

Defending Human Rights

Thomas Hammarberg

IS VOICE WAS HEARD THROUGH CRACKLING RADIO RECEIVERS in distant countries. It was January 1941, and US President Franklin D. Roosevelt was reading a speech that was to give hope to millions of listeners during the darkest days of World War II.

He spoke about four freedoms: freedom of speech, freedom of worship, freedom from want and freedom from fear. He gave people a vision of a future where the rights of each individual would be respected. The four freedoms, he said, were the necessary conditions for peace and a world lacking aggression, "a definite basis for a kind of world attainable in our time and our generation."

His words were echoed by other leaders of the Allied front opposing the forces of the world's fascist and totalitarian regimes. Jointly they declared their commitment to defend "life, liberty, independence, and religious freedom, and to preserve human rights and justice in their own lands, as well as in other lands."

They were responding to a widespread cry: Never again! Never again should the world allow a dictator to march people into slavery. Never again should Jews, Gypsies or any "undesirables" be herded into crematoriums, or should prisoners die of disease, malnutrition or torture.

This spirit was rekindled in San Francisco in 1945 when the United Nations was founded. Nongovernmental groups and dedicated individuals—many of them invited by the US government to serve as consultants—lobbied delegates from 51 governments. They managed to convince the doubters among the delegates that respect for human rights should be a major goal of the UN and that this should be spelled out in the organization's charter.

The founders of the UN moved quickly after the adoption of the charter. A Commission on Human Rights was set up in early 1946. Its first task was to draft an International Bill of Human Rights.

PREVIOUS SPREAD *Haitian Army soldiers hunt for anti-government demonstrators in the city of Cap-Haïtien during rioting that preceded the fall of François "Baby Doc" Duvalier in 1986.*

ABOVE *Survivors of the Buchenwald concentration camp on the day it was liberated in 1945. Responding to atrocities that took place in camps like this, the authors of the UN Charter insisted that basic individual freedoms be part of a plan for world peace.*

RIGHT *In a radio address to the nation, President Roosevelt defined what he believed were the basic rights to which all people are entitled. That message set the tone for the UN's advocacy of human rights, an effort that Eleanor Roosevelt would eventually lead.*

STRONG PERSONALITIES WERE APPOINTED TO THE COMMISSION. THERE was Eleanor Roosevelt, the president's charismatic widow. Unopposed, she was asked to take the chair. A vice-chair was offered to René Cassin, a French law professor who had fought in the Resistance and survived a German death sentence. He became a key member of the commission, his contributions belatedly recognized in 1968, when he was awarded the Nobel Peace Prize. John P. Humphrey of Canada, an international lawyer and professor, was asked to serve as secretary. He became the first head of the Division of Human Rights.

The post of rapporteur was given to Dr. Charles Malik, a humanist Christian from Lebanon, who emphasized the importance of ethics and the freedom of spirit. A Chinese diplomat, Dr. P. C. Chang, also belonged to the inner circle; he talked about Asian values, advancing the view that the new human rights standards should reflect more than Western ideas. The most pragmatic member of the team, Chang was the architect who deftly designed several important compromises.

The working atmosphere was at times informal. On one occasion, Eleanor Roosevelt invited fellow commissioners to her apartment for discussion over tea, which she hoped would speed up the work. However, the meeting ended in a lofty debate between Dr. Chang and Dr. Malik on the comparative merits of the teachings of Confucius and Thomas Aquinas.

John Humphrey and his secretariat began work on the human rights bill, producing a documented outline of more than 400 pages.

But I am getting far ahead of my journey to London. One day, as I was walking down the passageway to my cabin, I encountered Senator Arthur H. Vandenberg, a Republican, and before the war a great champion of isolationism. He stopped me.

"Mrs. Roosevelt," he said in his deep voice, "we would like to know if you would serve on Committee Three."

I had two immediate and rather contradictory reactions to the question. First, I wondered who "we" might be. Was a Republican senator deciding who would serve where? And why, since I was a delegate, had I not been consulted about committee assignments? But my next reaction crowded these thoughts out of my mind. I realized that I had no more idea than the man in the moon what Committee Three might be. So I kept my thoughts to myself and humbly agreed to serve where I was asked to serve.

"But," I added quickly, "will you or someone kindly see that I get as much information as possible on Committee Three?"

The senator promised and I went on to my cabin. The truth was that at that time I did not know whom to ask for information and guidance. I had no idea where all those blue documents marked "secret" that kept appearing in my cabin came from; for all I knew, they might have originated in outer space instead of in the Department of State.

—**Eleanor Roosevelt, from**
The Autobiography of Eleanor Roosevelt

Members of the US delegation to the United Nations arriving in Southampton, England, aboard the Queen Elizabeth in January 1946 for the first General Assembly session include Eleanor Roosevelt (center), chief US delegate Edward Stettinius, Jr. (center right) and Senator Tom Connally (second from right). During the crossing, Eleanor Roosevelt accepted a place on the committee that would draft the UN's Universal Declaration of Human Rights.

RIGHT *René Cassin acted as advisor to the French delegation during the first session of the UN General Assembly in 1946. He won the Nobel Peace Prize in 1968 for his human rights work.*

BELOW *Members of the Drafting Committee of the UN Commission on Human Rights meet for the first session in Lake Success, New York, in June 1947. They include, from left to right, Dr. P.C. Chang, Henri Laugier, Eleanor Roosevelt, John P. Humphrey, Charles Malik and Professor Vladimir M. Koretsky.*

The original concept called for a three-part project: a declaration defining the general principles; a covenant, which would be more detailed and legally binding; and, finally, suggestions for implementation.

The declaration was to be tackled first. René Cassin pulled together a revised proposal, an amended version of which was ready for the General Assembly meeting in Paris during the fall of 1948. Two months later, after a preparatory committee had held 81 meetings and dealt with 168 proposed amendments, the Universal Declaration of Human Rights was adopted by the full Assembly. The historic vote was taken on December 10, now celebrated as Human Rights Day.

No country voted against the declaration, but there were significant abstentions. The Soviet Union and its allies wanted human rights to be treated as an internal matter; Saudi Arabia saw a conflict with the Koran; and South Africa was not prepared to extend equal rights to its majority black population. The declaration had a wider audience than the member nations themselves, however. Eleanor Roosevelt said it could "serve as a guide and inspiration to individuals and groups throughout the world…" Indeed, it became an inspiration for nongovernmental organizations in several countries. And it became a tool they could use when approaching governments to discuss human rights violations.

THE COMMUNITY OF NONGOVERNMENTAL ORGANIZATIONS URGED governments to press the United Nations to adopt an activist human rights program. The response was tepid. The commission, for its part, concentrated almost exclusively on formulating standards.

Even so, there were problems. Since the declaration was only a statement of principle and not legally binding, it was urgent that work

on the second stage proposed, the covenant, be completed. Eleanor Roosevelt promised that a final draft would be produced by 1949. But major political differences had come to the fore, and the commission needed five

248

more years. It was not until 1966, 18 years after the adoption of the declaration, that the General Assembly got around to approving the legally binding articles.

In the process, it had been necessary to divide the various rights into two separate covenants—one on civil and political rights, the other on economic, social and cultural rights. It was to take another 10 years, until 1976, for these treaties to be ratified by a sufficient number of member nations to enter into force.

For two decades, during the 1950s and 1960s, the Human Rights Commission had been virtually paralyzed as the result of political disagreements. It could not agree on how to respond to the great number of human rights concerns that had begun to flow in from individuals and organizations. It could only acknowledge that they had been received, state that it could not take action and inform the governments concerned about the complaint (after deleting the names of the complainants). Several attempts to define standards for freedom of information and of the press were shot down; a special subcommission on the problem was short-lived.

The failures were basically rooted in disagreements on two specific issues: Should the international community be authorized to take positions on human rights violations in individual countries? Could economic and social standards also be formulated as rights?

The protagonists in the debate over these issues were the Soviet Union and the United States. As early as 1948, when the draft declaration was discussed, Soviet delegate Andrei Vyshinsky argued that its adoption would violate an important principle of the UN Charter. He was referring to an article of the charter that was to become a theme in the UN's discussions on human rights. It says that the United Nations should not intervene in matters that are "essentially within the domestic jurisdiction of any state."

Soviet delegates raised this point at meeting after meeting for years. The most articulate response came from René Cassin, who said that the responsibility for safeguarding human rights was both the nation's and the international community's. Human rights were a special case and different from domestic political questions; international action was sometimes justified. In fact, he pointed out, the charter itself enabled the United Nations to recommend steps for the protection of human rights within member states.

While this debate raged within the United Nations, the mood in the United States began to shift. The American Bar Association campaigned against the Universal Declaration and other UN initiatives for human rights on the grounds that they contravened the Constitution. Repeated Soviet denunciations of the United States—for its treatment of blacks, for instance—may also have contributed to isolationist tendencies.

The full impact of this US shift in mood became clear when, in 1951, the Senate refused to ratify the new international treaty against genocide—a stunning refusal, coming as it did so soon after the Holocaust. The decision had, Eleanor Roosevelt thought, "made many people in the world wonder whether it is possible for us to understand the intent of a humanitarian document and to accept it without fear that it will step on our toes."

Soon afterward, she received a letter from the newly elected president, Dwight D. Eisenhower, informing her that her services would no longer be needed.

For many years, the positions of the two superpowers prevented

BELOW *Chilean students, some of the 7,000 people rounded up by the military in the aftermath of the 1973 coup, await their fate in Santiago's National Stadium. Many were never seen again.*

The United Nations has been working on behalf of women since the principle of equal rights of men and women was proclaimed in the charter in 1945 to a world emerging from a devastating war. Despite the contribution of women to the war effort, discrimination against them in 1945 was widespread both in law and in practice; and in many of the original 51 UN member states, women had yet to win their political rights on equal terms with their male colleagues.

On February 27, 1946, Eleanor

the Commission on Human Rights from naming human rights violators. As late as December 1973, when Amnesty International organized a conference on torture in the United Nations Educational, Scientific and Cultural Organization's headquarters in Paris, it was expelled from the premises only hours before the conference was scheduled to begin. UNESCO feared—not without reason—that individual countries would be mentioned in the discussions.

Yet the United Nations was not consistent. Its strong response to the atrocities that followed the 1973 military coup in Chile showed that, on occasion, it could single out an egregious human rights offender. South Africa was cited for its racist policies, although the violations there were discussed in the context of the country's apartheid system rather than as the manifest violations of human rights they were.

THE OTHER BATTLE WAS OVER ECONOMIC, SOCIAL AND CULTURAL rights: Were they as important as other rights? Were they indeed rights? Again, the divisions reflected the polarized positions of the Cold War.

The Universal Declaration includes rights to social security, employment, education, rest and leisure, health care and an adequate standard of living. Could these aspects of "freedom from want" be framed as legally binding? The US government early on took the position that the implementation of these rights depended on domestic, political and economic consideration, and that they could not therefore be imposed from outside. Economic and social rights were described as "ambitions."

The Soviet position was the opposite: Economic, social and cultural rights were at least as important as civil and political rights. This split contributed to the decision to divide the package of norms into two covenants, albeit with some common articles.

New member states from the developing world sided with the Soviets in this debate. Resolutions were passed asserting that both categories of rights were equally important; that they were, indeed, interdependent and indivisible. Still, less priority and fewer resources were given to the promotion of the International Covenant on Economic, Social and Cultural Rights, and little emphasis was put on those rights within the Division for Human Rights (later renamed the Centre for Human Rights).

The UN family as a whole, of course, did not ignore civil and political rights. Important programs were run by, among others, the International Labour Organization, the World Health Organization, the United Nations Children's Fund and UNESCO. However, the programs were not officially regarded as human rights activities and thus were not well coordinated with the human rights operations.

THE MID-1970S MARKED THE BEGINNING OF A NEW ERA. THE COLD War was not over, yet the international climate was changing. The US had pulled out of Vietnam; Willy Brandt was trying out his new Ostpolitik of dialogue; dictatorships had fallen in Greece and Portugal and another dictatorship was ending in Spain.

In Latin America, however, the mid-1970s saw a rise in military regimes—such as the brutal junta that seized power in Chile in 1973—and an increasing number of "disappearances," political murders and incidents of torture. Changes were also occurring in Africa—for instance, the fall of the despotic emperor Haile Selassie of Ethiopia, who was replaced in 1974 by another government of terror.

During the 1970s, another phenomenon increasingly influenced the human rights debate. Already in 1968, the year he received the Nobel Peace Prize, René Cassin had highlighted the importance of non-governmental groups as links between ordinary people and official international bodies. By the mid-1970s, Amnesty International was fully established and was publishing chilling reports on what had happened in Greece, Spain and Portugal and on what was then going on in Brazil, Uruguay, Argentina and Chile.

Meanwhile a number of small nations—among them, Costa Rica, the Netherlands and the Scandinavian countries—were encouraging their delegates on the Commission on Human Rights and the General Assembly to take an activist stand on human rights.

The United Nations, after due deliberation, banned torture. Special procedures were also created to monitor such violations as "disappearances" and arbitrary executions. It became possible to put countries other than South Africa and Chile on the commission agenda. Rapporteurs were appointed to monitor specific human rights concerns, give recommendations and offer advisory services.

Only by early 1976 when enough countries had ratified the two covenants could they take full effect, making possible open discussions on how individual countries would implement them. Such implementation was the third step—following principles and legal norms—in the human rights agenda laid out many years earlier by Roosevelt, Cassin and Humphrey. Nonetheless, a number of countries, including the United States, still had not ratified the covenants.

The new working methods made the Centre for Human Rights more dependent on good information, hard facts. This, in turn, enhanced the role of the nongovernmental organizations. Dutch law professor Theo van Boven, who directed the center from 1977 to 1982, saw their importance and developed positive relations with them. His activist and principled approach, however, rubbed some governments the wrong way, and his five-year contract was not extended.

Bearing witness: "Mothers of the Disappeared" hoist journalists trying to take pictures over the gate of a women's prison in San Salvador in 1985.

Governments resorted to a variety of ruses or arguments to try to keep from being put on the Centre for Human Rights' agenda. Some argued that other nations were more deserving of being named than they. They criticized the procedures as selective. And, indeed, there was no denying that some countries had escaped being named for political reasons. The nongovernmental groups pressed for nonpolitical criteria, and the procedure did mature during the 1980s: The selection process became more objective and less partisan.

The discussion on implementation was reopened—and in a more fundamental way—during preparations for the 1993 World Conference on Human Rights in Vienna. Some governments argued that no single human rights standard could be applied globally because of differences in conditions and cultures.

Just prior to the conference, UN Secretary-General Boutros Boutros-Ghali enlivened the discussion. "We must remember that forces of repression often cloak their wrongdoing in claims of exceptionalism," he declared. "But the peoples themselves time and again make it clear that they seek and need universality. Human dignity within one's culture requires fundamental standards of universality across the lines of culture, faith and state."

The conference concluded that the universal nature of the UN standards on human rights was "beyond question" and that their promotion and protection was "a legitimate concern of the inter-

national community."

The human rights conference also took on the discussion of economic, social and cultural rights, stating that all human rights are indivisible and should be treated "on the same footing." Thus, the meeting responded to both of the issues that had long divided the United Nations: Yes, the United Nations could react against violations within countries. And, yes, economic, social and cultural rights should be regarded as just that, rights.

A mother stands vigil for her son in 1984: She is one of the Madres de la Plaza de Mayo in Buenos Aires, Argentina, who still gather every week in memory of the 15,000 "disappeared" from the so-called Dirty War in the late 1970s. Her son, Armando, was among them.

254

United Nations human rights observers investigate a shooting in San Salvador in 1991. The UN's mission in El Salvador included the creation of a Truth Commission that assigned responsibility for major human rights abuses during the war and purged abusers from the military.

WITH THE MORE DYNAMIC ERA THAT BEGAN IN THE 1970S, THE UN agreed on new treaties to combat torture, discrimination against women and violations of the rights of children. Committees were appointed to encourage their implementation. The commission also appointed experts to investigate freedom of expression, religious freedom, child prostitution and violence against women. In 1993, nearly 50 years after the founding of the United Nations, a High Commissioner for Human Rights was appointed.

The human rights debate was also carried on in such regional fora as the Organization of American States and the Council of Europe. Furthermore, declarations and conventions were adopted within the International Labour Organization, UNESCO and other specialized agencies of the United Nations.

Finally, in response to mounting criticism that the United Nations was failing to address a vast array of human rights violations, major programs were developed in countries such as El Salvador and Cambodia. They were part of a larger effort to foster or maintain peace and/or to supervise elections. By establishing a visible presence, the United Nations sought to influence an unfolding human rights situation. And in the 1990s, efforts were made to address gross violations in the former Yugoslavia, including a resolution to set up a war crimes

ABOVE *Unspeakable horrors: At a Rwandan refugee camp in Kibuma, Zaire, in 1994, bodies are removed for burial. Continued atrocities between warring factions in Rwanda are so severe that the UN Security Council has established a tribunal to investigate war crimes there.*

RIGHT *Bosnian prisoners at a Serbian camp in Manjaca, north-west of Sarajevo. More than 3,000 men were held at this camp in 1992, deprived of adequate food and sleeping on the floors of old cattle sheds.*

tribunal. Such developments represented an important extension of previous activities.

———————

COLD WAR POLITICIZATION OF THE HUMAN RIGHTS DEBATE IS GONE, but human rights are still highly controversial within the UN system, which seems to be one reason the budget for the UN human rights program remains lean. Some governments object to being scrutinized, but ideological differences exist as well—such as the relationship between the individual and the collective. The continuation, and even deepening, of the human rights dialogue is no small achievement.

However, the drafters of the Universal Declaration clearly aimed at concrete improvements for ordinary citizens in the member nations. To what extent has the United Nations contributed to the freedom and protection of such people? The UN's procedures for individuals to report human rights complaints have improved, and its response to large-scale violations has at times had an impact. On the other hand, individual complaints have rarely led to significant relief, and governments have often closed their doors at the specter of outside human rights investigators. Still, the awareness that violations of human rights no longer go unnoticed and that they can have serious repercussions may serve as a deterrent.

Through its evolving human rights mechanisms, the United Nations has allowed outside organizations to express their concerns, be they the rights of minorities, of children, or of women. In this manner, the United Nations is serving, in the words of Eleanor Roosevelt, as a "guide and inspiration to individuals and groups throughout the world."

CHAPTER TWELVE

Recording UN History

Recording UN History

Michael Littlejohns

EVEN BEFORE AN $8.5-MILLION GIFT FROM JOHN D. ROCKEFELLER, Jr., enabled the United Nations to acquire a length of East River frontage for its permanent home in Manhattan, there were practical reasons why New York was favored over other US cities that bid. For one thing, in 1946 ocean liners were the principal means of intercontinental passage, and at the Hudson River piers travelers could debark just a few blocks from the city's heart—a great advantage for busy diplomats. On her maiden voyage from Southampton to New York, the giant Cunarder *Queen Elizabeth* alone carried some 150 delegates to the first UN General Assembly, then about to reconvene in temporary quarters at Flushing Meadow following an inaugural session in London.

Oceangoers' convenience aside, Manhattan was attractive because of its reputation as the nation's information and communications center. The United Nations knew that to succeed it must command wide attention. The League of Nations had failed in part for want of public interest and support; its successor organization had to avoid a similar fate. Already, there were good omens: As early as 1943, a citizens' association dedicated to educating Americans about the organization-to-come was thriving under Eleanor Roosevelt's leadership.

Radio listeners had become accustomed to hearing the advancing Allied troops referred to as "United Nations Forces" in frontline dispatches by Edward R. Murrow, William L. Shirer, Robert Trout and other American reporters. With victory secured and the media beginning to assess the UN's capacity to implement its charter aim to end "the scourge of war," there was a ready-made public-relations advantage. Having mothballed their uniforms, correspondents fresh from the war fronts joined established domestic commentators like Walter Lippmann, Arthur Krock, Dorothy Thompson and Edgar Ansel Mowrer to feed public interest in this political novelty.

Not all of them were favorably impressed by what they saw. In an

LEFT *Actress Myrna Loy gets the attention of UN correspondents more accustomed to meeting diplomats than Hollywood stars.*

PREVIOUS SPREAD *CBS News reporter Mike Wallace interviews chief UN spokesperson Benjamin Cohen in a TV broadcast outside the Secretariat in 1951. At the time, CBS-TV produced a daily show called "UN In Action."*

TOP *The international press turns out for Soviet Foreign Minister Vyacheslav Molotov at Geneva's Palais des Nations in 1954.*

ABOVE *Harold Stassen (center), governor of Minnesota and a US delegate at the UN founding conference, is surrounded by reporters hunting for news in the corridors of San Francisco's Fairmont Hotel in 1945.*

261

April 1946 column titled "Nightmares and Daydreams," the conservative Thompson wrote: "Wisdom begins with facing the facts, the first of which is that UNO is a house built on the shifting sands of impetuous, childish assumptions." On radio, Ed Murrow opined: "A good American debating policy at the [Security] Council table is not necessarily a good American foreign policy."

Tabloid tattler Walter Winchell (whose readers and radio listeners exceeded 50 million), Ed Sullivan and others weighed in with their two cents—the price of a newspaper in those days. Fervent UN-backer Eleanor Roosevelt was a widely read columnist. The new diplomatic crowd in town was the focus of many an E. B. White contribution to *The New Yorker*'s "Notes and Comment" department. As delegates gathered on Long Island, the United Nations could announce that "nearly 600 newspapermen drawn from every country of the world and including some of the greatest names in international journalism" would occupy what was grandly designated "the nerve center for international news."

ABOVE Secretary-General Dag Hammarskjöld holds an informal press conference in Caracas, Venezuela, for reporters at an Inter-American Conference in March 1954. Hammarskjöld's assistant, Bill Ranallo, stands directly behind him and the UN's chief spokesperson, Benjamin Cohen, is on his right.

TOP RIGHT India's Ambassador to the UN Krishna Menon (right) is interviewed by Bill Oatis (left) of The Associated Press and Max Beer (center) of the Swiss newspaper Neue Zürcher Zeitung. While doing a stint as AP correspondent in Czechoslovakia, Oatis was tried and jailed for 25 months on espionage charges; Beer had escaped the Nazis in Europe before becoming a reporter at the United Nations.

The opportunity to cover the Foreign Ministers [conference, which was held in conjunction with the first UN General Assembly at Lake Success] came about most unexpectedly and for a very unique reason, not particularly unique in these days but it was in those days, because I was a woman. You see at that particular time broadcasting, which was merely radio then—no television—felt that women should not be heard on the air because they did not have authority in their voices, and therefore they could not discuss serious subjects, like international affairs, which was what I wanted to discuss. So I had been sent out on various and sundry nonsensical things, in my view: fashion shows and a forum on how to get a husband, and so on.

And one night I was sort of hanging around the newsroom hoping something would happen and there was a male correspondent there who was on staff—I was at that time merely a freelancer—and the editor looked up and said, "you know, there are two stories to be covered tonight. One is a truck strike meeting and the other is the Council on Foreign Ministers. He looked at me and he said, "You're a woman. I don't think I should send you to the truck strike meeting because there might be violence. I think you'd better cover the Council of Foreign Ministers."

—Pauline Frederick, UN Oral History Collection

RIGHT *Waiting to interview delegates as they emerge from a disarmament conference at UN headquarters in 1954 are correspondents Sven Ahman of Swedish newspaper* Dagens Nyheter, *Dan Harvey of the US Information Service, Joseph P. Lash of the* New York Post; *K. Rainey Gray of* The Greenwich Times, *Sam Bennett of Reuters, Anne Weill Tuckerman of Agence France-Presse, A. M. Rosenthal of* The New York Times, *Bill Oatis of The Associated Press and William R. Frye of* The Christian Science Monitor.

However, a cautious Benjamin Cohen, the UN's first assistant secretary-general for public information, was not convinced that the media love affair would last. Fearing—presciently, as it turned out—that once the novelty wore off the UN would wind up among the truss ads except in times of crisis, he traveled to Chicago on the eve of the resumed General Assembly session to deliver a pep talk to national broadcasters at their annual convention and to appeal for their long-term interest. Before anyone had heard the term "spin doctor," Cohen also pledged that, for its part, the department would eschew propaganda and make no attempt to cover up the inevitable UN failures to come.

As he spoke, stars of the US media (and stars-to-be, like A. M. Rosenthal of *The New York Times*) would soon be joined on the UN beat by correspondents returning from abroad, many of whom had reported on the recent war or fought in it. Some remain members of the press corps to this day. Louis Foy, who represents *France-Soir* and French radio network Europe No. 1, was a ship's purser in 1940 when he was stranded in New York by the fall of France. After finding work in the French pavilion at the World's Fair, he enlisted with General Charles de Gaulle, served in North Africa and, after demobilization, decided to try journalism. He joined the Agence France-Presse's bureau at Flushing Meadow, which included one of the few women UN correspondents,

ABOVE Correspondents Anne Weill Tuckerman of Agence France-Presse (left), A. M. Rosenthal of The New York Times (center), Frank Carpenter of The Associated Press (right) and others take notes during a press conference.

TOP RIGHT Vijaya Lakshmi Pandit of India meets with the UN press corps shortly after being elected the first woman president of the UN General Assembly in 1953. Andrew Cordier, executive assistant to the secretary-general, is in the foreground to her right.

RIGHT Racing to meet their deadlines, UN reporters file their stories over teletype machines in the press room during the 15th session of the General Assembly in 1960.

Ever since the UN was set up, it has been the world's favorite sitting duck. It's been blamed for what it hasn't done, blamed for what it has. It's been blamed for spending too much money, and it's been blamed for being penny-wise and stingy. It's been accused of taking too much authority on itself; it's been accused of doing nothing while the world slid into another war. It's been denounced as a sort of home base for Communist spies; it's been scolded for not having a full quota of Russians on staff....

[P]eace in Indonesia, peace in Kashmir, peace in Palestine, groping moves in the Balkans. The UN can take credit for them all....

This is the score card: World war, delayed, postponed, side-tracked or prevented: one. Regional wars, stopped: three. Armament races, stopped: none. Atomic agreements reached: none....

The men and women who don't make much news, just plug away every day in their windowless cubbyholes, can tell the rest of the story: of epidemics met, of children fed, loans made, trade agreements bargained out, food production stepped up, travel made safer, human rights set down on paper, backward regions given "know-how," refugees housed and clothed, mass murder outlawed by convention, narcotics rigidly controlled. That is the do-gooders' part of the story....

Last year, Mr Lie asked the 58 member nations to give him $33,469,587. For the 1950 financial year, he may ask for a few hundred thousand dollars more to meet increased expenses of missions overseas. In September, one of the Assembly's committees will go over the budget line by line, question every expenditure, haggle, and then decide it is worth it.

So for 1950 the United Nations will cost the world about $18,000,000 less than the Department of Sanitation costs New York City.

—A. M. Rosenthal, *Collier's*, 1949

Anne Weill. (NBC's Pauline Frederick and Kathleen Teltsch, of *The New York Times*, were others.)

Other press corps luminaries included: Bernard Person, a household name to Dutch radio listeners; Paul Sanders of *Het Parool*, which grew out of Amsterdamers' fierce resistance to Nazi occupation; Arnold vas Dias; and Fred vas Dias were just four members of the Netherlands press corps. The Netherlands press corps remained a substantial presence until the UN, in the name of anti-colonialism, forced the surrender of Dutch New Guinea to Indonesia. The cast of Fourth Estate characters in the first decades of the United Nations included Max Beer, a cigar-chomping caustic wit who fled Nazi Europe for New York by way of Central America and contributed insightful dispatches to Switzerland's *Neue Zürcher Zeitung*; Peter Freuchen, a large, spade-bearded Viking with a peg leg that had replaced the one he lost in an encounter with polar ice or a wild beast (it was never clear which); and the voluble Ruggiero Orlando, who reported to Italian radio before he gained a senate seat in Rome. Sven Ahman translated into English some of Secretary-General Dag Hammarskjöld's dense prose, when he was not writing for his Stockholm newspaper. He shared office space with the dapper Eric Britter of *The Times* of London, whose sartorial

elegance matched the elegance of his dispatches. Arne Thoren reported for the Swedish Broadcast Corporation before achieving fame on national television for his vivid descriptions of the first space flights and the moon landing. Swedish-born American David Horowitz has observed every UN session. At 91, he still contributes regularly to the *World Union Press*.

At the founding, relatively few correspondents were from what we now call the developing nations, but with the creation of the non-aligned movement in 1955 their numbers increased. India, a founding member of both the United Nations and the movement, has had among its media representatives Krishnamachari Balaraman, who later became deputy editor of *The Hindu of Madras*; The Press Trust of India's Raghavendra Chakrapani (now of *The Hindu*) and Chakravarti Raghavan (still active in Geneva); and Jogindra Banerji of the newspaper *Amrita Bazar Patrika*, to mention a few. Attesting to their colleagues' respect, each of these reporters was elected president of the United Nations Correspondents Association, formed at Lake Success in 1948. UNCA was formed "to maintain and protect the freedom and prestige of press, radio and television correspondents in all their relations with the United Nations." John G. Rogers of the old *New York Herald Tribune* was founding president.

ABOVE *Soviet Premier Nikita Khrushchev (left) addresses a luncheon at the United Nations delegates dining room hosted by the UN Correspondents Association in 1960.*

TOP RIGHT *Journalists cover a UN press conference in Leopoldville, the Congo in 1960.*

RIGHT *Major General E.L.M. Burns of Canada, commander of UN Emergency Forces, is interviewed by reporters on his arrival in the Gaza strip only after UNEF assumed control of the area from the Israelis in 1957.*

The long UN work days stretching into weekends led to informality, sometimes with unexpected twists. So it was that Thomas J. Hamilton, the long-time UN bureau chief for *The New York Times*, helpfully offered his personal car to Hernan Santa Cruz, Chile's chief delegate. But Hamilton, notoriously forgetful, then went looking for his vehicle in the parking lot and finding it missing, reported the car stolen to the local police.

George Barrett, another long-time *Times* reporter, acquired a 40-year-old Rolls, a yellow open touring car in which correspondents on wintery days would wrap on mufflers and bundled in lap robes would make the 22-mile trip to Lake Success crawling along the parkway at top speed—about 30 miles an hour—to the amusement of diplomats but not the traffic police. On one occasion, an Indian VIP, the Maharajah of Nawanger came racing along in his limo and seeing the journalists, ordered his chauffeur to draw alongside. The two vehicles then completed the trip with the Indian potentate making wildly encouraging gestures to the Rolls passengers to step on the gas.

And then there was the visit paid by President Harry Truman, after he left office, to see the Manhattan headquarters he once dedicated. Yes, he would meet with the correspondents but only for a friendly chat in their press coffee bar. Still, the international press corps was determined to wring some serious comment from the President and the questions turned political. That lasted only until Peter Freuchen, a towering bearded Dane, broke in and asked how "farmers in Truman's native Missouri manage to keep apples from rotting in winter?" The press members tittered or groaned but the President stopped them cold.

"That's a very good question. We put them in barrels using layers of straw," he answered gravely.

—Kathleen Teltsch

Among his successors was Rudolf Stajduhar of the Yugoslav news agency Tanjug. Stajduhar, a former companion-in-arms of Tito, transferred to the UN's department of public information and was for several years Secretary-General Kurt Waldheim's spokesperson. Journalists from the former Yugoslavia remain a sizable group in the UN press corps.

It was not until Kwame Nkrumah came to power in Ghana that black Africa sent a reporter, the national news agency's George Enninful. Although African states long have made up the largest single regional bloc of nations in the United Nations, Nigeria and South Africa are the only black-ruled African countries with correspondents who cover the UN regularly.

The bullpen, as the press area was called, launched several American journalistic careers. A. M. Rosenthal went on to become executive editor of *The Times*. Joseph P. Lash, whose intimate knowledge of the wartime White House and close friendship with Eleanor Roosevelt was the basis of his Pulitzer Prize-winning biography on the Roosevelts, cut his teeth as a *New York Post* correspondent. Max Frankel, Rosenthal's successor in *The Times* chief editor's chair, did a UN stint, as did Earl W. Foell, who became editor of *The Christian Science Monitor*. Pauline Frederick of NBC, a passenger along with Soviet Foreign Minister

ABOVE *In less formal days: The UN Correspondents Association (UNCA) held a 60th birthday party for Secretary-General U Thant in 1969. Reporters include, from left to right: Jogindra Banerji of the Indian newspaper,* Amrita Bazar Patrika, *who later became UNCA president; Sam Friedar of various Latin American publications; UNCA President Michael Littlejohns; and K. Rainey Gray of* The Greenwich Times *(far right).*

TOP RIGHT New York Post *and* Washington Post *correspondent Michael Berlin (center) questions Kurt Waldheim at the press conference in 1972 announcing Waldheim's appointment as the fourth UN secretary-general. On Berlin's left is Sam Friedar (near left) and Don Shannon of the* Los Angeles Times. *ECOSOC Secretary Rafeeuddin Ahmed is on Waldheim's right.*

Vyacheslav Molotov and those other delegates on the maiden voyage of the *Queen Elizabeth*, broke the networks' barrier preventing women from reporting "serious" news. For years she was a regular in the list of America's 10 most-admired women, and she led the way for other women journalists. (Today a number of chiefs of UN news bureaus are women, including *The Times*'s Barbara Crossette and Reuters's Evelyn Leopold.) Malvin R. Goode, reputed to be the first African-American TV network news reporter, added to his laurels at an ABC bureau headed by former Blue Network war correspondent John MacVane, a Down-Easter who had been a Rhodes scholar.

In this downsizing era, it is hard to believe that *The New York Times* once had a half-dozen or more UN reporters, while the Red-baiting tabloid *New York Daily News* maintained a staff of four. Sam Pope Brewer was a long-time *Times*man. William N. Oatis was an Associated Press celebrity. Arrested, tried and imprisoned for alleged espionage while Prague correspondent for the wire service at the height of the Cold War, he was freed in return for America's unfreezing of blocked Czechoslovak assets. The AP's Francis W. Carpenter, whose prematurely white hair, courtly manner and southern accent conferred a kind of senatorial aura, went on to work for the US mission as Henry Cabot Lodge's spokesperson. Reuters bureau chief John W. Heffernan, a British former sports reporter who often out-quoted the competition because he could write shorthand, moved from the United Nations to Washington and became the first non-American president of the National Press Club. Bruce W. Munn's many UN scoops for the United Press erased the memory of a communications foul-up when he was London bureau chief. The agency flashed an erroneous dispatch that Queen Elizabeth II's first-born was a girl.

Al Goldstein, covering the UN for the *St. Louis Dispatch*, had a

Pulitzer to his credit. Pierre J. Huss, among the last American correspondents to leave Berlin after Hitler declared war on the US, headed
a Hearst news team that included Millicent Phoebe Hearst, a grand-
daughter of "the Chief." She found romance, marrying Algerian delegate
Rauf Boudjakdji, and accompanied him on his posting to New Delhi.

Reminiscing about what he called those early "zestful" UN days,
A. M. Rosenthal recalled an informality at the organization's temporary
homes in the Bronx and on Long Island that today's diplomats and
bureaucrats might find unthinkable, if not downright objectionable. "If
you wanted to get in touch with somebody you didn't send your card or
make appointments in advance, you just knocked on his door or called
him up," he wrote in a 1961 *New York Times Magazine* article, in which
he also recalls telephoning Trygve Lie, the UN's first secretary-general, at
home at 2 a.m. for comment on some news development. Few reporters
nowadays would have the temerity to awaken Secretary-General Boutros
Boutros-Ghali.

Confirming the broad interest that the United Nations generated a
half-century ago, Rosenthal mentioned his own exhilaration about
working there. "It was new and you talked about it all the time—at
work, at home, at parties; what's more, people wanted to hear about it."

THE UNITED NATIONS BEGAN WITH 51 MEMBER STATES; TODAY THERE
are 185, and the Secretariat staff worldwide numbers nearly 34,000,
including more than 10,000 at the New York headquarters. The old col-
legiality, memories of which Rosenthal and some other old-timers cher-
ish, could hardly have been expected to survive in this virtual mini-state.
Maintaining this easygoing style became all but impossible with the

Brennon Jones

The decade-long conflict
which crippled UNESCO and
ricocheted through the UN was
known to aficionados as the New
World Information Order.

I became deeply involved in
analysis and debate about it in
1976 when I discovered two "confidential" working papers for a
UNESCO regional conference
intended to spur governments to
alter what was perceived to be an
"imbalance" of global news flows.
The papers decried the great volume of news sent from four Western services to the developing
world with little reciprocal
exchange, and alleged distortion
of "Third World" coverage.

This analysis did not disturb
me nearly as much as the "cure."
Variously described, though never
officially by UNESCO itself, proponents would create press performance codes, license journalists,
police their coverage and penalize
those who violated the press code.

I began to analyze these programs, writing about them on five
continents. I tried to balance my
analysis by separating valid criticism of Western journalism from
the censorious cures proposed by
hardline advocates of the New
World Information and Communication Order. But only heard—by
both sides—was my criticism of
the cures.

I played an activist role as vice
chair of the US Commission for
UNESCO and as a delegate to the
1983 General Conference of
UNESCO, even helping to negotiate alternative phrasing for the
already overburdened litany officially described as the New World
Information and Communication
Order. It became a "continuous,
evolving process"—not the impo-
sition of predigested cures.

Within a month, the United
States announced it would withdraw from UNESCO in January
1985. I lobbied Congress and the
press to avoid the pullout. I
believed the US should stay in
and fight. The confrontation over
international news and information was not the only reason for
the US withdrawal. But years of

bitter debate over UNESCO's alleged censorship prepared the way for virtually the entire US press to support withdrawal. The following year, the British left.

Ten years later, both countries remain out. In the interim, UNESCO has changed dramatically. From 1990 to 1994, UNESCO initiated press-freedom programs on four continents. Their purpose: to help create diverse, independent news media in developing and newly liberated countries. In recognition, the International Federation of Newspaper Publishers—for the first time—honored a non-journalist for significant contributions to journalism: Frederico Mayor, director-general of UNESCO.

—Leonard R. Sussman, Senior Scholar, Freedom House

LEFT *The press room at the 1979 UN Conference on Trade and Development in Manila: Mario Dujisin, a Chilean journalist with Inter Press Service bangs out an article. Inter Press is one of a number of news agencies that provides steady coverage of the UN and its activities to a large audience of readers in the developing world.*

TOP RIGHT *With the United Nations brokering a peace agreement in El Salvador in 1991, the only TV in Santa Marta, Cabanas, El Salvador is carried to the town center so all the community can watch news of the UN-sponsored negotiations ongoing in New York.*

huge influx of new nations—many of which brought cultural, religious and political values somewhat different than those of the former Judeo-Christian majority. Diplomats have always socialized, and correspondents with them. But some things that were considered perfectly normal a few decades ago are a bit less respectable today—for instance, alcohol as a lubricant in diplomacy. It was President John F. Kennedy's UN ambassador, Adlai E. Stevenson, who advised that a good delegate needed equal parts of protocol, alcohol and Geritol.

Dag Hammarskjöld, Trygve Lie's successor, may not have welcomed 2 a.m. phone calls, but he did continue a Nordic tradition of accessibility and was maybe the last of the secretaries-general to hold regular news conferences when in New York. Inevitably, the United Nations and its relations with the press corps have changed over the years, some might say for better, others for worse. A visitor from the Lake Success era sitting in on today's news briefings by the secretary-general's spokesperson likely would be dismayed by their sometimes confrontational tone, and occasional lapses of good manners, when reporters sense stonewalling.

Understandably, the UN wants to be admired, but officials often become very resentful when the media pries. Many of them were deeply offended when the popular CBS television program "60 Minutes" ran a segment on the UN—one of the very few it has done on the organization—that discussed waste and abuse in the Secretariat, at a time when Secretary-General Boutros-Ghali was pleading with the US to free up more than $1 billion in budget arrears. Not long after, other scandals reached the public prints—ones that the organization would have pre-

...ered to unreported: Almost $4 million cash missing from an insecure filing cabinet at the main UN office in Somalia, and a $900,000 New York headquarters security system never made fully operational because of poor design blamed on a bureaucratic snafu. It is charitable to observe, however, that comparable bureaucratic lapses have long been known to occur in member states that long ago progressed beyond the growing pains that afflict the rapidly expanding United Nations system.

Even before those scandals broke, the Western press had found cause to perceive the UN as something less than a knight in shining armor. The General Assembly's adoption in 1975 of a resolution that determined Zionism to be "a form of racism and racial discrimination" marked a turning point. Few UN actions have had a more profound effect, particularly in the US media where many editorial writers are sensitive to any whiff of anti-Semitism. And this was regarded as an alarming sign that an emotional developing world more inclined toward Moscow than toward Washington was threatening to take control and lead the organization in dangerous directions with untold consequences. It took 16 years and many earnest appeals to UN conscience and common sense, but the resolution eventually was revoked, a very rare event. Deputy Secretary of State Lawrence Eagleburger, leading the US delegation, hailed the decision to "consign one of the last relics of the Cold War to the dustbin of history." By then the UN's useful role in ending the Iran-Iraq war, in gaining freedom for Western hostages in Lebanon, blessing the US-led coalition's military campaign during the Gulf crisis, and deploying blue helmets to restrain the combatants in 13 separate areas of conflict was already restoring public and media recognition. For all its faults, the organization remains indispensable and deserving of support.

Emerging from a meeting with US President Bill Clinton, UN Secretary-General Boutros Boutros-Ghali chooses his words carefully in an informal press briefing outside the White House in 1993. His chief spokesperson, Joseph Sills (left), and Alvaro De Soto, assistant secretary-general (upper right) listen in.

Nongovernmental Organizations

Nongovernmental Organizations

Karen Polk

IN THEIR COMMITMENT AND PASSION FOR PEACE AND JUSTICE, THE nongovernmental organizations (NGOs) have been standard-bearers of the principles that guide the United Nations; in their constant cajoling and needling, encouraging and lobbying, they have been the Greek chorus that forever reminds the UN and its member nations of their human and moral responsibilities.

In the spring of 1945, at the UN founding conference in San Francisco, 42 NGOs were invited to participate in the process. Their involvement in the creation was acknowledgment by the UN founders of their contributions in areas that would concern the new international forum—human rights, peace and international trade, among others.

Now, 50 years later, NGOs that have an official relationship with the United Nations number in the thousands. Meanwhile thousands more, pursuing their special area of interest, work in cooperation with the UN. Whether their link to the world body is official or unofficial, these on-the-ground groups help to extend its influence to the farthest corners of the planet year after year. At the same time, they give people from around the world a voice at the United Nations.

Some see NGOs as shrill advocates of a narrow agenda; others as the keepers of the flame of such causes as human rights, disarmament and economic justice. Some within the United Nations regard them as pests who pursue delegates down the halls—or even scale the Secretariat walls, as members of Greenpeace have done—trying to persuade them to take a stand on a given issue. Others see NGOs as invaluable allies in advancing controversial issues on their own agenda. With increasing recognition, however, NGOs are considered credible and sophisticated sources of information, analysis and action in most every policy area.

A look at the list of agencies of the United Nations gives a quick overview of the myriad issues and constituencies the UN is called upon to deal with around the world. Population control, disarmament,

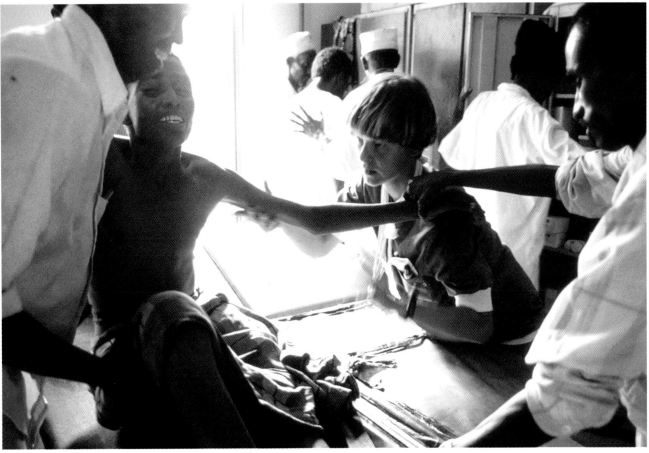

Frank Fournier/Contact Press Images

United Nations

David Hugill

PREVIOUS SPREAD *A half-mile-long scroll, with the signatures of 200,000 Americans who swear their "complete faith in the United Nations as an instrument for world peace," is presented to Oswaldo Aranha of Brazil, president of the General Assembly (center), and Secretary-General Trygve Lie by Clark M. Eichelberger (left), director of the American Association for the UN in 1947.*

TOP *At a Mogadishu hospital in 1992, French nurse Sabine Brunello of Médecins sans Frontières (center) and Somali health workers receive a patient.*

ABOVE *US Ambassador Andrew Young greets Danny Weiss, the secretary-general of a four-day Model UN session in 1977 that gave 1,100 students from around the United States a chance to experience the world of the UN diplomat.*

ABOVE *An anti-apartheid rally in England in the 1980s.*

refugee and relief work, human rights, international trade and commerce, decolonization, peacekeeping, economic development, health and nutrition—the tasks the UN undertakes on a daily basis are virtually infinite, beyond the ability of one institution to carry out. In reality, few UN programs could be implemented and fewer still sustained without the assistance of nongovernmental organizations. Sometimes the determined efforts of just one person can have an impact. While the delegates in San Francisco debated the official agenda, a passionately committed individual became, in effect, a one-man NGO and succeeded in making the United Nations heed his message and act on it.

A professor at Yale Law School, Raphael Lemkin had been an adviser to the US prosecutor at the trials in Nuremberg of those held chiefly responsible for Nazi war crimes. Members of his own family had been killed in the Holocaust. Appalled by the lack of enforceable laws that could be used to convict Nazis of crimes against groups of people, Lemkin introduced the word "genocide" into the English language. And through relentless lobbying in the halls of the United Nations, he saw that the term made its way into international law.

On December 11, 1946, the General Assembly unanimously adopted a resolution that defined genocide as "the denial of the right of existence of entire human groups," and called upon member states to legislate against it. Two years later the General Assembly adopted a convention outlawing genocide. It was under this convention that, in February 1995, a UN tribunal charged a Serbian commander of a concentration camp in Bosnia with the crime of genocide against Bosnian Muslims. The indictment was the first of its kind ever issued by an international tribunal.

SOME OF THE FIRST NGOs to work with the United Nations were those whose purpose was to develop public support for it. Most prominent among them is the World Federation of United Nations Associa-

were NGO consultants to the US delegation at the UN founding conference in 1945. At right is Genevieve Schaffer of the National Women's Business Council.

BOTTOM LEFT At a UN youth forum sponsored by The New York Times at Lake Success in 1948, students scramble for autographs from some of the panelists.

RIGHT The people of Wolfeboro, New Hampshire, play host in 1954 to UN delegates from Greece, Indonesia, Panama, New Zealand, Egypt and Yugoslavia, even making them honorary selectmen at a town meeting and treating them to a barbecue dinner. Local youths, in foreground, wait their turn to entertain the UN delegates with a Greek folk dance.

BOTTOM RIGHT The contingent of UN delegates that visited Wolfeboro went home with something more than memories. Each received a tractor and other farm equipment. Here, local kids give the once over to a tractor similar to those donated.

278

In early 1953, Mrs. Eleanor Roosevelt began her new role as a volunteer with the American Association for the United Nations. One day, soon after settling in at her new AAUN office, she invited several staff members (including me) to lunch in the delegates dining room at UN headquarters.

As we walked toward the entryway between the public area to the delegates' section, Mrs. Roosevelt paused, flustered. "I've just realized that I don't have an official pass anymore, so I will have to ask for one at the visitors' entrance," she said. The security guard just stared in awe at the lady who had been a frequent attendant at UN meetings for a number of years. We assured her that she would have no problem walking to the elevators to take her to the dining room.

After lunch, Mrs. Roosevelt insisted that she stop in at the UN security office to request a nongovernmental organization pass. She believed in living up to the rules. We finally convinced her that a courtesy pass would be issued for her use, and it was so arranged. She carried it with her whenever she came to UN headquarters.

—Estelle Linzer

tions, whose headquarters are in Geneva. Founded in 1946, it now has member associations in more than 80 countries. Its chapters sponsor international education campaigns, cultural exchanges and training programs for chapter leaders, all designed to advance the ideals of the United Nations.

One of the federation's largest members is the United Nations Association of the USA, created in 1964 with the merger of the American Association of the UN with the US Committee for the UN. Among the American Association's early leaders was Eleanor Roosevelt, who volunteered to work with it when her term as a US delegate to the United Nations ended in 1952. Among this group's many contributions was the multilingual tour-guide program at UN headquarters in New York. Now UNA–USA counts among its supporters both ordinary citizens and giant corporations such as Boeing, Pepsico and IBM.

RELIGIOUS ORGANIZATIONS PLAYED A CRUCIAL ROLE IN SUPPORTING THE fledgling United Nations both during its creation and during the post-

war years, as the polarization of the world into ideological blocs imperiled the founders' sense of unity. In 1943 the United States Federal Council of Churches produced a document whose formal title was "Statement of Political Positions," but which was com-

...monly known as the "Six Pillars of Peace." Almost all the ideas laid out in this document, which reflected earlier church efforts to assure a just and durable peace," found their way into the draft proposals for a United Nations Charter developed in 1944 at Dumbarton Oaks.

John Foster Dulles, who had chaired the commission that drafted the "Six Pillars" statement, was a member of the US delegation to San Francisco. Reflecting on his UN experience, Dulles, who went on to become secretary of state under President Eisenhower, observed, "It was the religious people who took the lead in seeking that the organization should be dedicated not merely to a peaceful but to a just order. It was they who sought that reliance should be placed upon the moral forces which should be reflected in the General Assembly, the Economic and Social Council, and the Trusteeship Council rather than upon the power of a few militarily strong nations operating in the Security Council without commitment to any standards of law and justice."

The work of religious NGOs has covered a wide spectrum of issues that concern the United Nations. In the 1950s and early 1960s, for example, church-based NGOs joined with others to assure passage of the ...

She was a college undergraduate, Lilli de Brito Schindler remembers, when she found herself standing at the rostrum in the UN's cavernous General Assembly Hall where the 1,800 seats were filled and every occupant seemed to be waiting for her words.

True, this was not a regular session but a Model United Nations, and for a span of time she was the chosen secretary-general. The experience was awesome, she recalls, even eight years later.

These days, Mrs. Schindler speaks in the UN not as a role-player, but as a staff member in the office of the spokesman of the secretary-general, Boutros

Boutros-Ghali—she adds very hastily, "a very junior spokesperson."

Still, it is a responsibility for which she seems distinctively qualified. She is the daughter of Dantas de Brito, a Brazilian-born official who served for 28 years in the UN and was a director in the Department of Political and Security Council Affairs. Her mother, known within her UN circle as "Henny," was a Dutch survivor of a Nazi concentration camp—most of her family perished. She wanted to work for the new peace organization. The pair met, married, and their wedding "celebration" was assignment as a couple to a tough overseas mission to Korea.

The UN always was a focal point of the de Brito household. Lilli as a teenager gravitated at school toward the "Model United Nations" movement and, eventually, won its highest honor of acting as secretary-general for the annual meeting. She was "conditioned" from birth, she says, to seek a career at the UN but before she succeeded, there were years of graduate work, honing her language proficiency and preparing for the UN's highly competitive written and oral examinations.

On the UN's 50th anniversary she finds herself dealing with the frequently negative image with which the United Nations is regarded by a large segment of the world press. It is not a new experience, she says, having lived through the "UN bashing years" of the eighties. Much of the disenchantment she encounters, she believes, stems from misinformation about what the UN can and cannot do. Also, the organization's achievements seem to be shrugged off as "not newsworthy." She does not see herself today as the wide-eyed optimistic undergraduate of earlier days. Not an apologist. But never a cynic either. "We feel it is our mission to get out the message as clearly as we can."

—Kathleen Teltsch

laration on the Granting of Independence to Colonial Countries and Peoples. The involvement of NGOs in that issue was not limited to public forums or button-holing delegates in the halls of the United Nations. It was often very down-to-earth and domestic. Cora Weiss, who now heads the

Samuel Rubin Foundation and was at the time a volunteer for the American Committee on Africa, often housed people like Oliver Tambo, Kenneth Kaunda and Eduardo Mondlane at her home in New York City to enable this new generation of African leaders to make its case for independence.

After staying overnight at the Weiss home, the leaders would head over to the United Methodist Church's UN office on First Avenue. There, Mia Adjali, who now heads the international affairs department of the Women's Division, provided the telephones and typewriters they needed to prepare speeches and testimony for presentation at the UN General Assembly, just across the street.

Methodist leaders themselves made a unique contribution to UN committee hearings on independence. In 1961 the Methodist bishop in Angola, Ralph Dodge, and his missionaries were expelled from that country by the Portuguese colonial government. Credible information from inside Angola and other African countries was hard to come by, and the United Nations welcomed the firsthand information provided

281

by Dodge and other missionaries. The testimony during hearings proved crucial to passage of the Declaration on the Granting of Independence to Colonial Countries and Peoples in 1960.

NONGOVERNMENTAL ORGANIZATIONS HAVE SHOWN THEIR METTLE IN the battle for human rights as well. NGOs and a handful of committed individuals pressed the delegates at San Francisco to include human rights as a goal for UN member nations. As a result the charter mandated the creation of a UN Commission on Human Rights (set up in 1946), and the General Assembly adopted the Universal Declaration of Human Rights in 1948. This landmark document, which for the first time outlined the basic rights and freedoms due every individual in every nation, was and remains the standard statement of principle used by NGOs around the world to promote human rights.

But despite the passage of the Universal Declaration and its legally binding Covenants such human rights violations as torture, "disappearances" and arbitrary executions remain widespread and stand as a

RIGHT *Waiting to testify at a 1960 UN Fourth Committee hearing on South West Africa are (left to right): Mburumba Kerina, Reverend Markus Kooper, Jarirentundu Kozonguizi, Reverend Michael Scott, Jacob Kuhangua, Reverend Sam Nujoma and Van Ismael Fortune.*

Thirty-eight years ago, in 1956, I helped found the United Nations Association in Westport, Connecticut, and organized the Hospitality Committee of the Town of Westport. Having received over 40,000 international visitors since then, I realize how much my life has been changed by these UN-related endeavors. A bachelor host became my husband! A fatherless Indian painter guest my adopted son.

Now expanded to comprise members in 23 towns of Fairfield County, our Hospitality Committee lists some 3,000 participating host families, and in every issue of the UN *Secretariat News* there is an invitation to UN staff and missions to spend the holidays and the last Sunday of every month with a Westport family which we take pains to match according to age, language, children, hobbies and interests.

The most memorable event to me, among so many, is the Thanksgiving weekend in 1960, when delegates from 17 new member states, mostly French speaking Africans, responded to our invitation. At that time before civil rights legislation had been enacted, black Africans, even distinguished diplomats were apt to encounter social discrimination in cities like New York and suffer from it. Our welcome into French-speaking American families for traditional Thanksgiving dinners and a gala ball at the Country Club showed them a different aspect of American life, and in its small way contributed to international understanding and fellowship. Which is our goal, isn't it?

—Ruth Steinkraus-Cohen

reminder of the limitations of formal declarations. Here again, the NGOs play a crucial supporting role. Groups like Vicaría de la Solidaridad in Chile, the Committee on the Administration of Justice in Northern Ireland and the Turkish Human Rights Association have worked independently to establish standards of behavior in their own countries. With the UN, they also push for compliance by other member nations.

These activists and NGOs, notably Amnesty International and Human Rights Watch, seek to make sure that human rights remain high on the UN's agenda. Curt Goering of Amnesty International USA points out that human rights NGOs serve as a gadfly, gathering evidence that will "expose the gap between rhetoric and action" among UN member nations.

It is often a dangerous undertaking. In 1990 Sebastían Velásquez Mejía, who worked with a rural human rights group in Guatemala, was kidnapped; his battered corpse was found in Guatemala City a few days later. Three witnesses who identified members of a local paramilitary group who carried out the

ABOVE *Doctors with Médecins sans Frontières struggle to find a vein to begin an intravenous drip for a severely dehydrated Kurdish child, one of thousands of refugees who made the long trip to camps in northern Iraq in 1991.*

RIGHT *A volunteer nurse from France cares for an undernourished Somali infant in 1993.*

abduction were shot three months later. Two died. Every year hundreds of human rights activists the world over are killed and hundreds more imprisoned.

In addition to being among the most committed of advocates, human rights groups are among the most sophisticated. Developing critical investigative reports and legal analysis of human rights issues, they work closely with the United Nations to ratify international treaties and conventions that give clear legal force to the Universal Declaration. Among the successes in which they have collaborated, at times prodding the UN and member nations, are the 1989 Convention on the Rights of the Child and provisions to enforce guidelines regarding torture, extrajudicial executions and "disappearances." NGOs are also credited with the creation in 1993 of a UN High Commissioner for Human Rights, a position whose goal is to centralize the rights activities carried out by UN agencies and coordinates their work with that of the NGOs.

FEW IF ANY OF THE UN'S MANY REFUGEE AND RELIEF SERVICES COULD function effectively without the active involvement of NGOs large and small. Among those whose names are recognized worldwide are the International Rescue Committee, the International Red Cross and CARE, Médecins sans Frontières, Save the Children and Catholic Relief Services. Then there are the innumerable grassroots groups, like the Organization of Rural Associations for Progress in Zimbabwe and the Association of Development Agencies in Bangladesh.

Robert P. DeVecchi, president of the International Rescue Committee (IRC), describes the connection between the NGOs and the UN as "a marriage of necessity. The UN cuts the red tape and provides funds for NGOs. We provide the services." In Nicaragua, for example, the United Nations High Commissioner for Refugees (UNHCR) sponsored a repatriation program in the early 1990s that included funds for rebuilding infrastructure. Using UNHCR monies for materials, a local

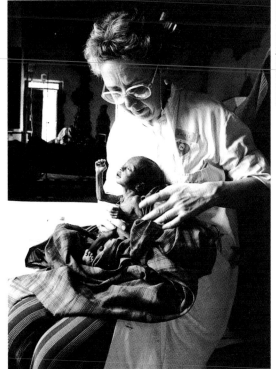

NGO, Fadcani, volunteered the labor to rebuild a bridge across the Tuapi River that allowed returning refugee farmers to bring their products to market.

The bond between relief NGOs and the United Nations was strengthened in the mid-1970s in response to the exodus of refugees from Southeast Asia. Before then, UNHCR had been a relatively small-scale operation whose primary responsibility was to provide legal protection for displaced persons. The boat people of the post-Vietnam War era and the flood of refugees from Laos and Cambodia created a refugee problem of unprecedented magnitude, requiring more resources, services and coordination than NGOs alone could muster. UNHCR became the central organizer, working with NGOs to assist refugees with humanitarian aid and to arrange the resettlement of hundreds of thousands of refugees in other countries.

Later the 14-year-long war in Afghanistan caused the long-term dislocation of some 6 million refugees and resettlement of 2 to 3 million —one of the the largest refugee movements in history. As a result of such catastrophic dislocations, NGOs were compelled to go beyond providing emergency services to set up education, health and training services for populations forced to live outside their homeland for years on end.

For example, in 1990, after civil war forced thousands of Liberians to seek refuge in neighboring Guinea, the IRC recruited 1,120 former teachers among the refugees to set up a school system for 60,000 exiled children—more than are in the school system of West Virginia. In 1993, as a result of such massive efforts— and of expectations that more would be required in years to come—the UN High Commissioner for Refugees launched a

Nairobi, 1985. The campus ground milled with people holding myriad viewpoints: Iranian women for and against Islamic law, Palestinian women for justice and freedom, some American women for sexual rights and others for civil rights, African women for economic power, Asian women for political power. Fifteen thousand women from all over the world meeting alongside the UN Conference on Women which concluded the women's decade launched in Mexico in 1975 and reconvened in Copenhagen in 1980. The contrast between the women's NGOs on the university grounds and the government representatives in the formal conference hall could not have been greater. At the former, there was life, color and information on the reality of women's lives. At the latter, there was sobriety, grayness and a preoccupation with paragraphs. Where was the better work done? Women NGOS cemented a growing understanding between North and South, East and West, and the networks that would carry the women's movement irrevocably forward. Governments had, over the decade, produced a Convention on the Elimination of all Forms of Discrimination Against Women and begun to collect data on women's real contributions to socioeconomic development. Both helped to promote the human rights of women. It's an ongoing process.
—**Nadia Hijab**

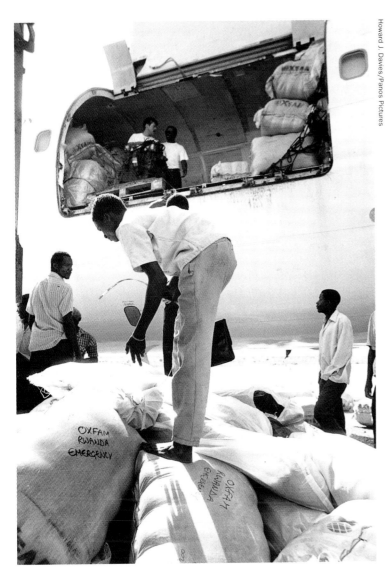

yearlong review of the NGOs' work, meeting with some 450 NGOs in Caracas, Katmandu, Tunis, Bangkok, Addis Ababa and Budapest, as well as in Canada, Japan and the United States. The review culminated in a 1994 declaration establishing closer working ties with NGOs and a commitment to provide further support for their efforts.

WITH DEMAND FOR THEIR WORK increasing worldwide over the past decade, nongovernmental organizations have gained greater credibility and influence, and along with their assertiveness, their numbers have grown. In 1978 the UN accredited 300 NGOs; now it registers thousands. Regions in which nongovernmental activity had for years been underground or virtually nonexistent, such as in Asia and Eastern Europe, have witnessed the proliferation of NGOs responding to social issues that national governments are sometimes ill-equipped or reluctant to address. Meanwhile, sophisticated global communications have made it easier for NGOs even in remote corners of the world to share information.

TOP LEFT *A young refugee sizes up a Medécins sans Frontières worker in a Zambian refugee camp in 1989 as he measures her height and weight to detect signs of malnutrition, part of a health program supported by UNICEF.*

LEFT *Delivering emergency supplies from CARE to rural villages in Somalia in 1993, required a Marine escort to avoid ambush.*

ABOVE *Emergency relief supplies, courtesy of OXFAM, make their way to Rwanda in 1994.*

In many cases, the issues themselves have demanded the unique contribution of NGOs, with their far-reaching constituencies, their ability to exchange and pool information, and the financial and technical resources that they may have at their disposal. This year the International Court of Justice has taken up the case of whether the use of nuclear weapons—or even the threat to use them—is illegal under international law. This case would never have come before the court were it not for a nearly 10-year international grassroots campaign by nongovernmental organizations to convince the General Assembly to take up the issue.

The campaign required extensive lobbying of some 83 UN delegations by NGOs, coordination of grassroots public support in every continent, and the expertise of legal and health professionals from dozens of countries. Only nongovernmental organizations had the knowledge, contacts, international reach and abiding commitment to have carried out this battle for so long.

KEENLY AWARE OF THE limitations of government leadership in environmental issues, Maurice Strong, secretary-general of the 1992 UN Conference on Environment and Development, encouraged NGOs to attend what was popularly known as the Earth Summit. Held in Rio de Janeiro, the Earth Summit was the largest conference in the UN's history. In addition to the representatives of the governments of 178 nations, nearly 1,500 NGOs were officially accredited to the conference by the United Nations. While they and the governmental representatives convened in a convention center outside the city, hundreds of other NGOs held their own Global Forum in a park in downtown Rio.

There, groups ranging from Greenpeace International and the Finnish Association for Nature Conservation to the Nairobi-based Green Belt Movement and Japan's Citizens' Alliance for Saving the Atmosphere and the Earth shared ideas and rallied support for conference proposals or coordinated critiques of them.

Whatever else it achieved, the Earth Summit helped to forge a closer connection between the United Nations and NGOs and stimulated the growth of these energetic, energizing citizens' groups. The March 1995 World Summit for Social Development held in Copenhagen accredited the highest number of NGOs to date—more than 2,000. Thousands of women's NGOs, which have been invaluable contributors in a wide spectrum of issues, and the most successful lobbyists at recent UN conferences, were involved in the Fourth World Conference on Women, in Beijing in September 1995.

TODAY UN OBSERVERS ARE LOOKING more closely at NGOs for answers to some

Donna DeCesare/Impact Visuals

ABOVE *Greenpeace maintained a highly visible presence in New York's East River, just below UN headquarters, during a 1993 conference on declining global fish stocks. The high-profile NGO was urging the 100 nations meeting within to hammer out stringent reforms on international fishing.*

of the problems facing the world body. Their flexibility, the breadth and depth of their constituencies, the resources they are able to muster—all are qualities that could benefit the United Nations. In the face of rapidly changing global politics, UN officials have been willing to reach out to all of the forces that can assist them in their mission, and have undertaken an extensive reviewing of the UN's working relationship with NGOs. Its starting point is acknowledgment of the essential contribution NGOs make to the United Nations.

In the spring of 1995, as that review of the UN/NGO relationship is near completion and a report of its findings readied for the secretary-general, hundreds of thousands of men and women in nongovernmental organizations throughout the world went about doing what they do best—building the foundations of peace, one issue, one person, one country at a time.

CHAPTER FOURTEEN

An Insider's Look

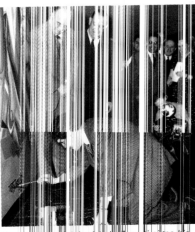

Dominican artist José Vela Zanetti signs his wall-sized mural in 1953, while Henry Allen Moe of the John Simon Guggenheim Memorial Foundation and Trygve Lie look on.

United Nations

What most often defines people who have been associated with the United Nations is a sense of idealism and commitment, be it tarnished or not, and a storehouse of anecdotes and reminiscences, some humorous, some passionate, and usually telling of larger truths about the world organization and its activities. Here are a few:

While being shown through the United Nations Building the other day, a young Middle Western matron who has friends on the UN staff was introduced to the secretary of Secretary-General Dag Hammarskjöld. She promptly asked the secretary of the Secretary if she could possibly get the autograph of the head man. In response, she was handed a small card. She was about to read it when Mr. Hammarskjöld himself strode into the office. Slightly flustered but still determined, the young matron thrust the card upon him and begged for an autograph. Mr. Hammarskjöld looked at her quizzically, murmured "This is rather unusual," and wrote his name. Not until she was on the way back to her hotel in a cab did she have a chance to examine the card. On it was printed, "The Secretary-General of the United Nations deeply regrets that the heavy burden of his official duties prevents him from complying with the many requests he receives for his autograph," and underneath was scrawled the signature "Dag Hammarskjöld."

—*The New Yorker*, May 24, 1958

I will never forget the shoe banging by Khrushchev. What I remember best about that episode was not just Khrushchev and his away from the interpretation booth, taking off his shoe and banging the table with it. What impressed me was the gloomy and positively mournful expression of Gromyko, who realized how gauche this cleaning was. Then a faint jaundiced smile appeared on Gromyko's sour face and he started banging the table himself with his shoe but with his hand.

—George Sherry, *UN Oral History Collection*

In past history, the Security Council served as a theater for impassioned speeches, sometimes hours in length....

In a dramatic case during the early years of the Palestine debate, the Egyptian representative, Mahmoud Azmi, collapsed from a heart attack on the Council's horseshoe table while making a virulent verbal attack on Israel. His grey form was transported immediately on a

Soviet Premier Nikita Khrushchev (center), with Andrei Gromyko (right), during the 1960 General Assembly meeting.

stretcher to the infirmary where his death was not announced for hours, pursuant to the laws of the state of New York which require prolonged resuscitation efforts when the victim's physician is not present....

During the endless—and still unresolved—conflict between India and Pakistan over Kashmir, Krishna Menon of India asked that a meeting of the Council be postponed [because of his being ill]. It was finally concerned, and Krishna Menon appeared, followed by his doctor who took a seat behind him. He spoke for over two hours in a wheezing voice which at times could barely be heard. The physician would then seize his arm and make his pulse. Having reached the end of his speech, Mr. Menon finally laid his head on the table. But when UN guards approached with a wheelchair, the Indian statesman rose with an angry stare and, leaning on his cane, made a slow exit proudly from the chamber.

—Annie Weill-Tuckerman, *UN correspondent for Agence France-Presse, 1946–1983*

At the end of the San Francisco conference, it was decided that there was no provision for safekeeping for the charts. The United Nations hadn't come into being, and the conference secretariat would be disbanded. And it was agreed that someone would keep it in the safe in the White House. Since the US had been the host, this would be appropriate. I

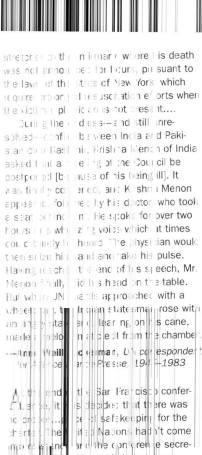

Alger Hiss, secretary-general of the UN founding conference, arrives in Washington with the charter—complete with parachute.

was therefore deputed to carry the charter to the White House and to deliver it to him for that kind of safekeeping. And the Army put a plane at my disposal for that purpose. The humorous aspect of this was that since the charter was so valuable it had a parachute attached to it—and I didn't!

—**Alger Hiss,** *UN Oral History Collection*

It was 20 years ago that my 12-year-old son and I spent a morning at the United Nations. While he was off and about, I wandered down to the UN gift shop where a silver pendant caught my eye. It had a peace symbol on one side and the UN symbol on the other. It pretty well summed up what I believed in.

As it was in December, just before Christmas, I bought it for my wife. It was then that I showed it to my son. He said "No, don't give her that. It's so ugly. She'll never like it!" We argued about it for some time, but I wasn't going to budge. I was going to give it to her for Christmas!

But there's a funny ending to the story. Came Christmas morning, and I'm opening my presents and lo and behold, what do you think I found? The exact same pendant. It was from my wife to me, and my son knew she had bought it for me! We've worn them every day since.

—**Sal Grittani,** *New York pharmacist*

As a United Nations administrator and later as one of President Lyndon Johnson's ambassadors, Arthur "Tex" Goldschmidt, was well known as an expert in helping the Third World spur its economic development. But even Goldschmidt, a favorite with the UN press corps because of his breezy disregard for UN pomp or protocol, had a tough time inducing correspondents to cover the doings of the Economic and Social Council.

Still, the correspondents suspected something was afoot when Goldschmidt casually mentioned over his customary sandwich lunch in the UN Press Club that he would be speaking later and intended to "have a little fun."

Other Council members, accustomed to being ignored, were puzzled when the usually empty press gallery was almost filled. They knew there wasn't anything riveting about the scheduled program—a dullish debate about experiments in developing cheap, high-protein resources, one of them a promising fish flour.

What Goldschmidt offered was a scholarly treatise on the merits of the newly developed fish flour being promoted by the United Nations Children's Fund. True, the flour was less than a culinary treat when tried in the laboratories, he said. But with a little ingenuity, it could win acceptance, said Goldschmidt, signalling to one of the prettier United Nations aides who began moving around the conference room serving the seated diplomats generous samplings of chocolate chip cookies made from the experimental flour, and baked according to Goldschmidt's instructions a few hours earlier in Washington and flown to Manhattan.

As photographers recorded the event,

Eleanor Roosevelt places an order at the UN cafeteria at Lake Success.

the smiling delegates responded with a round of applause—except, in those bad, old, pre-Perestroika days, for the Soviet representative, who frostily refused to taste the cookies and had some cutting remarks about the exercise as an example of American high jinks.

No matter—the others were pleased for once to be seen as newsworthy. And the Japanese representative was so enthused, he stayed behind at the meeting's end and carefully collected the crumbs in an envelope that went into his dispatch case.

—**Kathleen Teltsch**

At an evening reception at the home of the Guinea Ambassador to the United Nations in Riverdale, New York, a number of us were gathered in the garden looking at a harvest sky and the full moon emerging. Andrei Gromyko, the Soviet Union's foreign minister and ambassador was standing with me.

As I pointed out the qualities of the full moon, Gromyko said to me, "That's Uncle Sam's moon."

—**Cora Weiss**

Tasting Technology: members of the Economic and Social Council sample a tray of Ambassador Goldschmidt's protein-rich fish-meal cookies in 1968.

The Falklands crisis of 1982 hit the Security Council like a ground-to-ground missile. When I called an emergency meeting on April 1st, only hours before the Argentine invasion, some of my colleagues thought I was perpetuating an April Fool's joke. The idea of war between Britain and Argentina was unimaginable. The American delegate even considered removing the Council by absenting her delegation from the proceedings.

After the invasion, we knew that we must secure a quick resolution demanding Argentine withdrawal. Only with such a resolution would the British Parliament and

the General Assembly, US Ambassador to the UN Madeleine K. Albright confers with an aide.

the majority of the international community support whatever policy London felt obliged to adopt. But Britain was a old imperial power and Argentina a member of the non-aligned movement which at the time dominated the Council's proceedings. In the debate, our tactics were to concentrate on the illegal use of force to settle a political dispute, leaving aside the question of sovereignty over the islands of which Britain

was in a minority. The debate was crisp and passionate: the dispute had never been to the Council before relating to the first time in my UN experience I saw delegations being swayed by speeches.

We got our resolution, although the outcome was uncertain until the last moment. The prime minister had to telephone a head of state in the small hours to secure his country's vote. The Soviet Union was close to vetoing but abstained when it saw the majority of the non-aligned might behind the British draft. Why did we win the day? Because the non-aligned members are hostile to the use of force. That vote gave the lie to the myth that Western powers were always outvoted by a mechanical Third World majority.

---Sir Anthony Parsons

On April 30, 1980, on the eve of May Day which was the great Soviet/communist/socialist revolutionary holiday, I was representing the United States in the Security Council in a debate on a question relating to the Middle East. Ambassador Oleg Troyanovsky, the Soviet primary representative, and I sat together talking until the president of the Security Council entered the room. We then separated to go to our respective chairs. At that very moment I was attacked from behind and a huge pail of red paint was thrown over me. I was covered from head to toe. As the incident happened, of course, I did not appreciate what the perpetrators were doing. I thought I might have been shot since the red flowing from my head downward was not identified as paint at that point. I stood still and looked around and saw that two men were then attacking Ambassador Troyanovsky in the same way

they had attacked me throwing a pail of red paint over him. The Security recovered from its surprise. The security forces rushed in, tackle the attackers and wrestled them to the floor. In the midst of this chaos, I walked over to Ambassador Troyanovsky to be sure that he was not injured. Both of us were dripping with red paint and Ambassador Troyanovsky was furious at what had happened. In a few minutes, some semblance of order was restored. I invited Ambassador Troyanovsky to go with me and perhaps, to go to our Mission which was located across the street where we might get a change of clothing and media attention if needed. He refused to do that, not wanting to leave the building until representatives of his own Mission arrived with new clothes. We walked out of the Security Council chambers. By that time a large number of press representatives had gathered trying to find out what had happened. I was asked what I had said to Ambassador Troyanovsky as we confronted the crime that had been done to us. I replied "I said to Oleg Troyanovsky that we would be better red than dead." There was a great laugh from the press corps and we went our separate ways freed from the incident.

A follow-up to this story occurred some months later. The perpetrators were arrested and indicted in federal Court for attack on federal officials. Their trial was held at which I was a witness. They were sentenced to some years in prison. It turned out that it was members of a Trotskyite/Maoist group in California that had used the event May Day to attack the representatives of the two great law-making powers of the world, the Soviet

Cleanup time after US Ambassador to the UN William J. vanden Heuvel and Soviet Ambassador Oleg Troyanovsky had red paint thrown on them in the General Assembly.

Union and the United States." My young daughter, Katrina, coming home from school one day some months after the trial was approached unwittingly by someone handing out leaflets and buttons. The leaflet and the button both read: "Free the UN Two"—so Katrina came home sporting the button to free those who had been convicted of attacking her father.

As far as I know, this attack upon Ambassador Troyanovsky and myself was the first and only attack on ambassadorial representatives on the premises of the United Nations.

—William J. vanden Heuvel

Not only words, but little matters of custom, such as food or even chitchat, cause rifts in international serenity. That we have discovered from some frank talks with UN delegates and Secretariat members about American hospitality; and contrarywise, with American hosts. Guests from abroad never have any complaints about the quantity of food at American tables (indeed, they deplore the daily waste of food that could be so well used abroad). But when it comes to culinary virtuosity, well—c'est autre chose. Some verdicts:

American sauces—lowest rating anywhere

Salad dressings—can't get the right kind

Desserts—lack of subtlety

Quiet after-dinner talk—impossible because of constant solicitous inquiries by the hostess.

Guests also get bored by repetitious questions. Some choice ones:

"What nationality are you?"

"Is this your first visit to the US?" (then, before there is time for an answer:

"I bet you're glad to be here.")

"Aren't you sorry your wife isn't here to have a good meal with you?"

Then the clincher: "I bet you are sorry to go home."

But hosts, too, have some grumbles. First of all, they say that many of the delegates affect a slight air of superiority which gets on their nerves. Also, the diplomats tend to speechify—they forget they're in a private home and not a Cabinet meeting, and they consider any interruption practically a "hostile act." Other little quibbles:

If addressed as plain Mr. So-and-so instead of "Mr. Ambassador" or "Your Excellency," diplomats of the old school often raise their eyebrows.

Representatives of newer governments resent it if their political theories are not accepted immediately or are criticized.

Guests become impatient if someone does not understand their English.

Above all, they love to hear themselves talk but hate to listen to others.

Since the US and UN will have to live together for a long time—if they are to live at all—how about hosts inventing a few more imaginative questions, about art, literature, politics, for example? And how about guests being slightly less pompous and more amenable to the new UN concept that equality of human beings applies even to diplomats?

—United Nations World, *1947*

It is, perhaps, only a slight exaggeration to suggest that the entire UN system runs not on money or international cooperation, as might popularly be believed—but on espresso. That's right, those tiny little cups of deadly black coffee that remove

US Ambassador George Bush confers with the delegate Radha Ramphul of Mauritius, in 1972.

the enamel from your teeth and chew their way through the inner linings of your stomach. This and this alone is the true stuff of diplomacy.

At the UN it is consumed by the gallon—no, by the ocean! If T. S. Eliot measured his life by teaspoons, it might rightly be said that UN diplomats, Secretariat officials, staff members and journalists all measure their lives by the number of espresso cups they lift each day. A trained Espresso Observer (an "EO" in UN parlance) can witness this particular phenomenon in any number of locations within the Secretariat building: in the voluminous and affordable staff cafeteria, located on the ground floor with its wonderful view of the East River; in the dramatic Delegates Lounge, with its soaring ceiling, comfortable leather chairs and enormous Chinese tapestry of the Great Wall; at the little known and sparsely furnished North Lounge, tucked away in an anonymous corner outside the Security Council; in the shabby quarters of the UN Correspondents

Paul Robeson (center, smiling) poses for an informal portrait at a UN reception.

At the opening of a UN art exhibition, Ralph Bunche's remarks draw some laughs.

Association, with its 1950s cafeteria decor and the photographs of past Association presidents as the chief (and only) form of decor.

But for my money (a very modest $1.25, by the way), the most delightful place to sip the ubiquitous black jet fuel is the Vienna Cafe—a curious little assemblage of tables and chairs tucked cozily under the large stairway that leads from the main floor to the first sub-level. Here, within easy distance of the Secretariat's many conference rooms, a pleasant little kiosk is open from September to December (ie, while the General Assembly is in session), and a simple sandwich, a piece of fruit or a very decent slice of carrot cake can be quickly purchased and consumed. To be washed down, of course, with a cup of espresso!

—John Tessitore, *director of communications, the UN Association of the USA*

The United Nations organization has two working languages, English and French, and a total of six official languages: Arabic, Chinese, Russian, Spanish, plus French and English.

The secretary-general is expected but not requested to speak fluently both English and French, and the French government has made it a policy of putting its veto, in the Security Council, to any candidate that does not speak French. However, there was an exception in the case of U Thant, of Burma, who was elect-ed following Dag Hammarskjöld's accidental death.

The present secretary-general, Boutros Boutros-Ghali of Egypt, is the first to speak English, French and Arabic fluently. He can shift without the least trace of hesitation from one to the other in his official duties.

But what does he speak at home with his wife, Lea?

"Well," says Boutros-Ghali, "we usually speak Arabic. But when we disagree we switch to English where words are more forceful. And when things go especially well we turn to French, the language of love and diplomacy."

—Louis Foy, *France-Soir*

Dear Dag Hammarskjöld,
Thank you very much for the wonderful dinner party last night. It will always remain in my mind as a moment of great significance....

I have tried to write to you for nearly two years to tell you how much we, as artists, all owe to you, and depend upon you, for art itself as well as for our lives. Every morning when I listen to the news, and read the papers, what you are doing and saying and creating is the one "reality" in a conflicting nightmare of unreality and disbelief.

In England the artists are deeply implicated because we are such a small and concentrated unit, and the impulse to create depends on the ability to resolve and establish what UN stands for is being an essential part of the true discipline of the creative imagination.

You have the fully integrated "vision" which demonstrates the naturalness and beauty of the spirit of man which all of us in varying degrees are striving to obtain by the unity of mind and imagination. These are halting words and I could only do better in the quietness of my studio, where I have, for a long time, thought of you and all you stand for, almost every day.

I could more easily express my thoughts by making you something. I have always wanted Single Form to be yours entirely, to give it to you, but hesitated to speak as I do not know whether this is what you would ever like! An alternative idea would be to carve you a special object just for handling, a more personal sculpture done after my experiences here.

Do not hesitate to say if you do not like either of these ideas—I am quite detached. Single Form belongs to you in essence anyway, and I shall do you a small carving also whether you see it or not!

With my sincere thanks.
Yours ever, Barbara

—Letter to Dag Hammarskjöld from Barbara Hepworth, October 16, 1959

Dear Barbara Hepworth
This is a report not on "progress" but on success.

Your sculpture—as strong as it is moving—arrived safely. An inconspicuous base was made and it was placed where I had hoped that it would come into its own and, at the same time, give me daily and, indeed, hourly pleasure.

Delegates at UNESCO headquarters in Paris.

I have now had it before me a couple of weeks, living with it in all shades of light, both physically and mentally, and this is the report: It is a strong and exacting companion, but at the same time one of deep quiet and timeless perspective in inner space. You may react at the word exacting, but a work of great art sets its own standard of integrity and remains a continuous reminder of what should be achieved in everything.

So you hear that your gift gives me great joy of a kind which ultimately is of great help, whatever our specific task may be. I believe that this is what you wanted to achieve and, if so, you have indeed amply succeeded.

Once again, thank you for what you have done and for your daily contribution to our work.

Dag Hammarskjöld

—Letter to Barbara Hepworth from Dag Hammarskjöld, *August 11, 1961*

Barbara Hepworth's "Single Form," in honor of Dag Hammarskjöld, is dedicated in 1964.

United Nations

Rene Burri/Magnum Photos

UN peacekeepers in the Gaza Strip in 1958.

The sun's not risen yet over the Hotel Cambodiana in Phnom Penh where our group and much of UNTAC are quartered. Unable to sleep, overenergized by the past 48 hours, I pad out to the pool. On the edge, alone, I reflect: Two days ago, I walked the far side of the Thai border, among 350,000 Cambodians about to be repatriated from the refugee camp of tin shacks and narrow dirt lanes that had been "home" for six, ten, thirteen years. Fear and anticipation—land mines, AIDS, hostile Khmer Rouge, poverty, farming their own acres, kin lost or found—were palpable in their words, the air. How could the UN, preparing to run Cambodia for the next year, pull off this extraordinary undertaking, resettling over a half-million citizens, effecting free elections, securing peace? Yesterday from the museumed school

where countless who didn't perish on the Killing Fields were tortured to death, we were summoned for tea with Prince Sihanouk in his jeweled palace. On silk divans we listened to the Prince—survivor, symbol of his country, beloved despite the decades of political madness and brutality, by today our one hope for holding Cambodia together after the United Nations departs, and we marveled at his blend of royal graciousness and defensiveness, the personal obsessions revealed. He had just dispatched Hun Sen (long hated, snubbed) to Washington to persuade Americans to pay their dues to the UN. Last night we ate at the hotel with a succession of journalists returning from still-dangerous regions of the interior. Mr. Akashi, the secretary-general's special representative who heads this incredible venture, joined us. Impressive, unemotional in his morning office, he was relaxed, humorously sanguine. In contrast, the UNTAC programs director, a Brazilian who had infected us with his optimism at noon walked by our table, head down, deep in thought. I'm anxious for them all.

About to plunge in, now, I realize I'm not alone. A tall broad-shouldered figure emerges from the shadows: General Sanderson, the Australian designated to command UN troops arriving in this capital from world ports. He nods hello and points out fishing boats silhouetted under the trees on the lightening horizon and tells me a bit of the river's and the countryside's history before he dives in, doing two laps to each of mine, leaps out, and strides off wet and confident as the sun illuminates the disheveled city, the pastel tiles on the glorious palace roof. I suddenly believe this will be a proud year for the keepers of Cambodia's peace.

—Rose Styron, *Diary entry, March 1992, Phnom Penh, 5:30 a.m.*

Henry Moore inspects his sculpture in UNESCO's courtyard in Paris in the late 1950s.

Pierre Boulat/Life

She was an ardent advocate of women's rights—a feminist—says Minerva Bernardino, the longtime delegate from the Dominican Republic, in an era when other United Nations diplomats seemed indifferent to her pleadings and demands. Today, she is acknowledged widely as one of the crusaders—with scores of awards, the most recent presented to her by Hillary Clinton from the Franklin and Eleanor Roosevelt Institute.

"I was a fighter, and I still am," said Señora Bernardino, recalling a few of the skirmishes:

There was the day in a UN Assembly debate when Saudi Arabia's representative, the voluble Jamil Baroody, made the mistake of addressing the committee's women members as "the ladies," instead of the customary "distinguished delegates."

It was in midsentence when Señora Bernardino suddenly pounded her fist against the desk on a point of order.

"You may refer to us as ladies when you buy us a drink, a cup of tea or dinner; here we are not ladies but delegates and should be addressed properly."

Her more serious and persistent protests were meant to persuade UN delegates drafting landmark declarations and conventions that it was not sufficient to pledge to uphold *human rights* without specifying these were rights belonging to *men and women.* "In many countries, there

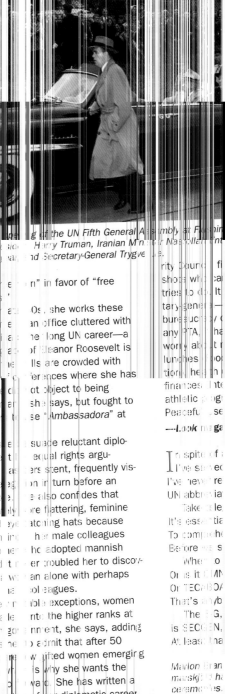
Minerva Bernardino (center), with other delegates, including Nobel Prize-winning poet Gabriela Mistral of Chile (left), prior to a 1953 UN session on the Status of Women.

was no acceptance of women, they were looked on as mere possessions like a pen, a paper or a cow," she says.

Always active in promoting voting rights for women in Latin America, she carried her crusade for equality to the newly organized United Nations. At the San Francisco conference, where she was one of four women who signed the UN Charter, she was influential in getting members to drop

Attended the opening of the UN Fifth General Assembly at Flushing Meadow in 1950 were (left to right) US President Harry Truman, Iranian Minister Nasrollah Entezam, president of the General Assembly that year, and Secretary-General Trygve Lie.

the phrase "men" in favor of "free human beings."

Now in her 80s, she works these days from home, an office cluttered with the memorabilia of the long UN career—a signed photograph of Eleanor Roosevelt is on her desk. Walls are crowded with photographs and conferences where she has presided. She did not object to being called "chairman," she says, but fought to get translators to use "*Ambassadora*" at meetings.

How did she persuade reluctant diplomats to accept the equal rights arguments? She was persistent, frequently visiting each delegation in turn before an important vote. She also confides that she deliberately wore flattering, feminine dresses and even matching hats because she was convinced her male colleagues detested women who adopted mannish clothes. And it never troubled her to discover she was a woman alone with perhaps 20 or more male colleagues.

With a few notable exceptions, women have not made it into the higher ranks at the UN or in government, she says, adding that it pains her to admit that after 50 years there are few qualified women emerging as leaders, which is why she wants the crusade to push forward. She has written a book, a chronicle of her diplomatic career at the UN. Its title, it is entitled: *Lucha, Agonía y Esperanza — The struggle, the agony, and the hope.*

—Kathleen Teltsch

What is the UN? It is an arena of quarrels, a kitchen of good works, a cathedral of hopes. It is not a world government or a super-state. It is more like a global PTA. It has a membership which meets in a General Assembly—99 members when the session started. It has a board of directors—11 members in a Secu-

rity Council, five of them permanent big shots who can veto anything the board tries to do. It has a president—the secretary-general — and his Secretariat, a bureaucracy of more than 4,000. And, like any PTA, it has a host of committees which worry about momentous parallels to school lunches (Food and Agriculture Organization), public health (World Health Organization), finances (International Monetary Fund) and athletic programs (Committee on the Peaceful Uses of Outer Space).

—*Look magazine, 1961*

In spite of all the years now I've served the United Nations, I've never quite mastered UN abbreviations.

Take cablegrams, for instance: It's essential we are able To comprehend the strangest words Before we send a cable. When do we say UNATIONS? Or is it UNMESS? Or TECABOARD or TECASSIST? That's anybody's guess. The SG, in a cable, Is SECGEN, quote unquote. At least that has a meaning

Marlon Brando and Secretary-General Dag Hammarskjöld have a chat prior to UN Staff Day ceremonies.

In a light moment, UN Secretary-General Trygve Lie examines the state of the world.

Which isn't so remote.
    UNFICYP and UNMOGIP—
I muddle up the two.
They sound very much alike,
At least I think they do.
    You all have heard of UNTSO
and UNEF, too, no doubt,
But which is which, you must confess,
It's hard to figure out.
    And don't forget there's OGS
As well as ESA,
But which does what,
and when and how

A UN political affairs officer files a report in 1950 from South Korea shortly after the conflict began.

Is not for me to say.
    The GA meets in session,
So does ECOSOC,
When one first hears such references,
It's really quite a shock.
For stamps, you go to UNPA,
For books, it's OPI;
Of course, I never get them right
No matter how I try.
    And then there's TARS and TAO,
There's also P and T;
To get things fixed, call BMS,
To get confused, call me!
    IAEA has caused me
Inestimable worry.
In order that you get it right,
Don't say it in a hurry.
    It's strictly UN jargon,
Whoever could have styled it?
I'd like to meet the character
Who actually compiled it!
    BE, UNPA, OGS, UN, NYC, USA
—Secretariat News, *1964*

One day [at the height of the Congo crisis in the early 1960s] a Congolese came saying, "I want to repair your telephone." I said, "It is working a bit haphazardly. Do what you can...." He worked and worked and worked and then said, "I can't manage it." I said, "What are you doing?" He said, "I am supposed to put in one of these listening devices but I can't get it screwed in in the right way."
—Sture Linner, UN Oral History Collection

Here's a modern fairy tale which happens to be true. Once upon a time, in the 1950s, the General Assembly's Fifth Committee was discussing a budget cut for the library. The reason given was that the room in the Secretariat building used to shelve books and periodicals could no longer absorb new acquisitions, short of creating a safety hazard. The Advisory Committee therefore recommended that the library be wound down and eventually dismantled. Among the "facts" cited in favor of this course of action was that within a radius of 10 miles from UN headquarters, there were at least five first-rate libraries which made it superfluous for the United Nations to have one. The members of the Committee were about to take a vote, which routinely adopted the Advisory Committee's proposals, when I, as the delegate from Israel, took the floor.

After explaining that my research had disclosed that within a radius of five miles of UN headquarters there were at least 50 excellent eating facilities—the delegates dining room and the staff cafeteria were therefore redundant—I suggested that they should be converted to make room for the library. Otherwise, the United Nations might well go down in history as having

A UN window washer gets a bird's-eye view of the General Assembly building under construction.

ushered in the New Dark Ages, just as the burning of the library in Alexandria began the original ones.

The chairman of the Advisory Committee, who was a Greek, Ambassador Aghnides, apparently felt it politic at that point to announce that his Committee's proposal was withdrawn, pending further consideration next year, whereupon the original allocation was approved.

For years thereafter, no cuts were made in the library budget. While this may have preserved the good name of the United Nations, it did nothing to solve the space problem. A solution came when the good fairy, known as the Ford Foundation, seeing the plight of the UN, offered to finance a separate building to house the library. This is the Dag Hammarskjöld Library, and this is the story of how it came into existence.

—Arthur C. Liveran

Dag Hammarskjöld chats amid a group of concert-goers on UN Staff Day.

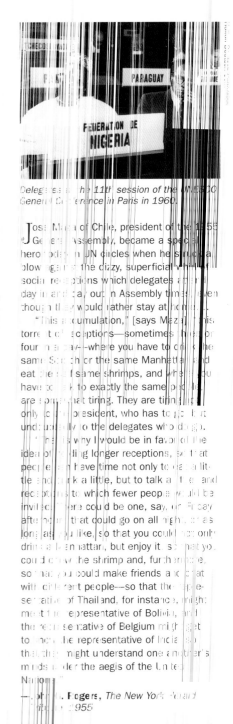

José María of Chile, president of the 1955 UN General Assembly, became a special hero today in UN circles when he struck a blow against the dizzy, superficial whirl of social receptions which delegates attend day in and day out in Assembly times, even though they would rather stay at home.

"This accumulation," [says María], "this torrent of receptions—sometimes three or four in a day—where you have to drink the same Scotch or the same Manhattan and eat the self-same shrimps, and where you have to talk to exactly the same people, are sometimes tiring. They are tiring, not only to the president, who has to go, but undoubtedly to the delegates who do go.

"That is why I would be in favor of the idea of holding longer receptions, so that people can have time not only to eat a little and drink a little, but to talk a little, and receptions to which fewer people would be invited. There could be one, say, on Friday afternoon that could go on all night, as long as you like, so that you could not only drink a Manhattan, but enjoy it so that you could chew the shrimp and, furthermore, so that you could make friends and chat with different people—so that the representative of Thailand, for instance, might meet the representative of Bolivia, and the representative of Belgium might get to know the representative of India, so that they might understand one another's minds under the aegis of the United Nations."

—*John N. Rogers, The New York Herald Tribune, 1955*

The highlight of my years at the UN was the uproar over the question of whether Chairman Yasir Arafat of the Palestine Liberation Organization would be permitted to speak from the rostrum in the Great Hall of the UN General Assembly in December 1988.

This issue hit headquarters and Foggy Bottom (the State Department) like a hurricane. Emotions on both sides of the question were boiling hot. From my vantage point, there was no question that under the Host Country Agreement of 1947 between the United Nations and the United States

of America), any speaker invited by the General Assembly to address it would automatically be granted a visa to enter the United States. Then Secretary of State George P. Shultz did not think so and was prepared to do full battle in denying the visa. The spirit in the General Assembly was totally adamant that Mr. Arafat be granted the privilege of addressing the body as he had already done in 1974. I could literally feel tension rising; he still had warned my fellow countrymen of the dangers and the certainty of dead.

Next I sat there riveted, surveying the raging, tumultuous Assembly. The General Assembly and the Host Country regarded one another with no one blinking. Conflict was inevitable and the outcome at hand was the only time in the history of the United Nations that every member state voted against the United States (save Great Britain which abstained) to extend an invitation to Chairman Arafat.

The rest is history, with the entire General Assembly being lifted from New York City and transported to Geneva where—at the oasis des Nations—Chairman Arafat was given rights and rank to address the General Assembly of the United Nations. And before that meeting started, my language prevailed that we were in the hall of the House of Peace, and the Chairman appeared without his ever-present gun.

—*Joseph Verner Reed, under secretary-general, special representative of the secretary-general for public affairs*

My first encounter with the UN was during its formation in San Francisco. I was then on active duty in the Navy, but

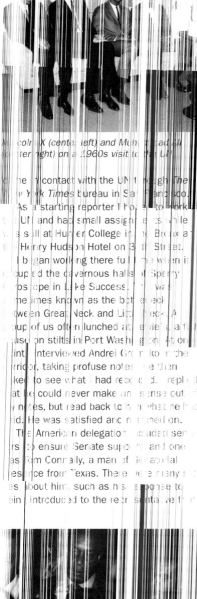

...contact with the UN through *The New York Times* bureau in San Francisco. As a starting reporter I had to work at the UN and had small assignments while I was still at Hunter College in the Bronx and the Henry Hudson Hotel on 38th Street. I began working there full time when it occupied the cavernous halls of Sperry Gyroscope in Lake Success. It was sometimes known as the bottleneck between Great Neck and Little Neck. A group of us often lunched at a little restaurant house on stilts in Port Washington. At one point I interviewed Andrei Gromyko in the corridor, taking profuse notes. He then asked to see what I had recorded. I replied that he could never make any sense out of my notes, but read back to him what he had said. He was satisfied and marched on.

The American delegation included senators to ensure Senate support, and one was Tom Connally, a man of senatorial presence from Texas. There were many stories about him, such as his response to being introduced to the representative from

298

UNESCO: "A small country, but a brave one," he said. Or then there was Warren Austin's alleged plea that the Arabs and Jews make peace "in a truly Christian manner."

By the time Israel was voted into existence, the UN General Assembly had moved to the New York State Building at Flushing Meadow (later a skating rink). It was a highly emotional scene. I remember a rabbi with flowing beard walking down the hall crying: "This is the day the Lord made!"

My assignment then was to follow construction of the new headquarters on the East River, where there had been a slaughterhouse and bocci court, patronized by

Salvador Dali was one of many artists and entertainers who performed in UN radio documentaries in 1950.

local Italians. I took pride in knowing the intricate tunnels and passageways of that complex.

My final UN assignment was the Paris General Assembly during the winter of 1951–52. The conference was held in temporary buildings at the Palais de Chaillot. My wife and I rented an apartment in Auteuil.

We have never lost faith that world peace will ultimately come through the UN.

—Walter Sullivan

Ambassador Shirley Temple Black served as public delegate with the United States Mission to the United Nations in 1965. She was a superb diplomat, earnest and dedicated. She did her homework and was always prepared.

At official receptions, when she entered a room, international statesmen and their ladies swarmed to the door ("like a ship listing to one side" an envoy observed). They were eager to exchange greetings and to be photographed with the former child star.

A diplomat remembered that he had seen *Little Miss Marker* and other Shirley Temple films on a white sheet with a battery-operated projector in a village square in Central Africa.

As UNICEF Public Information Officer, I had the honor one day in 1965, to escort Ambassador Black who was to address a

luncheon at UN headquarters. We were running late and rushing from the elevator and heard the unmistakable and frightening sound of fabric ripping. The seam at the back of her dress had torn. We draped my jacket over her shoulders while searching for a quiet corner to assess the damage. It was sizable. Nonplussed, the Ambassador searched through her attache case among the documents and files and came up with a couple of small safety pins with which I attached the rip. As I recall, I did a pretty good job. At least it held. And it didn't show.

She patted my hand, smiling her thanks as we continued on to the luncheon in the delegates dining room where, as always, she was terrific.

From my seat at the table I beamed, pleased that in the crisis, I had provided emergency technical assistance in the finest tradition of the international civil servant.

—David Sureck

[I]t was because I felt that not talking would contribute to violence and bloodshed, that I thought the risks of talking to the PLO were nothing compared to the risk of the bloodshed, the violence, the possible destruction and disruption of the relationships which we enjoy with many, many people in that region of the Middle East.

I've said that it's a ridiculous policy not to talk to the PLO, and I think it is a ridiculous policy. But if it's ridiculous not to talk to the PLO on the part of the United States and the nation of Israel, it's also ridiculous

UN security guards in a training session.

for many of you around this table not to have good relations with the nation of Israel. For ultimately if we are going to have peace in that region, people have got to approach each other as friends and as brothers and not as enemies, blood-thirsty for the destruction of each other.

And so I would say that in the experience of my nation, though many in my nation would not agree with me, that violence has almost always failed.

—Andrew Young, *former US Ambassador to the United Nations, excerpt from a 1979 speech to the Security Council*

The early years of the United Nations have been difficult ones, but what did we expect? That peace would drift down from the skies like soft snow? That there would be no ordeal, no anguish, no testing, in this greatest of all human undertakings?

—Adlai E. Stevenson, *1952*

In the UN delegates lounge: Taking a break between sessions.

The UN and Its Agencies

UN Principal Organs

GENERAL ASSEMBLY *New York, NY*

The Assembly is the UN's main deliberative body where each member nation is represented with one vote. Meeting from the third week of September until mid-December, the General Assembly discusses a wide-range of international issues, from questions related to international peace and security, disarmament, international law and human rights. Following consultation with its seven Main Committees, the General Assembly issues recommendations most approved by a simple majority ("important" recommendations which member admittance or security issue require a two-thirds vote). General Assembly decisions have no legal weight beyond the force of world opinion.

SECURITY COUNCIL *New York, NY*

Responsible for maintaining international peace and security, the Security Council is the only UN body with the power to back up its declarations with action. There are 15 members of the Security Council, 10 of which are elected by the General Assembly to two-year terms. Five members — the US, Russia, UK, France and China — are permanent members. Any substantive Security Council decision requires nine votes. The five permanent members have veto power. The Security Council's mandate is to investigate international disputes and recommend resolutions of reconciliation. Its primary concern is to bring disputes to an end or achieve cease-fires among fighting sides. If further measures are required, the Security Council may call on UN members to apply economic sanctions or take military action against an aggressor. In its 50-year history, the Security Council has taken action in 35 international disputes.

ECONOMIC AND SOCIAL COUNCIL (ECOSOC) *New York, NY*

ECOSOC coordinates the economic and social work of the United Nations and of its specialized and affiliated institutions. The council meets once a year in a one-month plenary session. Its 54 members are elected by the General Assembly to three-year terms. ECOSOC facilitates cooperation between UN agencies, consults with nongovernmental organizations on pertinent issues and oversees its own regional commissions (representing areas like Africa or Europe) and six functional commissions (covering areas such as population, human rights and the status of women).

TRUSTEESHIP COUNCIL *New York, NY*

Founded to administer the Territories in the UN's trust — most in Africa and the Pacific — the Council's process has led to its dissolution: one territory after another gained independence or joined neighboring nations. The last Trust Territory, a Pacific island group in the Pacific, gained independence in 1994 and became the 185th member nation. The five permanent members of the Security Council — France, Russia, China, the US and the UK — likewise make up the five members of the Trusteeship Council.

INTERNATIONAL COURT OF JUSTICE *The Hague, Netherlands*

Known as the World Court, the ICJ is the one judicial body that can settle disputes between nations. When disagreeing countries agree to accept its jurisdiction, the court will decide legal disputes. The Court also issues advisory opinions on international legal matters to the General Assembly or the Security Council. Fifteen judges — elected by the Security Council and the General Assembly for nine-year terms — use a variety of grounds on which to decide cases. In order of preference, the court relies on international conventions and customs, general legal principles and, in some cases, the judicial decisions of highly qualified jurists of various nations.

SECRETARIAT *New York, NY*

The United Nations Secretariat serves UN bodies, administering the multiple programs and policies established by the manifold UN organs. Headed by the secretary-general, the UN's chief administrative officer, the Secretariat is staffed by some 25,000 citizens of many member nations — a figure that includes not only those at UN headquarters in New York, but also the UN's Geneva office and the many technical and economic advisory workers. In practice, the Secretariat is involved in all aspects of the UN's work, from conducting development studies and surveying economic trends to disseminating information and translating speeches. Since 1992, the Secretariat has been undergoing a restructuring intended to consolidate departments and reduce redundant operations.

Subsidiary Organs

IAEA International Atomic Energy Agency *Vienna, Austria*

Set up in 1957, the International Atomic Energy Agency serves as the world's central intergovernmental forum for scientific and technical cooperation in the field of the peaceful uses of atomic energy. It also helps countries to satisfy their energy needs with international policies meant to ensure that nuclear material are not diverted to military purposes. IAEA safety recommendations are used by countries to establish standards and rules. Some 200 inspectors are deployed worldwide to monitor some 900 installations and other locations.

INSTRAW International Research and Training Institute for the Advancement of Women *Santo Domingo, Dominican Republic*

The International Research and Training Institute for the Advancement of Women was established in 1976 to develop new methods for increasing women's contributions to development and for making the overall process more attuned to the needs of women. The Institute aided the works of women's organizations, research institutions and national focal points, working to raise awareness of issues of concern to women.

UNCHS United Nations Centre for Human Settlements (Habitat) *Nairobi, Kenya*

Established in 1978, UNCHS (Habitat) is the focal point for global action to improve shelter for the poor and for coordinating human settlement activities in the United Nations system. Within the development of shelters, UNCHS (Habitat) is responsible for the planning, financing and execution of human settlement projects. Activities include technical cooperation, research and organizing expert meetings, workshops and training seminars, development and information services.

UNCTAD United Nations Conference on Trade and Development *Geneva, Switzerland*

UNCTAD was established in 1964 to accelerate trade and economic development, particularly in developing countries. The Conference works in four major areas: increasing participation in the world economy of developing countries and countries undergoing transition to a market economy, strengthening global interdependence and reducing global economic imbalances, examining international development experiences to derive useful lessons for future action and promoting sustainable development. UNCTAD has met for national conferences. Meeting according to principles of international trade and to reach agreements on commodity prices and practices. In 1971, UNCTAD adopted a Generalized System of Preferences, granting tariff concessions from industrialized countries to developing countries, a system still in effect.

In 1980, UNCTAD instituted general guidelines for debt restructuring, so that indebted countries might still benefit from full trade partnerships.

UNDP United Nations Development Programme *New York, NY*
Established in 1965, UNDP is the world's largest multilateral source of grant technical assistance for sustainable human development, as well as the central coordinating organization for United Nations development worldwide. Cooperating with governments, nongovernmental organizations and individuals in 175 developing countries, and with approximately 40 UN bodies, UNDP works to enhance developing countries' capacity for sustainable human development through the allocation of funding for technical assistance. Recent successes include providing access to electricity to 24 million people in Western China, retraining 6,500 Salvadoran guerillas in farm management and marketing, and participating in a multilateral effort that established a basic sanitation and sewage system in Dar es Salaam, Tanzania.

UNEP United Nations Environment Programme *Nairobi, Kenya*
UNEP was founded in 1972 to provide leadership and encourage partnership in caring for the environment by inspiring, informing and enabling nations and peoples to improve their quality of life on a sustainable basis. UNEP works in three broad priority areas: capacity-building, catalyzing governmental responses, and assessing environmental quality. UNEP acts as one of the implementing agencies of the Global Environment Facility, serves as the secretariat for several international environment conventions, works with other UN bodies and governments in the development of international environmental law, promotes the prevention of coastal and ocean degradation and raises public awareness and encourages local problem-solving through information, education and training activities. It was instrumental in identifying increasing risks to the ozone layer and negotiating with major chemical producers to phase out production of chlorofluorocarbons.

UNFPA United Nations Fund for Population Activities *New York, NY*
Established in 1969, UNFPA plays a leading role in the UN system in promoting population programs. Major areas of UNFPA assistance include family planning, information, education and communication, basic data collection, formulation of population policy and promotion of the status of women. This assistance places emphasis on the role of maternal and child health in safe motherhood, the importance

of attention to young people's reproductive health needs and on facilitating the needs and concerns of women when planning development and population programs.

UNHCR Office of the United Nations High Commissioner for Refugees *New York, NY*
UNHCR was established in 1951. Its two main functions are to provide international protection to refugees and to find durable solutions to their problems. Having won the Nobel Peace Prize in 1954 for work on behalf of the 2.2 million refugees in postwar Europe and in 1981 for aiding refugees in Afghanistan, Ethiopia and Vietnam, UNHCR continues to work to promote the granting of asylum and to prevent forced repatriation of refugees to countries where they fear persecution. UNHCR also provides emergency relief with basic essentials like food, shelter and medical aid, and local integration assistance to help refugees become self-supporting in their country of residence or of first asylum.

UNICEF United Nations Children's Fund *New York, NY*
UNICEF was established in 1946 to meet the emergency needs of children in postwar Europe and China. In the years since, UNICEF has championed the health, education and sanitation needs of children throughout the world. Working with governments, other UN agencies, nongovernmental organizations and local communities, UNICEF emphasizes community-based programs that directly assist the needs of children. UNICEF promotes the universal ratification and implementation of the Convention on the Rights of the Child. It aims to achieve child survival protection and development goals for the year 2000 adopted by the 1990 World Summit for Children. UNICEF was awarded the Nobel Peace Prize in 1965 for "the promotion of brotherhood among nations."

UNIFEM United Nations Development Fund for Women *New York, NY*
UNIFEM was established in 1976 as the Voluntary Fund for the UN Decade for Women, 1976–1985. It provides direct financial and technical support to low-income women in developing countries who are striving to raise their living standards. It also funds activities that bring women into mainstream development decision-making and addresses issues on the international agenda that critically affect women as beneficiaries of, and contributors to, the development process.

UNITAR United Nations Institute for Training and Research *Geneva, Switzerland*
Since 1965, UNITAR has provided educational instruction for United Nations and member state officials on practical matters

related to the UN's many programs and agencies. UNITAR's goal is to ensure that a well-trained UN staff will be more efficient and that cooperative ventures among UN agencies more effective. If, for example, an UNCTAD official needs instruction on debt management, UNITAR provides the training. If a UNEP project needs their staff to be proficient in Geographic Information Systems, they bring in UNITAR. From international economics and dispute settlement to drafting legal documents, UNITAR works with other UN entities to provide training programs suited to their specific needs.

UNRWA United Nations Relief and Works Agency for Palestine Refugees *Vienna, Austria*
UNRWA was established in 1949 to give assistance to some 750,000 Palestinian refugees who had lost their homes and livelihood as a result of the 1948 Arab-Israeli conflict. It also covers such services as education, health, relief and social services to over 2.9 million Palestinian refugees registered in 1994 with UNRWA in Jordan, the Syrian Arab Republic, Lebanon, the West Bank and the Gaza Strip. UNRWA operates 641 schools for over 390,000 pupils, offers health service through a network of 119 health centers, improves health conditions in refugee camps and provides food and cash aid to about 165,000 refugees. In addition, it also promotes self-sufficiency through income-generation projects, constructs new schools and clinics, renovates old shelters and works with community-based youth and women's activities centers as well as rehabilitation centers for the disabled.

UNU United Nations University *Tokyo, Japan*
Since 1975, The United Nations University has engaged in research, postgraduate training and the dissemination of knowledge on pressing global problems of human survival, development and welfare that are the concern of the United Nations and its agencies. Though UNU headquarters are located in Tokyo, it has research and training centers in Finland, the Netherlands, Macau, Ghana and Venezuela.

WFC World Food Council *New York, NY*
The World Food Council was an outgrowth of the 1974 World Food Conference in Rome which addressed the growing crisis in food production and distribution worldwide. In the 20 years since, the WFC has been assessing and coordinating food needs for an ever-growing world population. The WFC does not administer project assistance; rather, the agency works closely with the Food and Agriculture Organization, World Food Programme and International

Fund For Agricultural Development to identify problems and... and sustenance efficient... The W... annually to report and to assess...

WFP World Food Programme...
Founded in 1963 to reduce... hunger, WFP provides food to develop- ing countries to promote economic and social development and to meet emer- gency needs in the case of natural or man- made disasters. Some millions of people worldwide benefit from... aid. In addition, WFP aims to... designed to promote rural development and increase agricultural production during land reclamation and improve organiza- tion and soil conservation for... road building... resource development... education, training and rural...

Specialized Agencies

FAO Food and Agriculture Organization
Rome, Italy
FAO is the largest agency of the United Nations system, founded in 1945 with a global mandate to... nutrition and standard of living, to improve agricultural productivity to better the condition of rural populations, FAO had developed over 2,000 pro- jects by the late 1980s. The agency cur- rently works to enhance food security, reduce post-harvest food losses, and sustain plant and animal genetic resources, reduce reliance on pesticides, protect aquatic life and develop fisheries, promote sustainable agriculture, and improve nutrition... food security and nutrition, especially for women, children and the elderly.

ICAO International Civil Aviation Organization *Montreal, Canada*
ICAO was created in 1944 to promote the safe and orderly growth of civil avia- tion. A specialized agency... interna- tional standards and regulations neces- sary for the safety, security, efficiency and regu- larity of air transport and... a medium for cooperation in all fields of civil aviation among its member states. ICAO, among other activities, develops, adopts and amends international standards in all matters related to the operation of air- craft. It also cooperates with states to estab- lish regional air navigation facilities, creates standards for global air navigation and aviation security, studies... migration and public health for international air-crafts.

IFAD International Fund for Agricultural Development *Rome, Italy*
The idea for IFAD was... at the 1974 World Bank Conference in Rome, with the IFAD officially established as a UN Specialized Agency in 1977. IFAD's objective is to mobilize resources for better food production and nutrition among low-income populations in developing nations. Collaborating with the World Bank, FAO, WFC and other UN agencies, IFAD com- bines financial efforts with local initia- tives to ward off hunger at the source. IFAD approaches the issue at the grassroots, providing loans for small-scale development at very favorable rates and terms. IFAD has invested some $8 billion in more than 300 such projects in... countries—all of which require local participation and take advantage of sustainable natural resources.

ILO International Labour Organization
Geneva, Switzerland
The International Labour Organization was founded in 1919 to advance the cause of social justice. A unique feature of its struc- ture is the representation of workers and employers as well as civil government repre- sentatives in the deliberations and delibera- tions of the Organization. Since its found- ing, ILO has laid down international labor standards to form a comprehensive code of law and... These standards cover basic human rights, employment promo- tion, social and working conditions, occupational safety and health and labor relations. The ILO has fought to eliminate child labor, promote democracy and protect working... In 1969 the ILO was awarded the Nobel Peace Prize.

IMO International Maritime Organization
London, England
Established in 1948 at a UN Maritime Conference, the IMO encourages coopera- tion between countries on technical matters in the shipping trade. By establishing inter- national conventions and legally binding agreements among member countries, the IMO encourages the highest standards for shipping safety, efficiency and for eliminat- ing pollution from ships.

ITU International Telecommunication Union
Geneva, Switzerland
Founded as the International Telegraph Union in the 1860s, the ITU is the world's oldest international organization. A UN specialized agency since 1947, the ITU attempts to prevent interference between sta- tions in different countries and to improve use of the radio spectrum by eliminating... interference. The ITU's authority... the management of the radio spectrum by allocating frequencies and maintaining registrations for border sta- tions. In recent years, the ITU has also worked to encourage the creation and improve- ment of telecommunications in developing nations.

UNESCO United Nations Educational, Scientific and Cultural Organization
Paris, France
UNESCO was created in 1945 to build lasting world peace founded upon the intel- lectual and moral solidarity of mankind. Its areas of interest include education, natural sci- ences, social and human sciences, culture, and communications. UNESCO... the sharing of knowledge... aim to promote... The programs focus on... education for all, pro- moting... research, supporting the exchange... and protecting the world's natural heritage... promote the free flow of information, the freedom and the development of... and to strengthen communication capacities of developing countries.

UNIDO United Nations Industrial Development Organization *Vienna, Austria*
UNIDO was established by the General Assembly in 1966 to promote and acceler- ate the industrialization of developing countries and to coordinate the indus- trial development activities of the United Nations system. UNIDO activities include encouraging, providing assis- tance to developing countries, develop- ment, assisting developing countries in the establishment and operation of industries, providing assistance in an industrial context to advance... industrialized countries in the... consultations and negotia- tions and to encourage cooperation between developing countries and developed coun- tries and... Within the United Nations, UNIDO coordinates industrial devel- opment...

UPU Universal Postal Union *Bern, Switzerland*
Established in 1874, the Universal Postal Union was made a UN agency in 1948, with the objective to provide for the reciprocal exchange of... between nations... member states, the UPU fosters... that nations transmit the mail of other countries by the best available routes. This is through a system of fixed... that mail might be delivered from one country to another as if it was its national postal... The UPU seeks to speed up mail delivery especially in rural areas, enlarge the number of goods to be paid and the use of air... and staff management. UPU provides technical... assistance experts, awards fellowships to... training and fur- nishes equipment... and demon- stration material.

WHO World Health Organization *Geneva, Switzerland*

WHO, established in 1948, is the premier institution working in the field of health. Its objective is the attainment by all peoples of the highest possible level of health. In 1977, the assembly declared "Health for All by the Year 2000" as WHO's overriding priority and since then, a global strategy has been worked out to reach this goal. The strategy is based on a primary health care approach and has eight essential elements: Information and education concerning prevailing health problems; proper food supply and nutrition; safe water and sanitation; maternal and child health, including family planning; immunization against major infectious diseases; prevention and control of local diseases; and appropriate and immediate treatment of common diseases and injury.

WIPO World Intellectual Property Organization *Geneva, Switzerland*

Stemming from the 1883 Paris Convention for the Protection of Industrial Property and the 1886 Berne Convention for the Protection of Literary and Artistic Works, WIPO outlines and maintains legal standards for intellectual property worldwide. WIPO's goals are twofold: to facilitate the transfer of technology and the dissemination of literary and artistic works; and second to protect the legal rights of those technology and works. WIPO focuses on two areas of intellectual property: industrial property, which entails the patents, trademarks and designs essential for sustained business and industry; and copyright property, which includes ownership of literary, musical, art, film and performance. WIPO promotes treaties among countries and provides legal technical assistance for developing countries building industry.

WMO World Meteorological Organization *Geneva, Switzerland*

Established in 1950, the World Meteorological Organization is a specialized agency of the United Nations. It provides the authoritative scientific voice on atmospheric environment and climate change issues. It aims to facilitate world-wide cooperation in the establishment of networks of stations for meteorological observations as well as hydrological and other related geophysical observations. WMO operates a number of programs, including the World Weather Watch, World Climate, Atmospheric Research and Environment, Application of Meteorology, Hydrology and Water Resources and Education and Training and Technical Cooperation Programs.

IMF International Monetary Fund *Washington, DC*

The IMF was designed at Bretton Woods, New Hampshire, in 1944, where economists recognized the need for a steady world economy, based on the cooperation of governments in trade issues. IMF provides its members with a permanent forum for consultation, advice on key economic policies, technical assistance and training and temporary financial assistance. Accordingly, the IMF has three major functions: to administer a Code of Conduct among member nations regarding exchange rates and payments; to provide financial resources for countries to observe the code and correct imbalances in payments; and to provide a forum for countries to consult and collaborate with each other on international monetary issues. Functioning as a kind of nest egg for all governments at once, IMF funds come with stipulations: they are available only for temporary payment problems, and are expected to be repaid as soon as possible, usually within three to five years.

World Bank Group *Washington, DC*

The World Bank was founded in 1944 to advance sustainable economic growth and reduce poverty in developing countries. The World Bank provides loans to developing countries to finance investments that contribute to economic growth. Though the World Bank and the United Nations were set up separately and the Bank has its own system of accountability and sources of finance, the memberships of the Bank and the United Nations are very similar and the Bank is a specialized agency of the United Nations. The World Bank is actually a group of four institutions. Each provides distinct services to member governments, with a common goal in mind: to raise the living standards of developing countries by making funds available for worthy projects.

International Bank for Reconstruction and Development (IBRD)

Organized at Bretton Woods in 1944, the IBRD grants loans to member countries, political subdivisions, or private businesses within member countries for development purposes. Loans from the IBRD come only with certain stipulations: the loan must be for a productive purpose, i.e., development, education, or heath initiatives; the loan must be guaranteed by the government concerned; and funds must be unavailable elsewhere.

International Development Association (IDA)

When the IBRD recognized that some countries needed loans on easier terms, the IDA was created as the World Bank's "soft-money window." There are four criteria for

an IDA loan: a country must be very poor (the cutoff in 1990 was $740 per capita); the country must show economic, financial and political stability; it must exhibit a difficult balance of payment problem; and the country must show a genuine commitment to development, as shown in national policies. The standard terms are exceptionally easy: 50 years, no interest, with a 10-year grace period before payments are due.

International Finance Corporation (IFC)

Unlike the IDA, which finances governments, the IFC finances private enterprise for development projects. Unlike the IBRD, the IFC needs no repayment guarantee from the country. The IFC's goal is to stimulate the flow of private capital in developing countries, both domestic and foreign. Most IFC loans go to the manufacturing industry, while some have funded mining and energy projects, agriculture and even tourism.

Multilateral Investment Guarantee Agency (MIGA)

The most recent World Bank entity, MIGA was formed in 1988 as a hedge against the political risks that jeopardize investment in developing countries. MIGA offers private investors and companies long-term political risk insurance, providing coverage against war, civil disobedience, or expropriation. Prospective policy holders must be conducting productive development initiatives in countries. MIGA also provides advisory and consultative services to member countries and investors.

Other

GATT General Agreement on Tariffs and Trade and **WTO** World Trade Organization *Geneva, Switzerland*

The General Agreement on Tariffs and Trade, a treaty among trading nations that went into effect in 1948, established a code of conduct for liberalized trade relations, including the principle that trade should be conducted on the basis of non-discrimination (the "most-favored-nation" clause) and that tariffs should be reduced through multilateral negotiations. GATT, administered by a secretariat, also functioned as a forum for trade negotiations. In 1995, following agreement on a final set of GATT provisions during the so-called Uruguay Round of talks, GATT's 128 signatories joined a successor entity, the World Trade Organization. The WTO's mandate is to oversee compliance with GATT principles; phase out protectionist measures; and administer trade rules in areas not covered by GATT, including services, intellectual property and investment.

Acknowledgments

Editors and Producers
Amy Janello
Brennon Jones

Art Editor
Jon Smith

Copy Editor
Leslie Nolte

Caption Writer
Karen P...

Editorial Researchers

Special thanks to the Ford Foundation for major financial support; to Bernard Rapoport and Associates for startup funding; and to continued support from the NGO Secretariat and to office assistance. We are also grateful to the many people who have shared their UN experiences and given generously of their time.

Steve Cohen
Ann-Christine Da...
Stacy... Da...
Jennifer Davis
T... J... E...en
Shelia Devan
Sarah Diani
Sharni Dougherty
Fred...
Seymour Edwards
Ma...e E...
Tahar El-...
Jul...n E...
Luc... Fish...
Inez...
Frank...
Rich...
Dav...
Mir...
Karin Ge...
Ron...nn
Susan Gold... k
Arthur Golds...
Elizabeth Gol...
Ian...
Mar... Gupta
V... Ha...
Steve Hayes
Paul...
...
...
Susan J...
...
W... J...
C...ine...
Sam... K...
Ro...
...
...
...
Sara... ongh...
...
Jed...
Veg... M...
Alex Ma...
Michael Glaser
Bert McClean
Marilyn M...
Michael M...
Sharon M...
... Michaels
L... M...
... Morelli
Thomas M...
... N...
Daniel N...
E... O...
E... P...
...d E. Pitt
N...
R...
T... Pr...
...
R...
...
...e R... bl

Nina Schoenbaum
June Shorall
Rick Smolan
Don Sugiarto
Alex Talukatch
Kitty Teltsch
John Tessitore
Valarie Vars
Annabelle Weiner
Cora Weiss
Chi Hung Wong
Tommy Wong

ABOUT THE WRITERS

Introduction Writer

Brian Urquhart, the former UN undersecretary-general for special political affairs, is currently scholar in residence at the Ford Foundation. He is the author of two books on the UN: *Hammarskjöld: A Life in Peace and War* and *Ralph Bunche: An American Life.*

Chapter Writers

Michael J. Berlin was UN correspondent for both *The Washington Post* and the *New York Post* during much of the 1970s and 1980s, and is currently a professor of journalism at Boston University.

Thomas Hammarberg is the former secretary-general of Amnesty International and a member of the United Nations Committee on the Rights of the Child.

William D. Hartung is a Senior Research Fellow at the World Policy Institute and writes frequently on disarmament issues for *The New York Times, Christian Science Monitor, Newsday* and other publications.

Michael Littlejohns is UN correspondent for the *Financial Times* of London, a former Reuters UN correspondent and moderator of *World Chronicle,* a UN TV news program.

**Karl Maier is Africa correspondent for *The Independent* of London and contributes to *The Economist* and *The Washington Post.* He is a former editor at the Inter Press Service.

Bhaskar Menon is UN correspondent for *The Times* of India and editor of *International Documents Review.*

David E. Pitt, a former reporter for *The New York Times* and a contributor to the *World Summit,* has been writing about social development issues for the UN since 1994.

Karen Polk is a freelance writer and former *Boston Globe* reporter who frequently covers international issues.

Claude Robinson was bureau chief and correspondent for Inter Press Service from 1978 to 1990. He is currently director general of the Jamaica Broadcasting Corporation.

Sheila Rule, a former foreign correspondent in Africa and Europe for *The New York Times,* is now senior manager of reporter recruiting for the newspaper.

Michael Ryan is a contributing editor of *Parade* magazine and a former correspondent for both *People* and *Life* magazines. He co-produced and directed the award-winning documentary film *Eagle Scout.*

Kathleen Teltsch was a UN correspondent for *The New York Times* for 30 years, the last four as one of the bureau chiefs, starting in 1946.

Vivienne Walt is a *New York Times* reporter who frequently writes about the United Nations and international affairs.

Francis Wilkinson is political and features correspondent for *Rolling Stone*

EARTH

An Introduction to Physical Geology